Country Roads of SOUTH CAROLINA

Drives, Day Trips, and Weekend Excursions

Dan and Carol Thalimer

COUNTRY ROADS PRESS

NTC/Contemporary Publishing Group

Library of Congress Cataloging-in-Publication Data

Thalimer, Dan.
Country roads of South Carolina : drives, day trips, and weekend excursions / Dan and Carol Thalimer.
p. cm. — (Country roads)
Includes index.
ISBN 1-56626-175-9
1. South Carolina—Tours. 2. Automobile travel—South Carolina—Guidebooks. 3. Rural roads—South Carolina—Guidebooks. I. Thalimer, Carol. II. Title. III. Series.
F267.3.T48 1998
917.5704'43—dc21 98-22014
CIP

Cover and interior design by Nick Panos

Published by Country Roads Press
A division of NTC/Contemporary Publishing Group, Inc.
4255 West Touhy Avenue, Lincolnwood (Chicago), Illinois 60646-1975 U.S.A.

Printed in the United States of America
International Standard Book Number: 1-56626-175-9
99 00 01 02 03 ML 20 19 18 17 16 15 14 13 12 11 10 9 8 7 6 5 4 3 2 1

In loving memory of Agnes Wooters

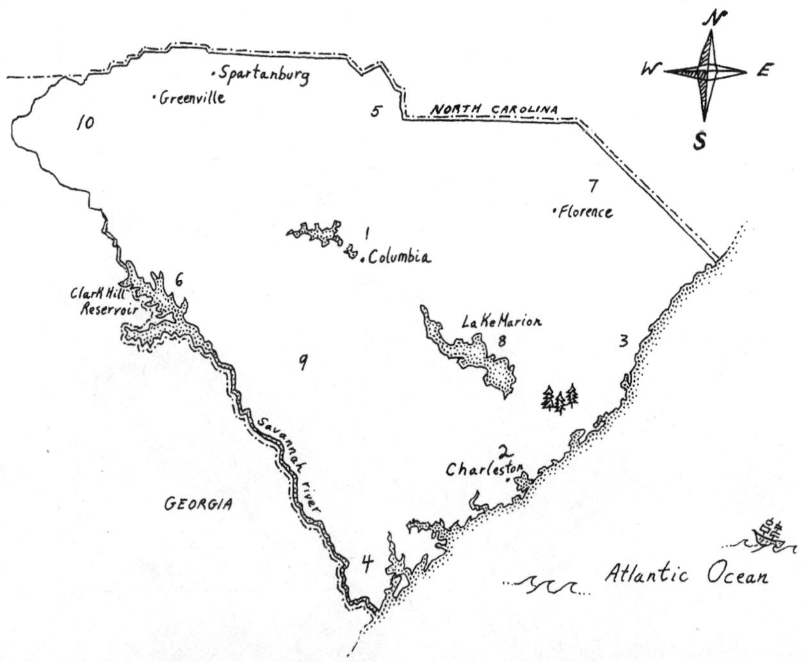

South Carolina Country Roads
(Figures correspond with chapter numbers.)

Contents

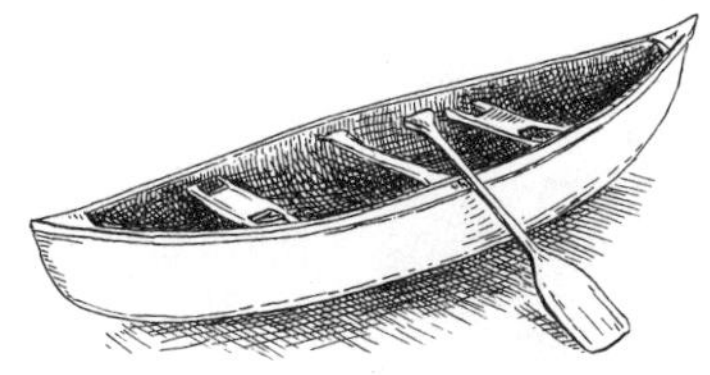

Acknowledgments

Special thanks are due to these special folks who acted as guides during the research phase of this book: Mary Beth Poston—Lowcountry; Brian Stevens—Point Historic Tours; Marilyn Thompson—Santee Cooper Country; Barbie Northrup and Colleen Yates—Sumter Convention and Visitors Bureau; Jane Scarborough and Sandra Varnadore—Olde English District; Tim Todd—Upcountry; Paulette Mims—Edgefield; Nancy Lindroth—McCormick County; Karen Thompson—Lake Murray Country; Dennis Adams, at the Beaufort County Library; and Wendy Staebler, whose intimate knowledge of Charleston and the Lowcountry is an invaluable resource.

The following planned itineraries for those visits: Amy Blyth, Charleston Trident Convention and Visitors Bureau; Fran Burr, Pee Dee Country; Miriam Atria, Lake Murray Country; and Barbara Ware, Old 96 District. Lou Fontana, Dawn Dawson, and Gwen Thurmond of the South Carolina Division of Tourism helped get us in touch with the regional representatives.

These hospitable innkeepers provided lodging: Mike and Patty Griffey, Abingdon Manor, Latta; Pat Clark, River Inn, Anderson; Judy and Mike Adamick, Southwood Manor, Ridge Spring; Steve and Marianne Harrison, Rhett House, Beaufort; Lawton O'Cain, John Lawton House, Estill; Carol and Buck Rogers, Magnolia House, Sumter; Melba and Jerry Peterson, East Main Guest House, Rock Hill; and Jack Branham, the Greenleaf Inn, Camden.

Introduction

My English and Scotch-Irish ancestors, like the majority of early South Carolinians, first came to this country by way of Pennsylvania, then migrated to Virginia, and finally settled in Camden before the Revolutionary War. In 1830 my great-great-great-grandfather Vincent Bell and six of his eleven sons, including my great-great-grandfather, moved on once again to Alabama, as did many others. The family tie to and fascination with South Carolina, however, has always exerted an inexorable pull. In the mid-1980s my sister Wendy Staebler completed the family circle by moving back to South Carolina. Living next door in Georgia as I do, I'm able to visit South Carolina frequently. This quintessential southern state is characterized by a sweet distillation of sun-kissed beaches, stately plantations, front porches, cotton fields, catfish, whippoorwills, and gracious hospitality.

Stretching from the Atlantic Ocean in the east to the foothills of the Blue Ridge Mountains in the northwest, compact South Carolina—only fortieth in geographic size among the fifty states but twenty-fifth in population—has not only played a major role in U.S. history for its three hundred years of existence, but is today a principal playground for modern tourists.

During antebellum times, South Carolina plantation society was based on romanticism. The coastal enclave between Charleston—considered the cultural capital of the region—and Savannah, Georgia, produced an aristocratic culture that was unique even for the Deep South. The interest in education and the arts, as well as the love of entertainment and gracious living that developed, are still very much in evidence today. It is believed that the first play produced in America was performed at the Dock Street Theater in Charleston in 1736. In Columbia the Town Theater claims to be the oldest continuously performing theater company in the country. Prolific novelist William Gilmore Simms, South Carolina's greatest antebellum literary figure, was instrumental in founding the prestigious *Southern Review* in 1828. Today symphony orchestras, opera and ballet companies, and other cultural institutions and events thrive, not only in the metropolitan areas, but in many small towns as well.

Descendants of slaves maintain several proud communities that speak the musical Gullah dialect, a curious combination of King's English, American English, and an African dialect. One of the prized mementos you can bring home from South Carolina is a sweetgrass basket woven by ladies from these close-knit communities.

Historical preservation is synonymous with South Carolina. Charleston organized the first preservation society in the country in the 1920s, and many other cities and towns quickly followed. The results of their Herculean efforts are on display in Charleston, Aiken, Abbeville, Beaufort, Camden, and elsewhere around the state.

South Carolina is not as geographically diverse as some of its southern neighbors, and early residents of the state began referring to the three significant regions as the Lowcountry, which is along the coast, the Upcountry, which is in the northern mountains, and the piedmont or the midlands, which includes everything else. Two-thirds of South Carolina is covered by the Atlantic coastal plain, a lowland that rises gradually from southeast to northwest. This area, locally known as the Lowcountry, includes a coastline of 187 miles. If the wide bays and inlets were also measured, the coastline would actually amount to 2,876 miles. The outer coastal plain, which contains some swamps, extends fifty to seventy miles inland.

Rolling, hilly terrain characterizes the inner coastal plain. The sand hills mark the western edge of the plain and indicate that the Atlantic Ocean once reached this far inland. Charleston is the major city in the Atlantic coastal plain, but surprisingly the plain extends inland to include Cheraw, Columbia, Florence, and Sumter.

Occupying a very narrow band in the extreme northwestern corner of the state is the Blue Ridge, part of the Appalachian Mountain chain. Known as the Upcountry, this forested area is characterized by peaks that reach up to 3,554 feet. The Upcountry has only two cities; the remainder of the region is made up of small towns such as Clemson, Walhalla, Pickens, and Westminster.

Much of the rest of South Carolina is in the piedmont plateau—an area marked on its eastern edge by the fall line where rivers tumble from the highlands to the lowlands. The piedmont is distinguished by land that varies in elevation from four hundred to fourteen hundred feet. The swift-flowing rivers are a major source of hydroelectric power and have helped make the region important for manufacturing. Cities include Columbia, Aiken, Camden, North Augusta, and Sumter.

The three principal regions contain plenty of natural attractions and outdoor recreational activities. The coast and the area of bays, inlets, and estuaries that empty into the ocean provide all types of water sports from boating to scuba diving. Gentle rolling hills in the pleasant midlands are perfect for biking, golf, and hiking, while inland lakes offer acres of water on which to fish or boat. The rugged Upcountry provides the challenges of wilderness backpacking and whitewater rafting.

South Carolina is blessed with a moderate climate. Summers can be hot, however, in the Lowcountry. More than one hundred years ago, planters began the tradition of summering on one of the barrier islands where they were cooled by the sea breezes or in the Upcountry where higher elevations provided some relief from the heat. The upcountry may even experience a dusting of snow in the winter. In the last century, wealthy northerners discovered that the areas around Aiken and Camden were ideal wintering spots for their thoroughbred and standardbred horses. Winter colonies based on raising, training, and racing horses developed and persist today. Winter "cottages" that may run to ninety rooms attest to the area's popularity with the horse set.

The Lowcountry boasts a cuisine all its own. Traditional Lowcountry fare includes red rice and beans, she-crab soup, gumbos, and stews, but the Lowcountry Boil consisting of shrimp, smoked sausage, ears of corn, beer, and seafood seasoning is world-renowned.

Throughout the year in every area of the state, a ceaseless whirl of activities gives you little time for quiet meditation. The state's premier event is Charleston's performing arts festival, Spoleto USA; however, myriad other festivals range from the frivolous to the sublime.

One of the best features of South Carolina is its small size—it's only a half-day's drive from the ocean's edge through the pleasant midlands to the Blue Ridge Mountains.

A Brief History

Although South Carolina's human history stretches back as far as ten thousand years, the period of recorded history begins less than thirty years after Columbus discovered the Americas. Spanish explorers sailed along the coast as early as 1514. An attempt in 1526 to establish a settlement on Winyah Bay near present-day Georgetown was doomed to failure because of a severe winter, Indian attacks, and disease. In 1540 Hernando De Soto explored the central part of the state and made peaceful contact with the Native Americans.

Conflict with France developed in 1562 when a group of French Huguenots established a colony on Parris Island near present-day Beaufort. When Jean Ribaut, founder of the settlement, returned to France for reinforcements and supplies, his remaining soldiers revolted and set sail for home. Their harrowing voyage finally ended when an English ship rescued the ragtag band.

Relieved to be rid of the French interlopers, the Spanish reinforced their hold on the region by building Fort San Felipe on Parris Island in 1566. They made Santa Elena, the settlement there, capital of the Florida Province. Attacked by Native Americans in 1576, Santa Elena was abandoned, but another fort was built the following year.

The next threat to Spanish dominance was posed by the English ten years later. After Sir Francis Drake destroyed St. Augustine, the Spanish were forced to mass all their strength in Florida. What is now South Carolina reverted to Native Americans for almost one hundred years.

King Charles II of England gave land in the region to eight English noblemen to create a colony. They established the first permanent European settlement at Albemarle Point in the Ashley River in 1670. Their colony set the tone for settlement in South Carolina for the next two hundred years. Indigo and rice plantations were formed, and Barbadians were imported to work them; thus South Carolina resembled the West Indian plantation economy more closely than any of the other North American colonies. In 1680 the English moved across the Ashley to the present site of Charleston. By 1708 the majority of the non-native inhabitants were African-American slaves. Native Americans, who were ravaged by the white men's diseases, could no longer significantly threaten the colony after 1715. In 1719 the colonists revolted against the noble proprietors who sold them their interests, and South Carolina became a royal province.

The success of the rice and indigo crops made the plantation owners the wealthiest men in North America. At the same time, white Protestants from Europe or from Pennsylvania, North Carolina, and Virginia were encouraged to settle the interior central and Upcountry regions. During this brief time period, whites were actually in the majority of the state's population. These German, Scotch-Irish, and Welsh settlers were different in both inclination and background from the tidewater planters. The majority of the new settlers farmed small pieces of property and weren't able to wrest control of the government from the landed aristocracy of the Lowcountry.

Whether rich or poor, however, most South Carolinians were staunch supporters of local rights. As such, they were in the forefront of resistance to the Stamp Act in 1765 and took an active role when difficulties with England escalated into the war for American independence. The initial overt act of the war involved the seizing of British property by American forces at Fort Charlotte in McCormick County in 1775. Repulsing the British fleet in 1776 at the palmetto-log Fort Moultrie on Sullivans Island near Charleston was the first decisive colonial victory involving land and naval forces. Charleston merchant Henry Laurens served as the president of the Continental Congress in 1777 and 1778. During the course of the Revolutionary War, more than two hundred battles and skirmishes took place on South Carolina soil—more than in any other state. Unfortunately, many of these conflicts occurred between South Carolinians themselves—those who opted for independence versus loyalists to King George. The victories at Kings Mountain in 1780 and at Cowpens in 1781 are considered to be turning points in the war.

In 1788 South Carolina became the eighth state to ratify the U.S. Constitution. Two years later the capital was moved to Columbia, a city created in the midlands specifically for that purpose. South Carolina continued to exert a major influence on regional and national politics. One of the state's most noted statesmen and state's rights advocates was John C. Calhoun, who in the course of his career served as a U.S. senator, secretary of war, and twice as vice president.

South Carolina was preeminent among the states in resisting the abolition of slavery and in supporting state's rights. As such, it is no surprise that South Carolina passed the Ordinance of Secession on December 20, 1860, as the first state to leave the Union. The following April, the first shots of the Civil War were fired at Fort Sumter, which surrendered to the Confederacy two days later. Although Union troops occupied the sea islands near Beaufort throughout the war and successfully barricaded the Charleston harbor, few military engagements occurred within the state until the spring of 1865 when General William Tecumseh Sherman marched north, fresh from his occupation of Savannah, Georgia. Columbia suffered the most devastating effects of his scorched-earth policy.

Immediately following the Civil War, South Carolina was occupied by Federal troops who remained until 1877. The economy was in ruins and poverty marked the state for generations. African-Americans played a prominent role in state government during Reconstruction, but the transition from a slave state to a free society was difficult, and corruption by carpetbaggers and scalawags left bad feelings that exist to this day. Return to a white-dominated government and disenfranchisement of blacks occurred in 1876 with the election of former Confederate General Wade Hampton III.

Rapid expansion of the textile industry in the 1880s and 1890s began the state's recovery. That industry, however, was still heavily dependent on the production of cotton, and the devastation wreaked by the notorious boll weevil gave the Great Depression a head start in South Carolina. It really wasn't until World War II that South Carolina began to pull itself out of the depths to which it had sunk. The war brought an expansion of military bases and, in the half century since then, domestic and foreign investment in manufacturing has revitalized the state and hastened the migration of residents from rural to urban areas.

South Carolina celebrated its tricentennial in 1970. Today, at more than 325 years of age, inclusion in the Sun Belt states coupled with plentiful natural attractions has made South Carolina preeminent in tourism—its number two industry.

Using This Guide

The South Carolina Division of Tourism has divided the state into ten regions, each based on similar typography, characteristics, historic significance, and other factors. We have devised a driving tour in each of these regions. Each begins or ends so that you can conveniently combine trips in other areas to make a longer vacation. Most of the tours can be comfortably accomplished in a long weekend, but a few of the regions have so much to offer, you'll need to allot a longer time to visit them, skip some of the attractions, or make multiple trips. Each attraction is listed with its address and telephone number, and we've included special lodgings, restaurants, and shops where possible. Chain motels and hotels can be found everywhere, so the overnight accommodations we recommend are primarily bed and breakfasts and intimate inns, as well as resorts and rustic cabins. In addition, we tell you about just a few of the major festivals in each area.

A mild climate and little difference in elevation make packing for a trip to South Carolina a cinch. Winter weather is almost nonexistent. Summers are hot, but are moderated by sea breezes along the coast, and nights may be cool in the higher reaches of the Upcountry, so you may need a sweater or jacket for evenings in those areas. South Carolinians dress casually, but you will probably want to pack one dressier outfit for upscale restaurants and resorts or for a cultural performance. Whether you're planning on long days of strolling through Charleston's historic district or strenuous hiking in the Upcountry, pack sturdy walking shoes. No matter where your destination, don't forget sunscreen, sunglasses, insect repellent, and an umbrella. Many hotels and resorts have indoor pools, so bring a bathing suit even in winter.

We do not give admission costs or hours of operation because they are so changeable. Major attractions are usually open daily, but the museums in small towns are often open only a few days a week or even a few days a month. Also, be aware that in the Upcountry, some attractions are closed during the winter season. It's always best to call ahead when planning your trip if your heart is set on seeing a particular attraction.

Sometimes more than one town or attraction claims to be the *first*, *oldest*, *biggest*, *smallest*, or other designation. We've tried to indicate that there may be room for dispute by saying that it is *claimed*, *believed*, *reported*, or *thought* to be whatever the designation is.

At the end of each chapter, we've listed the primary contacts with tourism organizations or chambers of commerce that might be able to answer questions that we haven't covered or which can give you up-to-the-minute information and schedules of events. In addition, for general information, you can contact the South Carolina Division of Tourism, P.O. Box 71, Columbia 29202, 803-734-0122.

Please note: The information in this guide was correct as of *January 31, 1998*. We recommend, however, that you call establishments before traveling to obtain the most current details.

1

Capital City/ Lake Murray Country

Columbia, a dynamic Sun Belt metropolis with a momentous past, is not only the seat of South Carolina's government, but the nucleus of the state's arts, education, and culture, as well as the gateway to the central heartland's small towns, Lake Murray, and numerous recreational opportunities.

In 1786 South Carolina's legislature decided to move the capital from Charleston to a more centrally located site in the midlands near the confluence of the Saluda and Broad rivers, but no city existed for such a move. The community of Columbia that was created became one of the first planned communities in the country. It took until 1790 for the first session of the General Assembly to meet in Columbia. By the 1820s, renowned architect Robert Mills, who later created the Washington Monument, was actively designing Columbia's beautiful courthouses, public buildings, residences, and canals. The Columbia Canal, which linked Columbia to Charleston, the sea, and the world, brought prosperity to the heartland by propagating numerous mills along the Broad River. By the Civil War, Columbia was a flourishing city. Although the city escaped action throughout most of the Civil War, in February of 1865, just two months before the war's end, Union General William Tecumseh Sherman's army burned Columbia practically back to the ground on its way north from Savannah. However, the city recovered quickly during Reconstruction and keeps on growing.

Begin your visit to the gracious southern city at the Columbia Metropolitan Visitors Center, 1012 Gervais Street (803-254-0479 or 800-264-4884), where you can see the award-winning orientation film *The Spirit of Columbia* and then pick up brochures about attractions, get recommendations on places to stay or eat, and purchase Columbia souvenirs. Brochures for walking/driving tours are also available from the Historic Columbia Foundation, 1601 Richland Street (803-252-7742). Columbia is an extremely easy city to tour on foot, because the historic district is broken down into three tours of one mile or less each.

Spend a leisurely day or two visiting Columbia's historic homes, buildings, and museums. You can tour the homes on your own or take a guided tour with Columbia Historic Homes Tour, operated by the Richland County Historic Preservation Commission (803-252-1770). Tours depart from the gift shop in the East Flanker of the Robert Mills Historic Home and Park, 1616 Blanding Street (803-252-1770). Before departing on a tour of the city, take in the Robert Mills house itself. Mills, one of early America's most noted architects, was the first to be named Federal Architect of the United States. His tenure as Federal Architect lasted through the administrations of seven presidents. Mills designed and built this Federal-Greek Revival brick house in 1823 for prominent Columbia merchant Ainsley Hall. Sadly, Hall never lived in the house; he died before it was completed, and his widow was forced to sell it. Over the years the house served as the Columbia Theological Seminary and the Columbia Bible College. When it became public knowledge that the house was going to be demolished, the women of Columbia formed the Historic Columbia Foundation and worked tirelessly to raise $350,000 to save it.

Set in a finely manicured park with a boxwood maze, the magnificent house features Mills's trademark Ionic portico, symmetrical columns and doorways, Venetian windows, twin parlors, ceiling ornamentation, and curved walls. Mills's dedication to symmetry sometimes ran to the eccentric. Look for the doors that don't go anywhere, but which were simply included to match a functional door. In complete contrast to the grand staircases of the day, Mills built simple stairways enclosed between brick walls and closed off by a door for fire safety. Four of the marble fireplaces are from other Mills buildings, and the re-created moldings and medallions on the fifteen-foot ceilings are copies of ones he did elsewhere. The museum house is sumptuously furnished with early-nineteenth-century English, Regency, French Empire, and American Federal antiques of the period 1820 to 1840.

On the first floor you'll tour the Morning Room (so named because it was on the east side of the house and received the morning light), a small parlor used as a game room, the formal dining room, and two stunning matching parlors, one used as a music room. Upstairs are several bedrooms, a trunk room, and the children's room, which spills over with toys that span the nineteenth century. In contrast, the ground floor was the working heart of the house. Ceilings are lower to trap heat and keep it warmer in the winter while the floors are brick to help keep it cool in the summer. Here you'll see the cozy, inviting family dining room, the warming kitchen, and the pantry, as well as many household implements. Take a few minutes to explore the formal boxwood garden.

The Historic Columbia Foundation also owns and operates three other historic homes that you can tour: the

Hampton-Preston Mansion, located directly across the street from the Robert Mills House; the Woodrow Wilson Boyhood Home; and the Mann-Simons Cottage. Allow at least a half day to see all four houses; you could easily spend an entire day to do them justice.

The Hampton-Preston Mansion, 1615 Blanding Street (803-252-1770), was the imposing town home of Confederate General Wade Hampton III, who later went on to become governor of South Carolina. The house, originally constructed in 1818 for Ainsley Hall, who had the Robert Mills House built, was bought by Wade Hampton I, once the wealthiest man in the United States with many plantations in South Carolina and Louisiana. During the next generation, his son Wade Hampton II lived among the thirteen thousand acres and private race courses at Millwood Plantation, while his daughter Caroline Hampton Preston lived in the townhouse. Wade Hampton III, who next lived in the house, raised the famous Hampton's Legion during the Civil War and his sisters helped provision it. Two of Hampton's female cousins were renowned during the Civil War: Sarah Hampton Preston, because she is reputed to have lost more beaux in the war than any other young lady, and Sally Buchanan "Buck" Preston, who is reputed to have been the most beautiful girl in America and whose hand was actively pursued by Confederate General John Bell Hood. The mansion was occupied by Union officers in 1865 as the headquarters of General John A. Logan and was thus spared destruction when Columbia was burned.

After serving as everything from a boarding house to the College for Women and Chicora College for Women, the house has been restored to its former grandeur. Unfortunately, Hampton's Millwood Plantation, Gaynor's Ferry Road (803-252-7742), did not survive the Civil War. Today all that remains are the graceful columns. Tours of the ruins are conducted, by reservation only, the last Sunday of the month from March through November.

Originally brick, Hampton-Preston House was stuccoed in the 1840s and scored to resemble stone. Inside, you'll be awed by the eighteen-foot ceilings and the sweeping spiral staircase. The mansion is lavishly furnished in pieces appropriate to the period 1835–55, as well as with some original family pieces. Among the Hall/Hampton/Preston family memorabilia, you'll see Ainsley Hall's top hat and carrying case, a collection of silver won in horse races, the riding crop given to Sally Buchanan Preston by Napoleon III, and a dress that belonged to Civil War diarist Mary Boykin Chestnut, who stayed for a period at the house when she was ill.

Woodrow Wilson's Boyhood Home, 1705 Hampton Street (803-252-1770), was the home of the future president from 1870 to 1874 when his father was teaching at the Columbia Theological Seminary as well as serving as the pastor of the First Presbyterian Church. Dr. Wilson's two salaries and an inheritance from his wife's brother made it possible for the family to design and build the spacious Victorian house and furnish it in a manner not within the reach of most teacher/ministers. Among the architectural details of special note are arched windows and doorways, elaborate latticework, bay windows, original slate mantels that are faux marbleized, and original gas lighting fixtures. Some family furniture is displayed, including the rosewood bed in which Wilson was born in Staunton, Virginia, in 1856; a desk Wilson used when he was governor of New Jersey; a dresser and sideboard of his mother's; a four-volume Bible that was a gift to Wilson's mother from his father; and several impressive Delft pieces. Beautiful mature magnolias were planted around the house by Wilson's mother more than one hundred years ago, and the gardens have been restored to resemble those she created.

A tribute to early African-Americans in Columbia, the Mann-Simons Cottage, 1403 Richland Street (803-252-1770), a raised cottage built at the beginning of the nineteenth century, became the home of Celia Mann, a freed slave. Mann was born into slavery in 1799, but later she bought her own freedom and walked from Charleston to Columbia to start a new life. She chose the Columbia of 1850 because it was a haven for free blacks, with 6 percent of its population free black. For Mann, part of beginning a new life included purchasing the cottage. A midwife by profession, Mann assisted at the births of many Columbia citizens both black and white. In addition, she played an important role in the formation of Calvary Baptist Church, allowing the congregation to meet in the basement of her home. Her descendants were seamstresses, laundresses, tailors, and grocers, and the house remained in the family until 1970 when the last descendant, Mrs. Bernice Robinson Connors, sold it to the Columbia Housing Authority. Listed on the National Register of Historic Places, the house now serves as the Museum of African-American Culture. Note the original carved front door, the mismatched upper-story dormers, and the extremely wide ceiling and wall boards in the midwife room. Furnished as would have been typical of a middle-class family's home, one room represents a sitting room, another the master bedroom, and another a sewing room. A display of artifacts discovered during archaeological digs on the property is exhibited in the basement, which served as the family dining room and kitchen.

Also from the Historic Columbia Foundation, you can pick up a brochure for the Arsenal Hill District Self-Guided Tour. With the exception of the Governor's Mansion, the buildings are not open to the public. Although the Arsenal Hill area was originally an eroded clay hillside with springs at the bottom, because of its elevation and its superb views, this neighborhood has always been a desirable place to live in Columbia. In addition, it was the site of early industrial and public-works projects. The city's first waterworks was developed here in the 1820s by Abram Blanding. Water was pumped from the springs at the bottom of the hill up to a holding tank at the top from which it was distributed throughout the city in cast-iron pipes.

Two of the earliest homes on the hill were the Caldwell-Boylston House, Richland Street, Governor's Green, built in 1825 by John Caldwell, a cotton broker and banker, and the Kenner House, Calhoun Street, owned by his sister, Sarah Caldwell Kenner. A gift shop is operated in the basement of the Caldwell-Boylston House. During the early 1840s Algernon Sidney Johnston, a publisher and city council member, developed a plan to beautify the hillside and supervised the building of a park, later named Finley Park (803-733-8331), that was a shady retreat with tall trees, walking paths, reflecting pools, benches, and bandstands. Today, bounded by Laurel, Taylor, Gadsden, and Assembly Streets, the park is an oasis of spectacular fountains, waterfalls, and pools. A concert series is performed in the park during the summer.

High atop the hill, the Arsenal Academy was founded in 1842 as a prep school for the Citadel in Charleston. Together, the two schools made up the South Carolina Military College, founded to prevent slave insurrection. A building constructed in 1855 as an officers' barracks was the only academy structure that survived destruction by the Union army in 1865. It was designated as the official Governor's Mansion, 800 Richland Street, Governor's Green (803-737-1710), in 1865 and after extensive renovation was occupied in 1870. From 1870 to 1878, it was the governor's choice whether or not to live there, but since 1879 the mansion has been continuously occupied by the governors of South Carolina and is open for tours. Also constructed in 1855, the Lace House, Richland Street, Governor's Green, is so named because of the ornate ironwork on the two-story porches. Although the house served over the years as a private home, a boarding house, and the state headquarters of the South Carolina Women's Christian Temperance Union, it is now used as a guest house for the Governor's Mansion and is not open to the public. Together, the Governor's Mansion, the Caldwell-Boylston House, and the Lace House make up the nine-acre Governor's Green complex.

Close by, the Palmetto Armory, Laurel Street, was built in 1850 and served as the Palmetto Ironworks during the Civil War when it produced great quantities of firearms and edged weapons. The muskets, rifles, and pistols produced there bore a palmetto-tree insignia. Rounding out the Arsenal Hill District is St. Peter's Roman Catholic Church, Taylor Street, the first Catholic Church in Columbia. The present structure dates from 1908.

Significant Columbia homes you can drive by include the Friday-Fields Cottage, 1830 Henderson Street, which typifies the "Columbia Cottage" style—full-brick raised basement, first floor, and a half-story under the roof; the 1820 DeBruhl-Marshall House, 1401 Laurel Street, which resembles the Robert Mills House although the architect is unknown; the 1874 Guignard House, 1534 Blanding Street, home of Jane Guignard, Columbia's first female doctor; the 1838 Crawford Clarkson House, 1502 Blanding Street, noted for its unusual pair of shelved glass columns once used to display rare plants; and the 1840 Lorick House, 1727 Hampton Street, a Gothic Revival noted for its gingerbread trim, window cornices, and ornate chimneys. While you're driving around, be sure to drive by Tunnelvision, Taylor and Marion Streets, an optical-illusion painting of a tunnel on the side of the Federal Land Bank Building. In Memorial Park, at Hampton and Gadsden Streets, is a Vietnam Memorial, the largest monument of its type outside Washington, D.C. The towering, five-sided pylon is carved in frieze motifs portraying contributions by each branch of the armed services. Two freestanding granite walls flanking the pylon are engraved with the names of South Carolinians who were killed or missing in action in Vietnam. Cruise by the former Big Apple Night Club, 1000 Hampton Street, originally built as a synagogue in 1916, but famous as the African-American night club where the "Big Apple" national dance craze got started during the 1930s and where the "Carolina Shag" got its start. Unfortunately, it is open only for special events.

In one fell swoop, you can see all that South Carolina was, is, and can be, but be sure to allow at least half a day to visit the South Carolina Museum, 301 Gervais Street (803-737-4921), where art, cultural history, natural history, science, and technology are covered at the state's largest repository. Containing one of the most important assemblages in the Southeast, the museum is housed in a renovated 1896 textile mill that was the first one in the world to be electrified. This is one museum that lives up to its claim that it has something for everyone. Exhibits include *Space Science*, artifacts used by South Carolina's five astronauts; *Native Americans*; *Civil War Arms*, which contains muskets, swords, sidearms, a cannon used in a futile attempt to protect Columbia from Sherman's army, and a replica of the Civil War submarine *Hundley*; contributions of slaves and their descendants; and several of the state's ecosystems where sound effects lend an air of authenticity to several re-created habitats such as a beach, salt marsh, backyard, and mountain cove. Transportation is traced from the dugout canoe through the railroad, horse and carriage, car, and airplane to the spaceship, but in a display depicting the state's love affair with the automobile, the stars of the exhibit include a 1904 Oldsmobile, a 1922 Anderson, and a 1934 Rolls Royce. Highlights of the exhibit on the state's prehistoric past are a life-size replica of a mastodon and a prehistoric giant white shark that is forty-three feet long and weighs six thousand pounds. Other exhibits explore the contributions made to South Carolina by agriculture and the textile, mining, shrimping, communications, and energy industries. Several short films are interspersed throughout the museum. Changing art exhibits rotate during the year.

Don't neglect Columbia's many other museums. Next take in the Confederate Relic Room and Museum, 920 Sumter Street on the campus of the University of South Carolina (803-734-9813). Although displays span the period from the Revolutionary War to the space age, emphasis is on the Civil War era. Exhibits include clothing, flags, newspapers, photographs, money, and other artifacts.

While you're on the campus, visit the McKissick Museum of the University of South Carolina, USC Horseshoe, Sumter Street (803-777-7251), actually a collection of museums housing art exhibits, science displays, regional history, geologic and gemstone displays including *Fluorescent Minerals and Gemstones*, and statesman Bernard Baruch's silver collection. The Historic Horseshoe area of USC is the original campus of South Carolina College, which began in 1801. The buildings, which have been restored to their earliest appearance, served as hospitals for both sides during the Civil War.

You can learn more about the history of the university at the University of South Carolina Visitor Center, 937 Assembly (803-777-0169), which also displays a variety of art created by students in the art department.

An eclectic collection that ranges from contemporary art to old masters fills the Columbia Museum of Art, located in a 1907 mansion at Senate and Bull Streets (803-799-2810). The museum's Kress Collection is one of the largest accumulations of Baroque and Renaissance art in the Southeast. The museum also contains a children's gallery. Live demonstrations and musical light shows are given at the museum's adjacent Gibbes Planetarium on weekends.

The historic State House, Main and Gervais Streets (803-734-2430), was still under construction as the Civil War wound down. It survived General Sherman's destructive march with minimal damage. Notice the bronze stars that identify pockmarks from Union cannonballs. Tours of the homes of the General Assembly members and the governor's office are available, and you can watch the proceedings of the state legislature from the brass-railed visitors' galleries.

Wander around the antique shops, trendy boutiques, artists' studios, and galleries of the Congaree Vista District/West Gervais Street Historic District, a converted warehouse area that has become the heart of the arts and antiques community in Columbia, as well as home to numerous restaurants and nightspots. Trustus Theatre, 520 Lady Street (803-254-9732), offers a regular show nightly and a Friday late-night happening. Columbia Brewing Company, 931B Senate Street (803-254-2739), really three nightclubs in one, features country, beach, and rhythm-and-blues music.

Riverfront Park and Historic Columbia Canal, Laurel Street (no phone), at the city's original 1906 waterworks and hydroelectric plant, is a tranquil setting for strolling, cycling, and jogging.

Don't leave town without stopping by the South Carolina Criminal Justice Hall of Fame, 5400 Broad River Road (803-896-8199), at the Criminal Justice Academy. Exhibits at the museum, created to honor law officers who died in the line of duty, detail the history of law enforcement. One highlight is the Melvin Purvis gun display—Purvis was the FBI agent who collared infamous criminal John Dillinger. Other exhibits include an antique moonshine still, a 1950s patrol car, and memorials to those officers killed.

Ranked among the top ten zoos in the country, Riverbanks Zoo, off I-126 at the Greystone Riverbanks Exit (803-779-8717), replicates microcosmic rainforest, desert, undersea, and southern farm environments for its two thousand animals. Water and light give the illusion of privacy and wild, unlimited space. Special programs include feeding the sea lions, experiencing a tropical rainstorm in the bird house, and scuba-diving demonstrations in the aquarium/reptile complex. Riverbanks Farm is a working farm with sheep, pigs, cows, and horses where you can watch milking demonstrations each morning.

Columbia abounds in places to stay. Claussen's Inn, 2003 Greene Street (803-765-0440 or 800-622-3382), occupies the historic 1928 Claussen's Bakery building located in the heart of the Five Points area near the University of South Carolina and the State House. Carefully preserved architectural features blend with an expansive vaulted skylight and terra-cotta tiles in a two-story atrium centered by a tinkling fountain to create an airy indoor courtyard. Each spacious guest room features a four-poster or iron-and-brass bed, traditional furnishings, and rich colors to create its own unique character. Some rooms boast hardwood floors and loft areas. Modern amenities include an outdoor Jacuzzi, complimentary continental breakfast, nightly turn-down service with chocolates and brandy, and complimentary wine and sherry served in the lobby. Chestnut Cottage Bed and Breakfast, 1718 Hampton Street (803-256-1718), is an 1850 Federal-style cottage that served as the Civil War home of Confederate General James Chestnut and his wife Mary Boykin Chestnut. One of the most historically significant homes in Columbia, the house was visited by Jefferson Davis in 1864, and he gave a speech from the front steps. A sofa and chair in the parlor belonged to the Chestnuts. Of the four rooms and one suite, naturally two are named after the Chestnuts: Mary's room features a queen-size canopied bed and a soft feminine touch, while James's room is tastefully decorated with a queen-size cannonball bed and Civil War memorabilia. Both the President Jefferson Davis Room and the Carriage House Bridal Suite feature whirlpool baths. Among the amenities are nightly turn-down service, luxurious robes, afternoon libations and refreshments, and a hearty breakfast. Tours of the house for nonguests are given on Friday afternoons at 2:00 P.M. with prior arrangements. So naturally does the Victorian Richland Street Bed and Breakfast, 1425 Richland Street (803-779-7001), fit in with its surroundings in the downtown historic area, including its neighbor the Mann-Simons Cottage, that you'd never guess that it is a newly built home specifically designed to serve as a bed and breakfast. The six guest rooms and bridal suite all feature private baths and king- or queen-size beds; two boast whirlpool baths. Guests are pampered with a deluxe continental breakfast and afternoon refreshments.

Among Columbia's numerous annual special events are: the March Carolina Craftsmen's Spring Classic, which features hundreds of craftspeople who set up shop at the State Fairgrounds (803-799-3387); April's Riverfest, an extravaganza of games, a fishing tournament, food, arts and crafts, a 5K run and walk, and a kayak classic (803-733-6210); Mayfest, the capital city's largest festival with national recording artists, arts and crafts, southern-food plaza, children's fun fair, and more (803-343-8750); from June through August, the Summer Concert Series at Finley Park, a thirteen-week series featuring jazz, country, rhythm-and-blues, and bluegrass (803-343-8750); early through mid-October, the South Carolina State Fair, which offers spectacular grandstand entertainment, agricultural exhibits, and a thrilling midway (803-799-3387); December's Carolina Carillon, the state's premier holiday parade (803-779-8203), and The Lights Before Christmas, when Riverbanks Zoo becomes a winter wonderland of 200,000 holiday lights (803-779-8717).

A few outstanding places to eat in Columbia include: Blue Marlin, 1200 Lincoln Street (803-799-3838), which features fresh seafood and Lowcountry specialties; Gourmet Shop, 724 Saluda Avenue (803-799-3705), a specialty food and wine store and cafe with indoor and outdoor seating; Motor Supply Co. Bistro, 920 Gervais Street (803-256-6687), which changes its menu every day, but features regional cuisine; Beulah's Bar and Grill, 902-C Gervais Street (803-779-4655), a casual restaurant and lounge in the Congaree Vista district; and California Dreaming, 401 South Main Street (803-254-6767), located in a gorgeously restored turn-of-the-century railroad depot.

For your evening entertainment, Columbia boasts eight theater groups including the Town Theatre, 1012 Sumter Street (803-799-2510). The oldest continuing community theater in the country, it has presented performances since 1924. The Capital City Bombers, 301 South Assembly Street (803-254-HITS), the minor league affiliate of the New York Mets, play at Capital City Stadium during the baseball season.

Take I-20 north of Columbia to Jackson Boulevard to visit Fort Jackson (803-751-7419), named for President Andrew Jackson, who was a South Carolina native. Fort Jackson is the U.S. Army's largest and most active initial-entry training facility, processing 50 percent of the men and women who enter the service each year. The fort instructs an average of sixty-two thousand soldiers in basic combat and advanced individual training annually. Exhibits in the fort's museum cover two hundred years of military history with emphasis on Fort Jackson's role in training and educating new American soldiers. Naturally, one display recounts the significant events in Jackson's life. Take US 1 to the southern outskirts of Columbia to Cayce, which sits on the site of Fort Granby, one of the earliest inland villages in South Carolina and the scene of two Revolutionary War battles. Make an appointment in advance to visit the Cayce Historical Museum, 1800 Twelfth Street Extension (803-796-9020, ext. 3030), housed in a replica of the old Cayce House, a mid-eighteenth-century trading post. The museum interprets the architectural, social, and cultural heritage of Cayce, as well as Old Saxe Gotha, Granby, and West Columbia with emphasis on Indian agricultural development, colonial trade, and transportation. Also on the grounds are an authentic kitchen house, smokehouse, dairy, and several railroad cars.

Take State 48 southeast of Columbia to Congaree Swamp National Monument (803-776-4396), a black-water wonderland known for its biological diversity and record-size trees. The park features self-guided canoe trails as well as a three-quarter-mile boardwalk for the disabled and eighteen miles of hiking trails. The last significant tract of old-growth, bottomland hardwood forest in the country, the monument occupies more than 22,000 acres.

Return to Columbia and take US 378 west to Lexington, founded in 1785 and named for the first battle of the Revolutionary War. Visit the Lexington County Museum Complex, Fox Street and US 378 (803-359-8369), which depicts pre–Civil War life in Lexington County through several antebellum buildings, including cabins, homes, a post office, and a barn housing decorative arts of the period, tools of self-sufficiency, handmade furniture, textiles, and toys.

Lexington's Old Mill, 711 East Main Street (803-356-6931), which produced mattress ticking and red fabric for prison uniforms at the turn of the century, now houses a festive marketplace, family-oriented restaurants, shopping, and the Patchwork Players, a nationally known dance theater group.

West of Columbia between I-26 and US 378 is Lake Murray, a fifty-thousand-acre impoundment of the Saluda River. Forty-one miles long and fourteen miles wide, the lake offers 525 miles of shoreline and all kinds of water sports. At the time of its construction in 1927, the dam was the largest earthen dam in cubical content for power purposes in the world. You can take a two-hour boat tour of the lake aboard the *Southern Patriot* (803-781-0399). Dreher Island State Park, State 571 (803-364-3530), has two- and three-bedroom fully-equipped villas on the shoreline, as well as a boat dock, store/tackle shop, fuel, and boat ramps.

From Lake Murray, either take State 391 or State 194 and US 78 to Batesburg, then turn west on US 1 to Ridge Spring, a sleepy southern country town noted for its fox hunts. South-

wood Manor B & B, 100 East Main Street (803-685-5100), is a 1918 Georgian plantation house surrounded by cotton fields and pecan groves. Peacocks wander freely on the grounds, while a horse or two nibbles beyond the paddock. In fact, should you own your own horse, you can bring it along, board it at the manor, and ride in the open spaces surrounding the farm. The manor boasts large comfortable rooms with four-poster beds and gas-log fireplaces, as well as a tennis court and an oversized swimming pool. Owner Mike, an aviation buff, can often be seen tinkering with his replica open-cockpit biplane, which he flies from the manor's two-thousand-foot grass airstrip. In her spare time, co-owner Judy creates lovely watercolors. These grace the house and are for sale.

Truly the heart of the state, Capital City/Lake Murray Country guarantees you numerous historical sites, architectural treasures, magnificent museums, cozy bed and breakfasts, great food, and boundless outdoor activities. This driving tour can be easily combined with all the tours in this book with the exception of the three coastal regions, although South Carolina's small size makes any combination possible.

For More Information

Capital City/Columbia Metropolitan Convention and Visitors Bureau, 1200 Main Street, Columbia 29202. 803-254-0479 or 800-264-4884.

Columbia Metropolitan Visitors Center, 1012 Gervais Street, Columbia 29201. 803-254-0479, ext. 1, or 800-264-4884.

Greater Columbia Chamber of Commerce, P.O. Box 1360, Columbia 29202. 803-733-1110.

Lake Murray Tourism and Recreation Association and Lake Murray Country Visitors Center, 2184 North Lake Drive (State 6), Irmo 29063. 803-781-5940 or 800-951-4008.

Lexington Chamber of Commerce, P.O. Box 44, Lexington 29072. 803-359-6113.

2

Historic Charleston and Environs

Although the undisputed dowager duchess of this region is Charleston, there are small towns and historical sights well worth the time of the traveler willing to venture beyond the bounds of the historic and plantation districts. Reams of books and articles have been written about Charleston, one of the most popular tourist destinations in the United States, but we can only give a broad overview with the limited space available here.

To understand South Carolina requires a background into Charleston's history because the state was born here. English colonists settled on the western side of the Ashley River in 1670, but in 1680 relocated to the present site of the city. By 1701 Charles Towne, surrounded by fortified walls for protection against pirates, Indians, Spanish invaders, and wild animals, was the only British walled city in North America. A semicircular half-moon battery projected from the wall and behind it stood the Court of Guard, a council chamber and jail. By the 1760s Charles Towne was a thriving port city in the royal colony of Carolina with a great deal of trade conducted with England and the West Indies as well as other colonial cities. Rice and indigo created an affluent class that made Charleston a cultural hub.

Charleston has survived not only hurricanes and earthquakes, the Revolutionary and Civil Wars, but also the encroachments of modern architecture and an invasion of interlopers known to natives as "people from off" to remain the proud, and unapologetically arrogant, civic aristocrat she is. Over the years, the city has been the scene of numerous and varied historic South Carolina firsts: the first decisive victory during the Revolution, the first regularly scheduled passenger train service, and the initial shots of the Civil War.

Ease into Charleston by starting at the northern or southern ends of this region—we've chosen to begin at the northern border with the Grand Strand region. Take a leisurely drive through McClellanville, located at US 17/701 and State 45. An authentic Spanish-moss-draped fishing village on the Intracoastal Waterway, quiet McClellanville was established centuries ago as a summer retreat by planters who lived along the Santee River. Visitors today enjoy the quaint atmosphere, the docks where the fishing fleet ties up, and the fresh seafood you can buy right off the boat.

In good weather, as you drive south on US 17, you'll pass ladies selling South Carolina's famous sweetgrass baskets from numerous individual stalls. Considered to be one of only three indigenous South Carolina crafts, these beautiful handmade baskets are created by artisans whose skills have been passed down through generation after generation in their families.

On the banks of the Cooper River is Boone Hall Plantation, US 17 (843-884-4371), dating from 1681. Its breathtakingly beautiful three-quarter-mile, live-oak-lined entrance drive to the house is recognizable from the TV miniseries *North and South*. The original magnificent trees were planted in 1743 by Captain Thomas Boone, and it is believed that the grave beside the avenue is his. The plantation received its name from Major John Boone, a member of the first fleet of settlers who arrived from England in 1681. Buildings on the cotton plantation were fashioned on the property and can still be seen in surviving structures. Prior to the Civil War, it took more than one thousand slaves to work the cotton plantation, which was one of the largest in the South. By 1904 Boone Hall Plantation had developed the world's largest pecan groves, acres of which are still productive. Using original bricks, woodwork, and flooring, the present house was constructed in 1936 to replace the seventeenth-century house. The grounds contain beautiful camellia gardens, an original cotton-gin house, and a slave row, one of the few remaining intact in the Southeast. Nine original slave cabins were used by house servants and the plantation's skilled craftsmen. Field slaves lived in clusters elsewhere, and none of those cabins survive. Craftspeople can often be found weaving sweetgrass baskets, such as those that were produced for use in daily plantation work. Each November the Battle of Secessionville is reenacted at the plantation.

Stop in the historic Old Village in Mt. Pleasant, just south of US 17. Founded in 1680, the old village affords as close to the archetype of classic small town southern living as may be found anywhere. A beautiful coastal town just across the Cooper River from downtown Charleston, the village's National Register Historic District consists of antebellum homes, a public park, and a magnificent view of the Charleston harbor. What's more, the village is a short bike ride to some of the area's finest beaches.

In the center of the old village is a historic building that began as a grocery store in 1888. Today it serves as the Guilds Inn, 101 Pitt Street (843-881-0510 or 800-331-0510), a bed and breakfast with two restaurants, Captain Guilds Cafe and Supper at Stacks. Guest rooms are furnished in period reproductions and feature modern amenities such as whirlpool baths. Quaint shops on the tiny main street include Complements, which produces handmade tiles and custom-made runners; an old Rexall Drug Store that still retains its soda fountain; and Tomorrow's Treasures and Antiques. Among the other interesting sites in town are a small Confederate cemetery on Carr Street and the Old Town Hall and Post Office at Banks and Pitt Streets.

Tucked away on quiet Lucas Street, near Shem Creek and just off busy Coleman Boulevard, The Common (843-849-1400) is a series of charming specialty shops in a setting reminiscent of an old-time village square. Among the shops is the Museum on the Common (843-849-9000), dedicated to the people and events that shaped the history of the East Cooper River region. Browse among the permanent and rotating exhibits that trace the history of the area from prehistoric times to the present. The largest display recounts the devastating five hundred minutes of Hurricane Hugo—eight hours that changed the face of the Lowcountry.

Mount Pleasant is noted for its wide variety of restaurants including several small cafes and seafood restaurants located on picturesque Shem Creek, the port for the area's shrimping fleet. Among them are the Village Cafe, 415 Mill Street (843-884-8095), and Slightly Up the Creek, 130 Mill Street (843-884-5005), which bills itself as a Maverick Waterfront Restaurant. A yearly event not to be missed is the Blessing of the Fleet each April. In addition to the parade of boats and the blessing, the festival also includes live entertainment, shrimp-eating contests, and an arts-and-crafts show. Call 843-884-2528 for more information.

The Old Pitt Street Bridge, which used to connect the town with Sullivan's Island, has been converted into an area for walking, fishing, or enjoying the peace and solitude of the marsh and harbor. Take State 703 to Sullivan's Island to see historic Fort Moultrie, West Middle Street (843-883-3123). It was from the original uncompleted palmetto-log fort in 1776 that Colonel William Moultrie and his men drove off a squadron of British warships during the Battle of Sullivan's Island. The third fortification on the site, the current fort was constructed in 1809. Trace the history of the fort through the changes that were made through World War II and see a video documenting the history of the 50th Massachusetts Infantry, a black regiment, and telling the story of Robert Smalls, a slave who captured a Confederate warship and turned it over to the Union fleet. Beyond Sullivan's Island is the Isles of Palms, home of the Wild Dunes Resort (800-845-8880).

Return to US 17 and proceed toward Charleston. Before you get to the bridge, you'll come to Patriots Point Naval and Maritime Museum, 40 Patriots Point Road, off US 17 (843-884-2727), the world's largest naval and maritime museum. A floating museum, the complex contains several ships open for tours: the aircraft carrier USS *Yorktown*, the submarine *Clagmore*, the Coast Guard cutter *Ingham*, and the destroyer *Laffey*. The size of three football fields, the *Yorktown* housed three thousand crewmen. The *Yorktown*, the famous "Fighting Lady" of World War II, was in many historic battles during that war. Her planes inflicted heavy damage on the Japanese at Truk and the Marianas, and she supported American ground troops in the Philippines, at Iwo Jima, and at Okinawa. Later, during the Cold War and Vietnam, she patrolled the western Pacific. She also recovered the crew of *Apollo 8*, the first manned spacecraft to circle the moon. The tour includes the flight deck, hangar deck, and many living and working areas of the ship, such as the hospital, bridge, and ready rooms. Bomber and fighter planes are displayed in the hangar bay where the Congressional Medal of Honor Museum is also located. Eight eras of Medal of Honor history are detailed from the Civil War through Vietnam. Panels list all of the medal recipients to date. Displays and artifacts relating to recipients are on view. The ship's theater regularly shows the Academy Award–winning film *The Fighting Lady*. The World War II submarine *Clagmore* operated in the Atlantic and the Mediterranean throughout her entire career. She patrolled the tense Cuban waters during the missile crisis in 1962. The tour route covers her control room, berthing and messing areas, engine rooms, maneuvering room, and displays of submarine warfare. The destroyer *Laffey* participated in the D-Day landing of Allied troops at Normandy and was then transferred to the Pacific, where she was attacked by five Japanese kamikaze planes and hit by three bombs within one hour off Okinawa. Her crew managed to keep her afloat and shoot down eleven enemy planes during the attack, earning her the appellation "The Ship That Wouldn't Die." After World War II, she served in the Korean War and the Atlantic. You'll see her bridge, battle stations, living quarters, and displays about destroyer activities during the tour. The Coast Guard cutter *Ingham* was one of the most decorated vessels in U.S. service, with eighteen ribbons over her fifty-year career. She took part in thirty-one World War II convoys, six Pacific patrols, and three Vietnam tours. She sank a German U-boat in 1942. In recent years, she tracked illegal boat immigrants and drug-runners. In addition, the park features a scale-model of a Vietnam naval support base showing living conditions and operational areas. Included are a river patrol boat, ammunition bunker, combat information center, gun and observation tower, medivac helicopter, displays, artifacts, and weaponry.

Return to US 17 and cross the Cooper River Bridge to Charleston, the jewel in South Carolina's crown. Let the traveler beware—there is no known antidote to the love-at-first-sight addiction that develops in all who visit this most innately southern of cities, which occupies a tiny peninsula by the sea.

The city has been vigorous in the preservation of its legacy and is best known as a living museum of important architecture. You can explore more than 800 historic buildings as you wander Charleston's cobblestone streets. Barely changed since its founding, the genteel port city boasts 73 pre-Revolutionary structures, 136 from the late eighteenth century, and more than 600 others built prior to 1840. Nor should a visitor overlook the city's intimate brick-walled gardens.

In September 1989 Hurricane Hugo pounded historic Charleston with a fury rarely experienced in this century. Although damage was extensive, most of the proud old buildings withstood the onslaught. Massive repairs were begun immediately and the city scarcely missed a beat in its tourism industry. In fact, Charleston has endured much, but the exquisite city always bounces back—better than ever.

There's a delightful story told about a wealthy matron that exemplifies the reason Charleston is such a magnet for tourists. When asked why she never used her money to travel, she answered, "But my dear, why should I travel when I'm already here?" Charleston has much to offer the visitor depending on the amount of time that can be spent there. If you have only a weekend, you will probably want to stay in the historic district where delightful hotels and bed and breakfasts put you within easy walking distance of sights, restaurants, and entertainment. You could, however, easily spend more than two days in the historic district and another day visiting the plantations on the Ashley River.

Begin your visit with a stop at the Charleston Visitors Information Center (843-853-8000), located at Meeting and Ann Streets in a nineteenth-century railway freight depot. A film, *Forever Charleston*, will introduce you to both the history of the city and the important sites in and around it. Staff members have information on hundreds of shops, restaurants, accommodations, tours, and services.

Located behind the visitors center is a replica of the Best Friend, 456 King Street (843-973-7269), a tribute to America's first passenger train with regularly scheduled service. Dubbed the "Best Friend" by enthusiastic merchants and Upcountry farmers, the train ran 136 miles from Charleston to Hamburg. Its premier run was on Christmas Day, 1830, and only six months later, a boiler explosion killed the train's fireman and engineer and destroyed the locomotive. The museum contains railroad artifacts, and its gift shop offers a variety of railroad merchandise.

Cross Meeting Street to the Charleston Museum, 360 Meeting Street (843-722-2996), which houses an eclectic mixture of exhibits. Begun in 1773, it is America's first and oldest museum. The city's natural history is reflected through exhibits of animal and plant life. Other collections focus on Native Americans, settlers, and African-Americans through clothing, furniture, ceramics, glassware, pewter, silver, games, vehicles, photographs, and other memorabilia. The Discover Me Room is full of things for children to touch, see, and do. Outside is a full-scale replica of the Confederate submarine, *Hunley*. The only thing we don't understand is why a city that lives off its history would have ever approved the nondescript modern building that now houses the museum collection.

The 1803 Joseph Manigault House (pronounced Manigo), 350 Meeting Street (843-723-2926), is considered to be one of America's most beautiful examples of Adam-style architecture. The stunning front hall boasts a beautiful curving staircase. A fascinating feature is the secret stairway between the second and third floors. An outstanding collection of Charleston, American, English, and French period pieces are used to furnish the house. The gardens are adorned by a gate temple.

Return to the visitors center, from which you can take a guided walking tour, a horse-drawn carriage tour, or hop aboard the DASH city transit system (843-724-7420), which allows you to park at the visitors center and buy an all-day pass to ride the trolley to explore on your own. Walking excursions offer a close-up glimpse into many prominent buildings and hidden courtyard gardens. Eagle Balloons, 100 Broadmarsh Court (843-552-3782), provides a bird's-eye view of the city. You can explore the harbor by boat and, in fact, can reach Fort Sumter only by boat. Although there are several sightseeing and dinner cruise boats that tour the harbor, our favorite is the schooner *Pride* (843-795-1180), on which one of our daughters had a lovely small wedding.

Whether you're exploring with a guide or on your own, look for Charleston's unique architectural features. One example is the seemingly ordinary front door. When you look at a historic house head-on, you'll see an unadorned house front broken by simple windows and a doorway to one side. You assume that the door opens directly into the interior. However, when viewing the structure from the side, you'll see that the door actually opens onto the first-floor porch or piazza that runs front-to-back along the side of the building. Each home usually has a piazza for each floor, so what looks like a plain, unassuming house from the front is magnificent and stately when viewed from the side. Also, look for circles, crosses, or stars on the facades of many buildings. Not just decorative, these are actually the end plates of metal earthquake rods that run completely through the structure to keep it stable.

Within the historic house museums are numerous pieces of Charleston-made furniture. Between 1720 and 1825, 250 London-trained cabinetmakers worked in Charleston. Their training allowed them to create pieces that pleased the largely English tastes of their clients. Although the first pieces made from local cedar and cypress were more functional than decorative, as the port city prospered, the demand grew for luxury items such as fine furniture. Charleston's proximity to the West Indies made it easy to import significant quantities of mahogany which they lavishly embellished with cypress.

Between 1768 and 1775, the workshop of Thomas Elfe produced fifteen hundred pieces, many of which survive.

There are so many examples of historic religious architecture in Charleston that it has earned the nickname the Holy City. Among the most significant churches are the French Huguenot Church, Church and Queen Streets; St. Philip's Episcopal Church, 146 Church Street; St. Michael's Episcopal Church, Broad and Meeting Streets; First Scots Presbyterian Church, Meeting and Tradd Streets; St. Mary's Roman Catholic Church, 89 Hasell Street; Beth Elohim Reform Temple, 90 Hasell Street; Emmanuel African Methodist Church, 110 Calhoun Street; and the Circular Congregational Church, 138–150 Meeting Street.

In addition to the Joseph Manigault House, several other house museums in Charleston can be toured. We suggest visiting them in chronological order beginning with the oldest so you can more fully appreciate the progression of architectural styles and innovations.

The Thomas Elfe Workshop, 54 Queen Street (843-722-2142), built prior to 1760 by the famous cabinetmaker, is a perfectly scaled miniature of a Charleston single house. (A single house is one room wide, while a double house has a central hall and is two rooms wide.) It is outstanding for its cypress woodwork. An extraordinary collection of eighteenth- and nineteenth-century American furnishings adds to the interest of the charming residence.

The Heyward-Washington House, 87 Church Street (843-722-0354), was the home of Thomas Heyward Jr., one of South Carolina's signers of the Declaration of Independence. Built as a double house in 1772 on the site of an earlier single house, the residence was located within the boundaries of the old walled city. When Charleston surrendered to the British in 1780, Heyward and twenty-eight others were arrested and exiled to St. Augustine, where they remained until 1781. By 1783 Heyward was back in Charleston and active in civic and

St. Michael's Church, Charleston

political affairs. Heyward, who by 1791 had turned the house over to his aunt to use as a boarding school for girls, leased the house to George Washington for a week during the president's southern tour. Later, the Grimke family lived in the house. Sarah Grimke, who, with her sister Angelina, was active in the abolitionist and evangelical movement of the mid-nineteenth century, was born there. Into the twentieth century the structure served as a bakery. The Charleston Museum acquired the house in 1929, and it was opened to the public in 1930. Of particular interest are the original heart pine floors and the original cypress trim painted to look like mahogany. Several pieces of Charleston furniture of the period 1700 to 1825 include some made by Thomas Elfe.

Today, the Heyward-Washington House contains a valuable collection of eighteenth-century Charleston-made furniture, including the Holmes bookcase, the finest extant American piece of furniture. Probably constructed around 1740, the original, restored kitchen building was divided into separate areas for cooking and washing by a huge double fireplace in the center, with servants' rooms above and a root cellar below. Also on the grounds are a carriage house and a small formal garden.

The early 1800s' Edmondston-Alston House, overlooking the harbor at 21 East Battery (843-722-7171), is a three-story Greek Revival mansion, still lived in by an eighth-generation Alston descendant. One of the city's most splendid dwellings, the residence is a gracious example of the early nineteenth-century commitment to elegance, style, and comfort. Charles Edmondston of Scotland, a successful merchant, built a late Federal-style mansion on the High Battery facing the harbor. Economic reversals during the Panic of 1837 forced him to sell his home to Charles Alston, a member of a rice-planting dynasty. Alston modified the appearance of the house to the fashionable Greek Revival style by adding a third-story piazza with Corinthian columns, a second-story iron decorative balcony on the east facade, and a parapet across the front on which he displayed the family coat of arms. It is reported that Confederate General Pierre G. T. Beauregard joined others on one of the piazzas to watch the bombardment of Fort Sumter and that Robert E. Lee took refuge at the Alston home when a spreading fire threatened his hotel farther uptown.

Memorabilia on display include documents, portraits, engravings, an outstanding library, furniture, silver, china, and other family heirlooms. Notice the unusual ball-and-rope woodwork.

The 1808 Nathaniel Russell House, 51 Meeting Street (843-724-8481), another outstanding example of Adam-style architecture, features an astonishing flying staircase spiraling from floor to floor and a tier of elliptical rooms. Completed in 1808 and set amid spacious gardens, the Carolina gray-brick and white-marble Federal-style mansion is recognized as one of America's most important neoclassical dwellings. Thirteen to fifteen bricks thick, the exterior walls are embellished with ornate iron balconies outside the drawing room and oval-shaped rooms. The graceful interiors feature elaborate plaster-work ornamentation and geometrically shaped rooms. Period antiques and works of art evoke the gracious lifestyle of the city's merchant elite as does the formal side garden.

Another noteworthy house is the 1817 Aiken-Rhett House, 48 Elizabeth Street (843-723-1159), residence of early South Carolina Governor William Aiken Jr. It was used as the military headquarters of Confederate General Pierre G. T. Beauregard during the 1864 Federal bombardment of the city. The beautiful entrance hall features a double staircase with decorative cast-iron banisters. Most of the wallpaper, paint colors, and furnishings are original. Wander through the kitchen, slave quarters, stable, and other outbuildings.

Then explore Charleston's other historic buildings and museums. The Old Exchange Building/Provost Dungeon, 122 East Bay Street (843-727-2165), built by the British in 1771, has served as a customs house, city hall, military garrison, and post office. As trade increased in the mid-1700s, the need became apparent for an exchange and customs house; it was the duty of the postmaster to collect a percentage of gunpowder, for defense of the port, and all the mail from arriving ships. Constructed in the Palladian style, the structure was completed in 1771 and is considered to be one of the three most historically significant colonial buildings in the country. The Exchange was designed with an open arcade trading floor on the first level, customs offices and an elegant assembly room on the second floor, and storage rooms in the cellar. At the time of completion, the building fronted directly on the water, but over the centuries, the land has been filled in, pushing the harbor back two blocks. During George Washington's presidential tour in 1791, several banquets and dances were held for him in the Great Hall of the Exchange. After 1896 the open arcade was enclosed and divided into rooms. In 1913 a developer wanted to buy the building, tear it down, and build a gas station. When the Daughters of the American Revolution (DAR) learned of the plans, the organization spearheaded one of Charleston's first preservation efforts, petitioning the federal government to deed the building to them to be preserved as a historic memorial. In 1913 the structure was conveyed to the DAR.

You'll notice in the elegant Rebecca Motte Room that the chairs don't match. When the DAR, which still owns the building, first met here the organization had little money for furnishings, so, ever resourceful, each member donated a chair or chairs from her own home. Note the ornate mirrors, which once hung in the palace of Queen Wilhelmina of the Netherlands. The South Carolina State Society NSDAR Room across the hall contains many artifacts and paintings from the state's colonial era. Upstairs is the Great Hall, where in 1773 the citizens of Charles Towne met to protest the Tea Act, after which the tea was seized, stored in the cellar, and later sold to fund the patriots' cause. In this room in 1774 South Carolina's delegates to the Continental Congress were elected. On March 28, 1776, South Carolina declared independence from Great Britain on the steps of the Exchange. These events earned the structure the title "The Independence Hall of South Carolina."

After a forty-two-day siege in 1780, the British marched into Charles Towne and occupied the city until 1782. They took over the Exchange and imprisoned leading citizens in the cellar, which became the Provost Dungeon. Colonel Isaac Hayne, for violation of parole, spent his last days in a small room off the Great Hall before his execution. As you enter the dungeon, you will see and stand at an excavated portion of Charles Towne's wall, the only surviving portion of that wall. The vaulted brick ceiling is constructed on the groin-arch principle in which two simple arches cross at right angles, joining the semisupporting column. Display cases show artifacts found during various excavations. In the northeast corner, you'll see a cutout into a room where ten thousand pounds of gunpowder were secretly stored by the patriots. The area was bricked, giving the appearance of an exterior wall. During the two-year occupation, the British never discovered the gunpowder.

Most popular with visitors, however, is the prison scene with mannequins representing imprisoned patriots held during the British occupation. The vignette depicts the cramped confinement, misery, disease, and death in the dungeon. It contains the figures of two signers of the Declaration of Independence, Arthur Middleton and Edward Rutledge, as well as one of the Sarrazin sisters who was suspected of spying for the patriots; Jonathan Sarrazin who aided the patriots; Christopher Gadsden, who led the South Carolina branch of the Sons of Liberty and was the lieutenant of South Carolina when it fell to the British; Richard Ellis, an officer in the First Regiment of South Carolina; and an African-American slave. (Although many slaves escaped their masters and served the British, they were often repaid by being sold into slavery again in the West Indies.) Overseeing the prisoners is the figure of Provost Master Sergeant Jarvis, who served in the king's Twenty-Third Welsh Fusiliers.

No trip to Charleston would be complete without wandering through the diverse merchandise in the Market, Market Street between Meeting and East Bay Streets. The Market stretches out for several blocks behind Market Hall. The one-story, covered open-air sheds filled with shops and stalls have operated for well over one hundred years. If you want the quintessential gift from Charleston, get a sweetgrass basket. These intricately woven containers preserve an art form brought to America by African slaves.

Check to see whether the Confederate Museum, housed in the upper story of the 1841 Market Hall, 188 Meeting Street (843-723-1541), is open. Since 1898 the Daughters of the Confederacy have run a museum featuring flags, uniforms, swords, and other Confederate memorabilia. It has been undergoing restoration, so it may be closed. If so, the collection is housed temporarily at 34 Pitt Street.

At the American Military Museum, 40 Pinckney Street (843-723-9620), you can see hundreds of uniforms, patches and insignia, and military miniatures and toy soldiers from the Revolutionary War through the Vietnam War.

Visit the Citadel Museum, 171 Moultrie Street on the campus (843-953-6846), to learn about the history of the Military College of South Carolina from its founding in 1842 to the present. Photographs, uniforms, documents, and other memorabilia portray the military, academic, social, and athletic aspects of cadet life. Don't miss the colorful dress parade every Friday at 3:45 P.M. during the school year.

Architecturally attractive, the Gibbes Museum of Art, 135 Meeting Street (843-722-2706), is located in Charleston's best example of Beaux Arts architecture. In addition to changing exhibits, the museum's permanent collection includes views of Charleston, portraits of notable South Carolinians, paintings, prints, and drawings from the eighteenth century to the present with a significant collection of Charleston Renaissance artists of the 1920s and 1930s.

One of the most priceless exhibits is a collection of miniature rooms, the Elizabeth Wallace Rooms, which demonstrate the remarkable world of microscopic craftsmanship. The late Elizabeth Wallace of Hilton Head, the donor, was a collector and maker of miniatures. The rooms, which follow the reduction rate of one-inch-to-one-foot, are exact replicas of eight historic Colonial- and two French-style rooms, with all the furniture and accessories rendered proportionally. Also housed in the museum is an outstanding collection of miniatures.

Delve into African-American history at the Avery Research Center for African-American History and Culture, which houses both permanent and visiting exhibits pertaining to the history of sea islands and the Gullah culture. On the campus of the College of Charleston, the center occupies the former Avery Normal Institute, which was one of the most prestigious black private schools in the nation.

Located at the corner of Broad and Meeting Streets is a group of buildings called the Four Corners of Law, a term coined by Robert Ripley, author of the "Believe It or Not" newspaper feature. The name refers to City Hall, which represents municipal government; the Charleston County Courthouse, representing county government; the U.S. Courthouse, representing federal government; and St. Michael's Episcopal Church, representing God's law. This is another excellent place to buy sweetgrass baskets.

To get a different insight into Charleston history, stop by the Historic Charleston Foundation's Visitors Center, Chalmers and Meeting Streets (843-724-8484), to see another outstanding film, *Dear Charleston*. Much of the narration in the prize-winning presentation is by descendants of Civil War–era planters and slaves. After seeing the film, you'll find the visitors center an excellent place to purchase quality Charleston reproductions and gifts.

When it fits into your schedule, spend a little time at Waterfront Park, located just off East Bay Street on Concord. The area, once a seedy neighborhood of derelict warehouses, is now a magnificent new park on the harbor. Blocks of grassy areas and sidewalks are punctuated by numerous park benches, trees, fountains, and flower-filled planters. The long wharf leading out into the harbor has covered arbors with old-fashioned swings in them. A popular time to visit the park is at night when it is lit up like a birthday cake.

Visit historic Fort Sumter National Monument via Fort Sumter Tours from the City Marina on Lockwood Boulevard (843-722-1691). A short boat ride takes you to the man-made island on which the fort was built to protect the harbor where the Ashley and Cooper Rivers meet. The fort catapulted from obscurity to international attention when the first shots of the Civil War were fired on it. Although South Carolina had seceded from the Union, Federal forces still occupied the strategic fort. The Confederacy demanded that Fort Sumter be vacated, and when the Union refused, South Carolina troops fired on the fort on April 12, 1861—the beginning of a two-day bombardment that resulted in the fort's surrender. Occupied by Confederate troops until it was evacuated on February 17, 1865, Fort Sumter experienced one of the longest sieges in modern warfare. For almost two years, from their position on Morris Island, Union forces bombarded the fort with forty-six thousand shells, estimated at more than seven million pounds of metal, reducing it from a three-story edifice to little more than a pile of rubble. In its present form, the fort has been restored to a one-story height. National Park Service rangers give guided tours of the fort, and a museum displays priceless artifacts. On the way to and from the fort, you'll hear a brief commentary about Charleston, the harbor, and the historic houses you'll pass along the Battery.

Once you have explored the historic district in Charleston, you'll want to venture back out into the countryside. Charles Towne Landing, up the Ashley River at 1500 Old Town Road (843-852-4200), a re-creation of South Carolina's first permanent English settlement, will give you insight into what the first residents found in 1670. There are several options for touring Charles Towne Landing, state-owned historic site and nature preserve. Although you can tour the facility completely on your own, we recommend that you see the film about the site and then take a thirty-minute tram ride through the grounds. After that, you can spend additional time wherever your fancy leads you.

Your guide will explain the significance of places you pass as the tram takes you first to the ship's wharf, where you'll see and can board a life-sized replica of the seventeenth-century trading vessel *Adventure* on which the colonists arrived. It is astounding that more than one hundred people could make a voyage of several months duration aboard this tiny fifty-three-foot ship. It's hard to imagine what the rigors of that voyage must have been. Near the wharf are the earthen walls of the original fortified town and a small section of reconstructed palisade walls. In the Settlers' Life Area—a reconstructed seventeenth-century village, costumed living-history interpreters portray the lives of the settlers and make candles and wooden spoons which are for sale. The simple wattle-and-daub residence found here also served as the print shop. (The printing press on display belonged to the partner of Benjamin Franklin.) Other structures include a small wood-working shop and a barn with blacksmithing tools. Several retired police horses live in the paddock. The early settlers experimented to see which crops would grow profitably, and in the re-created 1670 crop garden, you can see rice, indigo, cotton, sugar cane, and other plants they tried.

After the tour, you can wander around the eighty acres of English-style park gardens featuring azaleas, camellias, and seventy-eight other varieties of trees and shrubs; stroll along the half-mile nature trail; or visit the animal forest where animals indigenous to South Carolina in 1670 reside in natural habitats. Puma, bear, elk, bobcats, bison, alligators, and others can be viewed here. A landmark/photographic-opportunity spot is the large carved totem called Landing Brave, the head of an Indian carved by Hungarian sculptor Peter Toth.

You'll want to take State Scenic Highway 61 along the banks of the Ashley River to visit some of Charleston's fabled plantations. Plantation life in the Lowcountry was once described as "quiet as Sunday." To absorb a sense of that tranquility, make a point to see one or more among the several that are open to the public.

Drayton Hall, 3380 Ashley River Road (843-766-0188), circa 1738, is considered to be the finest example of unusually sophisticated Georgian Palladian architecture in this country. The style of the immense two-story brick house is characterized by the classical use of order, symmetry, and bold detail. The two-story portico is believed to be the first of its kind in America. Native materials were used freely, and English limestone and West Indian mahogany were imported to enhance details. Through seven generations of Drayton ownership, the house remained in nearly original condition. Despite changing tastes, periods of disuse, and occasional repairs, the house has hardly been altered. It was the only home along the Ashley River not vandalized by Union troops in 1865. In contrast to the sumptuously furnished and decorated townhouses in Charleston, Drayton Hall, now jointly owned by the state of South Carolina and the National Trust for Historic Preservation, is presented without furniture or embellishments of any kind so that visitors can appreciate the mansion's exquisite proportions and rich handcrafted detail work. Take time to stroll around the grounds. On a still day, a perfect reflection of the house is captured in the mirror surface of the pond and makes a striking photograph.

Magnolia Plantation and Its Gardens, State Scenic Highway 61 (843-571-1266), has been in the Drayton family since

Thomas Drayton arrived from Barbados in 1671. In pre-Revolutionary days, it was primarily used as a summer retreat. Destroyed during the Civil War, the plantation house was replaced during Reconstruction with one of Victorian style. Surrounding the house is this country's oldest colonial estate garden including an eighteenth-century herb garden, a biblical garden, a topiary garden, and a horticultural maze. Long famous for its springtime beauty with 250 varieties of azaleas, the garden is resplendent with 900 varieties of camellias from fall through late winter and provides extensive seasonal bloom every month of the year. In addition, the twentieth-century plantation also features a restored antebellum cabin, petting zoo, miniature horse ranch, and 125-acre waterfowl refuge, which you can explore by rental bicycles or canoes. Adjacent to Magnolia Plantation is the Audubon Swamp Garden—sixty acres of primeval black-water cypress and tupelo trees, punctuated by flowers and ferns and traversed by bridges, boardwalks, and dikes. There are separate admissions for the house tour, garden tour, and swamp-garden tour.

Middleton Place, State Scenic Highway 61 (843-556-6020 or 800-782-3608), circa 1740, was built by Henry Middleton, president of the First Continental Congress. Among the descendants of the Middleton family were Henry's son Arthur, who signed the Declaration of Independence; his grandson Henry, who served as a minister to Russia; and his great-grandson William, who signed the Ordinance of Secession. The part of the plantation open to the public comprises evocative house ruins, a restored house wing, a stableyard, and the most magnificent grounds and gardens in the Lowcountry. America's oldest formal landscaped gardens, they reflect the elegant symmetry of seventeenth-century European design. From the river's edge, you encounter butterfly lakes, then terraces that sweep up to French- and English-style gardens featuring intricate walks and exquisite plantings of roses, camellias, azaleas, and magnolias—some of which are original from the construction of the gardens in the mid-1700s. Paths lead from the Reflection Pool, past the ancient Middleton Oak, the family tomb, and a secret garden. The one wing of the plantation house that wasn't destroyed during the Civil War was constructed in 1755 as a gentlemen's guest wing. Considered by today's visitors as a quite sizeable house in its own right, it became the family residence after the war. Open for tours, the house interprets the Middleton family from 1741 through 1865 with priceless family silver, china, furniture, and art, such as portraits by Benjamin West and Thomas Sully. In 1870 newly freed slaves who wanted to remain and work on the plantation built their own houses. One of those, Eliza's House, remains. Interpreters describe living conditions in the authentically furnished cottage.

Periodic demonstrations by the blacksmith, potter, weaver, and carpenter are given in the stableyard. Even when these artisans aren't on duty, agricultural displays, horses, mules, hogs, cows, sheep, goats, and guinea hens bring the plantation to life. Exhibits in the Rice Museum document that crop's influence on the affluent plantation economy. If you have time, have lunch in the plantation's restaurant.

One of the things we find so delightful about the collections of floriculture at both Middleton and Magnolia is their endless variety. The flora isn't only glorious in the spring—throughout the winter, the gardens are splashed with brightly colored winter berries and camellias bloom from fall through spring. At Middleton you can walk down long *allées* with camellia bushes towering overhead, meeting above the path. Masses of red, pink, white, and variegated blossoms brush your hair and create luxuriant carpets underfoot. In January or early February you're likely to find azaleas, jonquils, and forsythia already starting to bloom. Magnolia Garden's peacocks strut across the lawns or perch on the roofs displaying their finery.

Although most tourists don't visit Charleston with the beach in mind, there is a fine beach just outside of town via State 171. Folly Beach is an oceanfront town with seven miles of wide, flat, sandy beach. In contrast to many of the trendy resort islands that have sprung from nothing along South Carolina's Lowcountry in the last quarter century, Folly Beach is a long-time family resort with the hodgepodge ambience of the forties and fifties. Just completed, the Folly Beach Fishing Pier is the longest in South Carolina. At more than one thousand feet in length, it offers plenty of room for serious angling and great sightseeing. A second-story observation shelter, a snack bar, a full-service restaurant, and a tackle shop round out the pier's amenities. Located in a restricted area on the island's east end, the Washout is considered one of the hottest surfing spots on the East Coast. It's the site of numerous tournaments throughout the year. Held each August, the Folly River Float Frenzy and Fish Fry is a fun-packed day consisting of a hysterical raft competition among homemade vessels of all kinds, followed by live entertainment and fresh seafood. Call 843-588-9258 to find out more.

Once you've explored Charleston's many attractions, you still find much more to keep you there. Charleston has so much to celebrate, the city seems like one long festival. The Southeastern Wildlife Exposition, which occurs in mid-February, is a three-day celebration of wildlife through the works of the world's finest wildlife artists, as well as through conservation exhibits. Call 800-221-5273 to find out more. From late March through early April, the Festival of Houses and Gardens is a legendary tour of treasured historic homes, courtyard gardens, and historic churches, as well as a plantation oyster roast. Call 843-723-1623 to learn more about it. From late May through early June, Charleston hosts the world-renowned Spoleto Festival USA, an international festival with more than one hundred events in drama, opera, chamber music, symphonic concerts, jazz, theater, dance, and art. Call 800-255-4659 for tickets or 843-722-2764 for information. Piccolo Spoleto, the companion festival to Spoleto USA features local and regional artists. Call 843-724-7305. In September the annual Candlelight Tours of Houses and Gardens provides nighttime tours of private homes. Saturday evening visits include champagne and music at one of the houses. Call 843-722-4630 or 800-968-8175. In December Christmas in Charleston includes tours of traditionally decorated homes, churches, and public buildings, as well as parades, including the Parade of Boats in the harbor, and other activities. Many hotels offer special packages (843-853-8000).

The city has so many good restaurants that it's hard to go wrong. Located in a historic-landmark building with a lovely courtyard is famed 82 Queen, 82 Queen Street (843-723-7591), known for its she-crab soup and other Lowcountry specialties. In addition, the restaurant features a raw bar, wine bar, and lounge. Lunch and dinner reservations are suggested. Carolina's, 10 Exchange Street (843-724-3800), is a casually elegant uptown bistro which serves a contemporary southern menu. Magnolia's—Uptown/Down South, 185 East Bay Street (843-577-7771), serves Lowcountry cuisine, as does Blossom's next door (843-722-9200), operated by the same company. Lafayette's, 276 King Street (843-723-0014), serves Cajun/New Orleans cuisine in a bistro atmosphere for lunch and dinner. Gaulart and Maliclet French Cafe, 98 Broad Street (843-577-9797), is a casual cafe with counter service specializing in French sandwiches, soups, quiches, and omelets. The restaurant is also well known for its great coffee. Anson's, 12 Anson Street (843-577-0551), features fine dining in a more formal atmosphere. Magnolia Restaurant, Calhoun and Meeting Streets (843-722-3391), features Lowcountry cooking. Pinckney Cafe and Espresso, 18 Pinckney Street (843-577-0961), an informal favorite of locals, serves lunch and dinner Tuesday through Saturday. Slightly North of Broad, 192 East Bay Street (843-723-3424), nicknamed SNOB, is billed as a "maverick Southern kitchen."

Most visitors to historic Charleston want to stay in a period hostelry. The city brims with such historic hotels, inns, and bed-and-breakfast establishments—more than forty in all. Each is an elegantly restored property overflowing with southern hospitality. Consider some of those listed below or contact Historic Charleston Central Reservations (800-686-2120) for a more comprehensive list.

Ansonborough Inn, 21 Hasell Street (843-723-1655 or 800-522-2073), is an all-suite inn located in a former stationer's warehouse convenient to the Market. Located on White Point Gardens overlooking the Battery, the Battery Carriage House, 20 South Battery (843-727-3100 or 800-775-5575), offers bed-and-breakfast accommodations. Some of the guest rooms, which are appropriately located in the carriage house in the garden courtyard, feature a steam bath or whirlpool bath. The John Rutledge House Inn, 116 Broad Street (843-723-7999 or 800-476-9741), is an elegant townhouse noted for its decorative ironwork piazzas. The Lodge Alley Inn, 195 East Bay Street (843-722-1611 or 800-845-1004), housed in a set of converted warehouses surrounding a courtyard, features rooms and suites furnished in authentic Charleston fashion. Most have a fireplace and minibar; some have kitchens. The inn also features an on-site restaurant and lounge. The Meeting Street Inn, 173 Meeting Street (843-723-1882 or 800-842-8022), features traditional decor with four-poster beds. Amenities include a private courtyard with whirlpool and afternoon wine service. The Mills House Hotel, Meeting and Queen Streets (843-577-2400 or 800-874-9600), built in the 1850s, features marble floors, priceless antiques, and impeccable service. The Planters, 112 North Market Street (843-722-2345 or 800-845-7082), dating from the 1840s, is ideally located in the heart of the historic district and next to the outdoor market. Afternoon refreshments, turn-down service. Two Meeting Street, 2 Meeting Street (843-723-7322), is a bed and breakfast located in one of the most beautiful houses on the Battery. The Vendue Inn, 19 Vendue Range (843-577-7970 or 800-845-7900), overlooking the Waterfront Park, features elegantly appointed rooms; suites with fireplace and Jacuzzi; afternoon wine and cheese with chamber music; and fine dining in The Library. For modern accommodations with an Old World attitude, stay at the Charleston Place Hotel (an Orient Express property), 30 Market Street (843-722-4900). The exterior blends well with the old buildings around it, while the interior replicates the high-ceilinged elegance of older lodgings.

If you aren't totally exhausted from your sightseeing and sated from your gourmet dinner, you might be interested in some evening entertainment. Check ahead to see if there are performances at the historic Dock Street Theater, 135 Church Street (843-723-5648); at the Coliseum, 5001 Coliseum Drive (843-529-5050); or at any of the other entertainment venues such as the Charleston Stage Company, 133 Church Street (843-577-5967); Charleston Ballet Theater, 280 Meeting Street (843-723-7334); Charleston Symphony Orchestra, 14 George Street (843-723-7528); or the Footlight Players, Inc., 20 Queen Street (843-722-7521). Serenade, located in an old passenger station at 37 John Street (843-973-3333), offers a two-hour variety show filled with music, dance, extravagant costumes, and comedy. Lowcountry Legends Music Hall, 30 Cumberland Street (843-722-1829), features authentic Lowcountry folk music, spirituals, and storytelling.

If you can tear yourself away from the beguiling charms of Charleston, there are more attractions nearby.

For another tour in a different direction, take I-26 north from Charleston, then take US 78 to Summerville. Twenty-five miles inland from Charleston, charming Summerville was originally populated by Lowcountry residents who retreated here in the summer to escape heat, humidity, and diseases common to Charleston and the coast. By 1891 Summerville's reputation as a health resort had grown nationwide. It was considered one of the best places in the country to recover from pulmonary diseases. Several inns and grand hotels were built, as well as many grand cottages. Prominent people such as William Howard Taft and Theodore Roosevelt wintered in Summerville. The town's abundance of lovingly preserved old homes and gardens reinforces the grandeur of the turn-of-the-century era and Summerville's reputation as "Flowertown in the Pines." You'll find a manicured town square surrounded by late nineteenth-century commercial buildings. During the annual spring Flowertown Festival, more than two hundred thousand visitors come to town to admire the azaleas and dogwoods in full bloom, as well as to see the works of local, regional, and national artists. Call 843-871-9622 for more information.

If you want to experience the gracious refinement of the Old South, arrange to stay overnight and/or have dinner at Woodlands Resort and Inn, 125 Parsons Road (843-875-2600 or 800-774-9999). Located on a superbly landscaped forty-two-acre estate, the plantation house is a classical-revival mansion built in 1906 by the Robert Parsons family who had selected Summerville as their winter retreat. Twenty magnificently appointed rooms offer every amenity: huge canopy rice beds with their four posters ornately carved with rice leaves and grains, gas-log fireplaces, whirlpools, and luxurious bathrooms. A full southern breakfast is included in the overnight rate. Woodlands' dining room features the finest in imaginative, contemporary Lowcountry cuisine served in an elegant setting and accompanied by the lilting strains of the grand piano. You can choose between the five-course chef's choice menu or, for a three-tiered set price structure, choose three, four, or five courses from the menu. Presentation is exquisite, the wine list extensive, and the service outstanding. The wonderful natural setting of the resort is enhanced with a pool, tennis, and croquet complex. Red-clay-based tennis courts are automatically hydrated by an underground reservoir system, and the lap pool is solar heated with a gas-powered back-up system.

Retrace your route to Charleston, from which US 17 heads southwest. You'll make detours off US 17 to see the remaining sites on this scenic driving tour.

First, take Main Road/Bohicket Road on Johns Island south toward Kiawah and Seabrook Islands, both controlled-access resort islands. Take a detour on Angel Oak Road to see the Angel Oak, a gargantuan live oak variously estimated to be as ancient as fourteen hundred years old. Some speculate that the tree got its name because some of its massive limbs rest on the ground and resemble angel wings; the true story, however, is that it was acquired from the Angel family, who owned the property and the tree around 1810. Angel Oak's measurements are astounding—height, 65 feet; circumference, 25.5 feet; canopy spread, 17,000 square feet; largest limb circumference, 11.25 feet; and largest limb length, 89 feet.

Kiawah is a ten-thousand-acre retreat with two resort villages, an inn, restaurants, shopping arcades, tennis, four championship golf courses, miles of bike trails, and ten miles of pristine beach on which the sand is packed hard enough for bicycling. Accommodations are available in the inn, luxurious villas, and rental properties. Seabrook features tennis courts, two golf courses, restaurants, an equestrian center, bridle trails, and bike trails. Accommodations are available in villas and rental properties.

Retrace Bohicket Road to Maybanks Highway/State 700 and turn east toward Wadmalaw Island. The island, still zoned as agricultural, is home, not only to many of the region's major tomato farms, including Planters Three where you can pick your own, but also to the only tea plantation in the United States. American Classic Tea Plantation, 6617 Maybank Highway (843-559-0383), gives tours in which the entirely fascinating history and production of tea is discussed by owners Mack Fleming, a horticulturist, and William Barclay Hall, a fourth-generation tea-taster and one of only eight tea-tasters in America.

Tea is the second-most-consumed beverage in the world—after water. Unlike the usage in other countries, eighty percent of the tea consumed in America is in iced tea—and the ratio is a staggering four-to-one of iced over hot. In realization of that fact, the American Classic Tea Plantation produces blends perfect for hot tea and a stronger, darker blend that remains tasty after the dilution factor of melting ice. The operation has recently developed a ready-to-drink tea as well, which is fresh-brewed and contains no preservatives, no artificial coloring, and no artificial flavors. Since 1987 American Classic Tea has been the official White House tea. "America imports some two hundred million pounds of tea a year, so that's well more than two hundred million dollars that wouldn't have to leave this country if Americans decided to take advantage of tea grown in this country," Hall points out. The real advantage to tea produced in this country is freshness, which translates into flavor. Imported teas can take up to one year to make it from the field to the store; American Classic Tea takes less than a month to reach the shelf. American Classic Tea is produced completely free of insecticides and fungicides—unlike imported tea. It is available in supermarkets around the Southeast and in gourmet and specialty shops in all fifty states. It can also be ordered by mail directly from the plantation along with tea jelly, mint tea jelly, tea honey, Benne wafers, and tea accessories such as shirts, tote bags, and note cards.

Tours of the plantation are conducted on the first Saturday of each month from May through October. The free walking tours begin every half hour from 10:00 A.M. to 1:30 P.M. and include a video about tea and the plantation, some time in the field with Mack, and time with Bill as he explains the different types of tea, the different stages in the process, and the types you'll be tasting. The tour concludes with a refreshing drink of hot or cold tea made with leaves less than a week old, accompanied by benne wafers, a Charleston specialty, and an opportunity to shop for the plantation's products. Approximately seven hundred people come to each of the popular tours.

Proceed to Rockville, the sleepy, picturesque Spanish-moss-draped village at the end of the island on which roads are still paved only by sand and oyster shells and where time has no relevance at all. In fact, Rockville has been described as the "End of the World." Watch out for wandering wildlife, peacocks, and hounds of all persuasions—in Rockville they have the right of way. Cruise along the few narrow streets to admire the stately homes. The anything-goes Rockville Regatta is held in August at the rustic Rockville Yacht Club. Call 843-559-1410 for more information. When Dr. Daniel Jenkins Townsend brought two of his slaves to build the Rockville Presbyterian Church in the 1850s, they fashioned a small white church in Greek Revival temple-style built high off the ground like Rockville homes, with support pillars made of tabby, a mixture of oyster shells, sand, and lime. Originally, steps led up to the front portico, which was supported by five large square columns and topped with a tall, handsome steeple. A slave gallery was built across the back of the sanctuary. During the Civil War, when Union gunboats sailed off the coast and up the rivers, the Confederate army used the steeple as a lookout. The church withstood both the war and the Charleston earthquake of 1886, but was heavily damaged by the hurricane of 1893. At that time the steeple was blown over, and it was never replaced. The pleasing little church you see today is little changed with the exceptions of the space under the church and the slave balcony being enclosed to create fellowship and Sunday school rooms. Despite the shading of overhanging live-oak trees, light streams through the tall windows and glints off the polished wood of the old pine pews and altar furniture.

Retrace your steps to Charleston and linger there a while to take advantage of the many museums, monuments, restaurants, and festivals. It's been said that Charlestonians consider their city the center of the universe, and visitors soon understand their attitude. Timeless Charleston is one of the most-visited cities in America and is particularly popular with foreign tourists. So mesmerizing is her allure that travelers find themselves rooted to the spot and unwilling to leave it or its environs.

For More Information

Charleston Area Convention and Visitors Bureau, P.O. Box 975, Charleston 29402. 843-853-8000 or 800-868-8118.

Greater Summerville Chamber of Commerce, P.O. Box 670, Summerville 29484. 843-873-2931.

3

Grand Strand

The Gulf Stream, a massive, warm, undersea river from the tropics, flows forty miles off the Atlantic coast, moderating the coastal climate of South Carolina for humans and nurturing an ideally balanced ecological environment for a vast population of marine life. The wide, enticing ribbon of sea-washed sand boasts pleasant temperatures—always cooled to the comfort zone by a salty sea breeze—that average in the low nineties in summer and rarely dip below the fifties in winter. The awe-inspiring sight of sunrise on the ocean and sunset over the marshes is the only measure of time that counts in these environs. Recreational activities are almost as limitless as the shells strewn upon the beach. Seafood from the ocean and estuaries abounds, and you may even catch some of it yourself.

US 17, the primary artery through the region, traces a precolonial Indian trail that came south from Massachusetts. To begin this tour, start at Little River, a quaint historic fishing village on the Atlantic Ocean near the North Carolina line. From Little River, many fishing boats head out to sea to angle for grouper and red snapper or to troll for amberjack and sailfish. The town's waterfront streets whisk you back to another era. Beautiful southern homes are situated on side streets in Little River and while many still serve as residences, others have been converted to bed-and-breakfast establishments, restaurants, and shops. The original Little River Methodist Church, for example, is now a popular gourmet restaurant. World-famous as one of the country's largest seafood suppliers, Little River's promise is that "you can't get it any fresher!" A popular activity is the sunset cruise down the Intracoastal Waterway.

Follow US 17 south, stopping as the mood strikes you at the beaches at Cherry Grove, Ocean Drive, North Myrtle Beach, Crescent, Atlantic, or Windy Hill—all of which at low tide present the widest shores in the area.

Of all of South Carolina's beach resorts, Myrtle Beach, the sun and fun capital of the Grand Strand, is the one most aggressively fixed on the amenities of modern life. Here you may lie back and relax, but here you'll also find the greatest number of activities for the Type-A personality—those who can't sit still for long. Fishing piers and deep-sea charters lure the avid fisherman. Golfers can tee off on one hundred courses while tennis buffs can ace on more than two hundred courts. Charted shipwrecks call from the ocean depths to the adventurous diver. Shopping options range from handcrafted treasures to outlet bargains. If all those choices are not enough, dinner cruises, helicopter rides, amusement parks, water parks, wax museums, dinner theater, several country music venues, and dancing the shag—South Carolina's official state dance—keep visitors up late at night.

Myrtle Beach is a party-hearty town, and special events go on year round. In mid-March Canadian-American Days welcomes snowbirds and others to town for "spring break" with sporting events, concerts, a St. Patrick's Day parade, and other activities. Call 843-626-7444 for more information. Stretching from November 1 to February 28, Treasures by the Sea—a holiday celebration—covers the area with images of mermaids, seashells, seahorses, and other nautical likenesses.

Call 843-626-7444 to find out more. Late September sees South Carolina's Largest Garage Sale, when a city parking garage is filled with items for sale. Call 843-448-8578 if you want to learn more.

If you're not too tired from all this frenzied action, take a detour on US 501 to Conway in Horry County (that's pronounced "O-ree"), a county rich in plantation history. One of the oldest towns in America, it was originally called Kingston for Great Britain's King George III, but after the successful Revolutionary War, it was renamed Conwayborough for a local American officer. For more than two hundred years, the community was a bustling little port city on the Waccamaw River. During the era from 1785 to 1860, the village was a major stop on the north/south stagecoach line. Today Conway is known as the "Gateway to the Grand Strand." You'll find archaeological and historic exhibits related to the area displayed at the Horry County Museum, 438 Main Street (843-248-6489 or 843-626-1282), located in the old post office. Admire the sturdy precision of the City Hall designed by premier South Carolina architect Robert Mills, who served seven presidents as Federal Architect of the United States. You'll want to enjoy the scenic views of the Waccamaw River seen from the 850-foot riverfront boardwalk. Attend an exciting auction at the Conway Tobacco Market, which is active between late-July and mid-October. Call the Chamber of Commerce at 843-248-2273 for schedules. For information about self-guided tours, call the Conway Chamber.

As you return to Myrtle Beach via US 501, make time to stop at the Traveler's Chapel, a tiny twelve-foot-by-twenty-four-foot structure, which is always open for meditation. Once you reach US 17, turn south and continue through Surfside Beach and Garden City to Murrells Inlet.

Known as the Seafood Capital of the South, Murrells Inlet is also noted as the home of famed mystery writer Mickey

Spillane. The picturesque fishing village is renowned for its charter fleet which departs daily from several docks for the open ocean or for the inlets that provide outstanding opportunities for fishing and crabbing. Murrells Inlet is justly famous for its numerous seafood restaurants, of which there are more than twenty on Restaurant Row alone. Dine outside on the wrap-around, screened-in porches overlooking the inlet or in one of the cozy, paneled dining rooms at Oliver's Lodge, 4204 US 17 Business (843-651-2963), a rustic, old summer cottage that is the oldest restaurant in the area. The regular dinner menu consists of seafood, prime rib, steaks, ribs, and chicken dishes. In May each year you can enjoy a day of family fun during the Blessing of the Inlet, sponsored by the Belin United Methodist Church. Call 843-651-5099 for more information.

While in Murrells Inlet, make time to visit Brookgreen Gardens/Huntington Beach State Park, US 17 (803-237-4218 or 800-849-1931). The gardens, located on the site of a colonial rice plantation, were the 1930s creation of Archer and Anna Huntington. Herself an artist, Mrs. Huntington gathered exquisite pieces of nineteenth- and twentieth-century American sculpture and developed an outdoor setting for them complete with two thousand species of plants. Today, the garden is the world's largest outdoor collection of American sculpture. Also on the grounds are an aviary and a wildlife park featuring native birds and animals. Across US 17 in what is now Huntington Beach State Park (843-237-4440) is the Huntington's former home Atalaya, a fortresslike thirty-room Moorish castle, now open for tours.

Keep going south on US 17 through upscale Litchfield Beach to Pawleys Island, one of the oldest beach resorts on the Atlantic Coast. Colonial rice planters and their families discovered early on that they could escape to the island in the summer to avoid the malaria which they believed stalked the woodlands, rivers, and marshes. In complete contrast to Myrtle Beach, Pawleys Island comprises individual cottages and almost nothing else except broad expanses of beach. In addition to recreation opportunities, the island retreat has two primary claims to fame. One is the Pawleys Island hammock—a woven-cotton creation in which to enfold yourself for a lazy summer nap. The hammocks have been handmade in the area for as long as anyone can remember and are available at several shops. The island is also well known for the mysterious Grey Man of Pawleys Island—the ghost of a colonial man who appears whenever danger, such as an impending hurricane, is imminent.

Follow US 17 south to Georgetown, a town that has raised the tradition of southern hospitality to new heights of excellence. Lying in the Lowcountry between Myrtle Beach to the north and Charleston to the south, the county has kept its allure under wraps. You'll enjoy discovering a perfect gem of a town, endless access to water, and grand plantations. Best of all, it isn't overrun by tourists yet.

Georgetown claims to be the first settlement in North America. Although an early Spanish colony, attempted in 1526, ultimately failed as a result of hostile encounters with a hurricane and with Native Americans, a permanent English settlement was established there in 1726. Originally a thriving center for rice and indigo plantations, for many years Georgetown was an important seaport serving the area, and Georgetown County was the wealthiest county in the nation. When the rice and indigo industries faltered, Georgetown County slipped into relative obscurity until recently.

The keystone of the county, the town of Georgetown's historic district dates back to the 1700s and is one of the best preserved and maintained we've seen anywhere. Founded by the Reverend Elisha Screven in 1730 and declared a port of entry in 1732, the entire district is listed on the National Register of Historic Places. The waterfront area of the historic district stretches along a harbor that opens into five bodies of water—the Black, Sampit, Waccamaw, and Pee Dee Rivers meet to form Winyah Bay, which ultimately flows into the Intracoastal Waterway. In the last century, these waters were often plied by pirates and Civil War blockade runners.

Most of the commercial structures were erected in the mid-1800s and are just as attractive from the back (along the waterfront) as they are in the front where they face the street. An ambitious revitalization project has converted the town's old docks into the charming Harbor Walk, a boardwalk stretching along the harborfront. It offers pleasant walking, access to tour boats, and comfortable places to sit and watch the world go by. Several restaurants have decks overlooking the harbor and boardwalk, creating perfect places to relax while savoring a drink, snack, or full meal. Several small, flower-filled parks meet the boardwalk and offer pleasant oases between buildings. Along Front Street, the street that parallels Harbor Walk, the roadway features a median lush with trees and flowers. Curbs and crosswalks are bricked to reflect the historic heritage of the city.

Before or after strolling along Harbor Walk, begin your investigation into Georgetown's history with the story of rice and indigo as it is told at the Rice Museum, Front and Screven Streets (843-546-7423), located in a quaint, raised brick building with a clock tower that reveals the time to both the street and the harbor. In days gone by, the open-air ground floor served as the town's market while the upstairs was variously a city hall, a jail, and offices. Eventually, the ground floor was bricked in and the upstairs was devoted to the Rice Museum. Realistic dioramas explain the operation of rice production. In addition, the museum has a small display about indigo, some history of the county, and other artifacts.

Then stroll through the historic district, sensibly laid out as a square with all the extra-wide streets parallel or perpendicular. Most of the houses were built between the mid-1700s and the mid-1800s and reflect the many styles that blossomed during that era. The best way to tour the area is to go on one of Miss Nell's Tours (843-546-3975). Because the district is about eight blocks wide by five blocks deep, it's particularly suited to a leisurely stroll along the Spanish-moss-draped streets with Miss Nell, a lifelong resident of Georgetown, as she recounts history, the fascinating background of former residents, and even some ghost stories. The cost of her tours is based on the area covered.

If you decide to tour on your own, you'll want to see the Kaminski House, 1003 Front Street (843-546-7706), situated on a bluff overlooking the harbor. The brick home, a pre-Revolutionary landmark built in 1760, is an excellent example of a townhouse owned by a plantation master and has an exquisite collection of antiques. Typical to houses of the era, it sits perpendicular to the streets with a terraced lawn sweeping down to the river.

Visit the Prince George Winyah Episcopal Church, 301 Broad Street (843-546-4358), established in 1721. Be sure to explore the church's ancient graveyard where some of the tombstones lean drunkenly or rest in the clutches of massive tree roots.

Take a cruise along the Intracoastal Waterway and into rivers and estuaries with Captain Sandy's Tours (843-527-4106). A garrulous local historian and naturalist, Captain Sandy is a veritable font of knowledge about legends of the area. During his leisurely flatboat cruises, he'll regale you with the history of the area, explain rice culture, and share his passion for nature and wildlife as he pilots you between the islands and abandoned rice fields of the Waccamaw and Pee Dee Rivers. If you're stout of heart, take one of his night tours when he'll mesmerize you with his Misty River tales. His spine-tingling ghost stories are guaranteed to make you shiver. Captain Sandy keeps an office at the Days Inn, but you'll more likely find him on his boat tied up at Harbor Walk.

Georgetown is surrounded by plantations—some still intact, others only ruins, and only a very few open for tours. The best way to see them is the annual spring Georgetown Plantation Tours, which also include colonial townhouses and magnificent gardens. Call 843-527-3653 for a schedule. One plantation that is open is Hopsewee Plantation, south of Georgetown on US 17 (843-546-7891). It was the 1740 home of Thomas Lynch, a delegate to the Continental Congress, and his son Thomas Lynch Jr., who was one of the signers of the Declaration of Independence.

With such an extensive historic district, it's no surprise that Georgetown offers overnight accommodations in eleven bed and breakfasts, two of which are Five Thirty Prince Street, 530 Prince Street (843-527-1114), and the 1790 House, 630 Highmarket Street (843-546-4821 or 800-890-7432).

From Georgetown, take US 17 ALT/US 521 northwest to Andrews, where you can visit the Old Town Hall Museum, 14 West Main Street (843-264-3715). Town memorabilia from the nineteenth century are displayed, including farm and railroad equipment and period furnishings.

Most visitors to the Grand Strand come for the beaches, the fishing opportunities, and the seafood, but many are pleasantly surprised by the historical towns, such as Georgetown, and astounded by Brookgreen Gardens. The region is conveniently located to explore Pee Dee Country, Santee Cooper Country, and Historic Charleston.

For More Information

Myrtle Beach Area Chamber of Commerce and Information Center, P.O. Box 2115, Myrtle Beach 29578-2115. 843-626-7444 or 800-356-3016.

Conway Area Chamber of Commerce, 203 Main Street, Conway 29526. 843-248-2273.

Georgetown County Chamber of Commerce and Visitor Center, US 17, Georgetown 29442. 843-546-8436 or 800-777-7705.

4

Lowcountry

The southern tip of South Carolina, which now includes Beaufort, Colleton, Hampton, and Jasper Counties, was one of the first explored and earliest settled areas in North America. French and Spanish explorers clashed over the area in the 1500s, but both eventually abandoned it. The first English settlements were among the sea islands in the late 1690s, but life was not peaceful. Yemassee Indians occupied the mainland areas and trouble was inevitable. Salted beef was a major export from the Carolinas to the West Indies and Atlantic islands. Settlers' cattle intruding on Yemassee lands, coupled with abusive traders, aroused hostility with the Yemassee and open warfare erupted. On April 15, 1715, Pocotaligo was the scene of the massacre which started the Yemassee Indian War. The Carolina Militia defeated the Yemassee at Salkehatchie and exiled them to Spanish Florida.

At the beginning of the Revolutionary War the allegiance of the area's inhabitants was sharply divided. British forces occupied Beaufort between 1779 and 1781, and established their main post at Pocotaligo. Following the Revolutionary War the Lowcountry became an important agricultural area. The primary crops were sea-island cotton on Edisto Island, short-staple cotton inland, and rice along the marshy coastal areas. Nathaniel Barnwell Heyward's Bluff Plantation was the state's largest producer of rice, making him one of the wealthiest rice planters in South Carolina.

Robert Barnwell Rhett, who was born and raised in Beaufort, led a strongly favored separatist movement beginning in 1842, earning him the name "Father of Secession." Practically as soon as the first shots were fired at Fort Sumter in 1861, Union forces captured the sea islands and occupied them throughout the Civil War. Beaufort and Hilton Head Island became respectively the chief base of the Loyalists Southern Atlantic blockading squadron and headquarters of the U.S. Army, Department of the South. During the years of Union occupation, agriculture was practically nonexistent. Although cotton production bounced back somewhat after the war, the infestation of the boll weevil in 1919 spelled the doom of the great long-fibered cotton from the sea islands.

The Lowcountry is noted for its beautiful beaches, its graceful, typically southern small towns, and its distinctive regional cuisine that developed here. Zesty Lowcountry dishes are distinguished by the use of seafood, especially shrimp, as well as grits or rice. Not only does the Lowcountry offer one of the longest hunting seasons in the nation, but it also contains the largest white-tailed deer population in the state.

Begin your exploration of the Lowcountry with Edisto Island, located southwest of Kiawah, Seabrook, and Wadmalaw Islands. To reach Edisto Island, take State 174 from US 17. Both the flags of the United States and the Confederacy have flown over Edisto Island, which has weathered countless hurricanes and one earthquake. Archaeological excavations show that the Edisto Indians inhabited the island far back into antiquity. The first Europeans were the French and Spanish, but eventually the island was bought from the Indians in 1674 by the British Lord Proprietors in consideration of "Valuable Cloth, Hatchettes, Brads and other Goods and Manufactures." Settled in 1690, the barrier island was once famous for growing the almost silky-textured long-staple Sea Island cotton. Rich alluvial soil was ideal for producing rice and indigo, as well as the world-famous cotton. It is said that Edisto's annual cotton crop was under contract to France before it was even planted. During this wealthy period, impressive plantation houses were erected, the oldest surviving one dating from 1735. In 1920 the boll weevil put an end to the island's lucrative cotton crop. Today, the island is still inhabited by descendants of former slaves, but is being discovered by tourists who come to enjoy the beach, the marshes, and the rivers, as well as the plentiful seafood. Edisto Beach is an unspoiled semitropical stretch of firm-packed sand, which is not only a shell-collector's paradise, but also a wonderful place for walking and jogging. Edisto Beach State Park, State 174 (843-869-2156), offers camping and cabins, as well as nature and hiking trails, bicycle and jogging paths, interpretive programs, and endless opportunities to observe the saltwater ecosystem.

Artifacts and storyboards at the Edisto Island Museum, State 174 (843-869-1954), give insight into the island's social history from Indian times to 1920, while the museum's natural history room displays fossils and shells found on Edisto Beach. The Edisto Island Historic Preservation Society operates the museum and each October offers the Annual Tour of Historic Plantation Houses, Churches and Sites. Another highlight annual event is the Summer Festival and Parade of Boats in July. Accommodations on Edisto Island are offered at the Fairfield Ocean Ridge resort hotel (800-845-8500), Bay Creek Villas (843-869-1848 or 800-533-7145), Cassina Point Plantation, Clark Road (843-869-2535), an 1847 bed-and-breakfast plantation, and several rental properties, as well as the campsites and cabins at Edisto Beach

State Park. Among the many restaurants from which to choose are The Old Post Office, Collins Pavilion, Dockside, Planters Oak Restaurant, Salty Mike's, and The Steamer.

Retrace State 174 to US 17 and go south to US 21 at Gardens Corner. Continue south five miles on US 17 to State Secondary Road 21 and turn right. Proceed 1.7 miles. On the right you will see the graceful remains known as the Sheldon Church Ruins, a haunting reminder of the tragedy of war. Built in 1753, Prince William's Parish Church, now known as Sheldon Church, was burned not once, but twice—first by Prevost's British troops in 1779 and then, after it was rebuilt, by Sherman's troops in 1865. Although the gable roof, pediment, windows, and interior have disappeared, the brick walls and pillars remain as a testament to the classic simplicity of the design. A photographer's dream, the site is a center for special religious observances.

Return to Gardens Corner and turn south on US 21 to Port Royal Island. Continue south on US 21 to Beaufort, the jewel of the Lowcountry, which you may recognize from such films as *The Big Chill*, *The Great Santini*, *Prince of Tides*, *Forrest Gump*, and *Daughters of the Dust*. This quintessential romantic southern town is graced with many antebellum homes, mellowed by years, located on narrow streets, and surrounded by quiet gardens shaded by ancient live oaks dripping with Spanish moss. In total, 304 acres have been designated a National Historic Landmark.

Beaufort, originally named Beaufort Town, was the second English settlement in South Carolina. Like the rest of the coastal area, however, it has a long history previous to that. The first inhabitants were Archaic Indians whose earliest traces date back four thousand years. Explorers and settlers from France and Spain came in the 1500s. Privateers and treacherous pirates also figure significantly in the area's history. The English Lord Proprietors began bestowing land grants on Port Royal Island in 1698 and agreed to build a seaport, which became Beaufort, in 1711. The fledgling town, however, was almost completely destroyed in the Yemassee Indian War of 1715. The Thomas Hepworth House, New Street, circa 1717, was one of the only survivors. Rebuilt, the affluent town became a haven for planters who built homes to take advantage of the summer breezes and to enjoy the socialization of fellow planters after months of isolation on their plantations. Beaufort suffered British occupation and ravages of war during the Revolutionary War, but it remained a cultural center for the Lowcountry—so cultural, in fact, that it was known as the most aristocratic town of its size in America.

At the outbreak of the Civil War, two forts were under construction to defend Port Royal Harbor: Fort Walker on Hilton Head and Fort Beauregard at Bay Point. Beaufort's position halfway between Savannah and Charleston made it vital to both sides of the conflict. Only a few months later, Union forces overwhelmed the uncompleted forts and Beaufort was occupied for the next four years. It took the Union Army three days to get to town from the forts, thus giving the residents time to flee. The town was abandoned and all the buildings commandeered for use as headquarters or hospitals, which resulted in the preservation of the historic structures. It was the only area between Savannah, Georgia, and Fayetteville, North Carolina, not burned to the ground by Sherman's advancing troops. The First South Carolina Volunteers—the first Confederate black regiment—was mustered in Beaufort. Harriet Tubman, founder of the Underground Railroad, served as a nurse to black soldiers in Beaufort. After the Civil War, the Reconstruction government imposed Direct Tax

Sales—enforced sales of properties with taxes owing. Ninety percent of the homes in town were sold for a pittance for back taxes of as little as twenty dollars.

Carriage, walking, trolley, and van tours of the Old Point Historic District leave from the Beaufort Visitor Center, 1006 Bay Street (843-524-3163), at Henry C. Chambers Waterfront Park on the Intracoastal Waterway, or you can explore on your own with a walking/driving tour map you can pick up at the visitors center. In addition to expert advice about sightseeing and recommendations for lodging and restaurants, the friendly staff at the visitors center will be happy to show you two excellent videos about Beaufort. We recommend taking one of the organized tours because you'll learn so much more about the important buildings than you can from the short piece about each one that appears in the walking-tour map. The centrally located park, scene of concerts and special events throughout the year, is an ideal place to watch boats go by, and in the spring and fall it is a favorite spot with locals for cast-netting for shrimp. You might want to plan your visit for spring or fall to take advantage of the much-anticipated Historic Beaufort Home Tours (843-524-3163); many of the homes are open to the public only then. A candlelight tour on Friday night is followed by a daylight tour on Saturday. Plantation and other homes ranging in style from Federal to Victorian are on tour during the St. Helena Spring Tour of Homes (843-524-6334). As you are exploring Beaufort, you'll come across signs that read "This View Preserved by the City of Beaufort." These signs indicate that it is permissible for you to walk onto the property to take pictures.

To learn more about Beaufort and the Lowcountry coastal area, visit the Beaufort Museum, 713 Craven Street (843-525-7077). One of the most important artifacts the museum maintains is the building itself. Once an arsenal, it was constructed of tabby, a material of burned oyster shells, whole shells, lime, and sand unique to the South Carolina and Georgia coasts.

After a national militia act created new military units, the Beaufort Volunteer Artillery (BVA) was formed in 1775—the fifth oldest military unit in the country. And in 1795 the state of South Carolina authorized building a powder magazine and laboratory in Beaufort for making shot and explosives. General Stephen Elliott, a Beaufort native, served as the first lieutenant and then captain of the BVA, which under his command saw action in four important Civil War engagements. In 1863 he was chosen as the commander of Fort Sumter and rebuilt the fort while repelling assaults by Federal landing parties. Elliott rose to the rank of brigadier general in the Confederate army. Wounded several times, he died of those wounds after the war ended.

The present castlelike building was completed in 1851 and continues to serve as the headquarters of the BVA. In addition, the Beaufort Arsenal garrisoned the Beaufort Light Infantry, an African-American militia unit which counted former slave and later U.S. Congressman Robert Smalls among its ranks. During both World Wars, the Arsenal served as a recreation and entertainment center for servicemen operated by women's auxiliary organizations. After an expansion in the 1930s by the Works Progress Administration (WPA), the arsenal became the home of the museum in 1939. Even so, the National Guard continued to muster at the Arsenal until 1966. On the parade ground is a bronze twenty-four pounder filed howitzer, cast in 1847, which was used aboard the USS *George Washington*, a ship that was attacked and destroyed by a Confederate battery in 1865.

Inside the museum are relics of nature, war, and early industry. A wide range of items reflects the personalities, interests, and diverse natures of local citizens. Residents have donated not only objects relating to the area's natural history and Beaufort's history, but also peculiar objects picked up elsewhere—such as souvenirs from service overseas brought home by military men. Artifacts range from fossilized sharks' teeth, bird-egg collections, and geological specimens to prehistoric Indian relics, artifacts from Spanish settlements, textiles, dresses, household furnishings, plantation handicrafts, and military objects from America's wars. Among the Civil War items is a portrait of Stephen Elliott by artist James Reeve Stuart, another Beaufort native, the presentation sword of Captain Hal Stuart, and a *Harper's* drawing of a party from the US *Seneca* destroying guns and gun carriages at the Beaufort Arsenal in 1861.

The Federal-style John Mark Verdier House (pronounced Verdeer), 801 Bay Street (843-524-6334), was built in 1790 by one of Beaufort's merchant princes, visited by the Marquis de Lafayette in 1825, and commandeered for use as a Union headquarters during the Civil War. Furnished in the style of the period, it is an excellent example of an early 1800s home. Take special note of the hand-carved rope molding. During December, Christmas at the Verdier House features beautiful decorations, songs and stories from the nineteenth century to the present, and light refreshments.

The flat tombstones of St. Helena's Episcopal Church, 501 Church Street (843-522-1712), were used as operating tables during the Civil War. Bricks brought from England as ship's ballast were used to construct the church in 1724, making it one of the oldest churches in the country. The silver altar service, which is still in use, was given by a grieving widower whose wife was carried off by the Yemassee Indians in 1715.

John Cross Tavern, 813 Bay Street, has been in continuous operation since 1720. Among the patrons were historical characters as diverse in nature as John Wesley, one of the founders of Methodism, and bloodthirsty pirates from Fripp Island. Today, the space is occupied by Harry's Restaurant, which can be reached at 843-524-3993.

In 1863 Abraham Lincoln created the Beaufort Veterans Administration National Cemetery, 1601 Boundary Street/US

21 (843-524-3925), as a place to bury black and white Union victims of the battles in the South. Eventually, the cemetery was used for the remains of 9,000 Union soldiers and 121 Confederates. A guide to the cemetery can be found on the office door.

Among the private residences that you'll want to walk or drive by are many that follow the Beaufort style of architecture: houses are raised off the ground for ventilation, roofs are flat so there is no attic to trap the hot air, T-shaped wings jut out from each side of the house so there are windows, and ventilation is available on three sides of the room. Most of the residences saw an important historical event or have an interesting story attached to them. The oldest house in town, the 1717 Thomas Hepworth House, New and Port Republic Streets, has musket slits in the foundation allowing the family to protect itself from the Yemassee Indians. The 1850 Joseph Johnson House, East Street, also known as the Castle, was used as a hospital by Federal troops. The 1814 James Robert Verdier House, off Pinckney Street, known as Marshlands, was the scene of Francis Griswold's novel *Sea Island Lady.* The 1853 Paul Hamilton House, Short and Laurens Streets, known as the Oaks, is the only house in town with a widow's watch (an enclosed belvedere). The 1850 James Fripp House, Short and Hancock Streets, also known as Tidalholm, as it is the only house in Beaufort with water on three sides, was used in *The Great Santini* and *The Big Chill.* The 1813 Milton Maxey House, Church and Craven Streets, is also known as the Secession House because a draft of the Ordinance of Secession was drawn up here. The 1785 Edward Barnwell House, Bay and Monson Streets, was used as an occupation headquarters by Federal troops. The 1811 John Joyner Smith House, Bay and Wilmington Streets, was used as a headquarters by Union General Stevens and also as a Union hospital. Pretty Penny, the house at 502 Prince Street, earned its name when it cost the owner far more than he had originally estimated. The house at 511 Prince Street was owned by Robert Smalls, a slave who later became the first black Congressman from South Carolina. Smalls, who was educated by the mistress of the house, purchased the house at a Direct Tax Sale after the Civil War and provided a home for his former owner until her death. He is commemorated with the Robert Smalls Monument on the grounds of Tabernacle Baptist Church, 907 Craven Street (843-524-2607).

You'll notice that many of the houses in Beaufort have pink foundations. This is not just an affectation on the part of homeowners—these foundations were constructed of tabby and painted white, but the pink color from the oyster shells bleeds through no matter how many times the foundation is painted.

Near Beaufort on State 280 are the ruins of Fort Frederick, a tabby fortress built by the English in 1732 to protect themselves from the Spanish, French, and Indians.

Beaufort abounds with excellent places to eat. The Bank Restaurant, 926 Bay Street (843-522-8831), is located in a 1916 bank building that is the only example of Beaux Arts classicism in town. In keeping with its former use, the restaurant features the original vault, utilizes the tellers' windows (now flush with the wall) as decoration, and fastens the napkins with money wrappers. Among the specialties are Carolina she-crab soup, Beaufort crab cakes, and Frogmore stew. The Anchorage, 1103 Bay Street (843-524-9392), is located in the pre-Revolutionary War William Elliott House, built by one of America's best-known early natural scientists and authors. From the understated but elegant dining room, the clubby tap room, or the terrace of the La Sirena, 822 Bay Street (843-524-2500), you overlook the seawall promenade, crafts market, gardens, and marina of the Henry C. Chambers Waterfront Park while dining on Italian cuisine, fresh seafood, and Low-country specialties.

Considering the number of exquisite historic homes in Beaufort, it's not surprising that several of them have been converted to use as bed-and-breakfast inns. Spend a romantic night in Beaufort at the Rhett House Inn, 1705 Bay Street (843-524-9030), one of the most renowned bed and breakfasts on the coast. Shaded by Spanish-moss-bearded live oaks and magnolias, the inn, which was the home of aristocrat Thomas Rhett and his wife, Caroline Barnwell, prior to the Civil War, is one block from the bustling waterfront and within easy walking distance of fine shops and restaurants. Filled with priceless art and antiques, the ten-guest-room Rhett House boasts all the modern amenities: private baths, television, telephone, afternoon tea, bicycles, and a dining room that serves gourmet dinners. TwoSuns Inn B&B, 1705 Bay Street (843-522-1122), named for the ending scene in the movie *2010* (the sequel to *2001: A Space Odyssey*), is located in a 1917 neoclassical-revival home overlooking the Intracoastal Waterway. The inn offers five delightful guest rooms—one with the restored 1917 brass full-body combined needle-and-shower bath. Two upstairs guest rooms share a screened porch overlooking the marsh. Rooms are simply named Chambers A–D because the original call-button box found in the basement labeled them that way. Carrol Kay, an accomplished weaver and craftsperson, created many of the bed coverings and window treatments used in the bed and breakfast. More of her creations are for sale in the gift area. Have her husband, Ron, tell you about his active participation in the International Banana Club. A Federal-style home built somewhere between 1790 and 1810, the Cuthbert House Inn, 1203 Bay Street (843-521-1315), located on a bluff overlooking the Beaufort River, was a wedding present from John Alexander Cuthbert to his bride, Mary Anne Williamson. Typical Beaufort style, it is constructed on a raised foundation with central hallways on both floors extending from front to back. The hallways and parlors feature rare hand-carved rope molding such as that found in the John Mark Verdier house museum. U.S. Army Brigadier General Rufus Saxton used the house as his headquarters during the Civil War, and General William Tecumseh Sherman spent the night of January 23, 1865, in the house during his march from Savannah to Columbia. Several Union signatures were discovered scratched into the black marble fireplace during a recent renovation. In addition to the antique Eastlake-furniture-filled guest rooms in the upper stories, Cuthbert House offers two ground-level apartment suites that sleep six. These apartments, featuring fully equipped kitchens, are ideal for families, small groups, or extended-stay guests. Bay Street Inn, 601 Bay Street (843-522-0050 or 843-524-7720), a filming site for *The Prince of Tides*, is located directly on the Intracoastal Waterway. The historic inn offers eight antique-filled guest rooms, seven with fireplaces. Amenities include a decanter of sherry, a fruit basket, evening chocolates, and the use of bicycles. Notice the cracks in the marble steps that lead up to the front veranda. These cracks were caused when the residents threw their trunks out the windows of the upper stories when making their hurried escape before the Yankees got to Beaufort. Old Point Inn B & B, 212 New Street (843-524-3177), was built in 1898 by William Waterhouse as a wedding gift for his wife, Isabelle Richmond, and is often referred to as the Wedding Gift House. The typical late-Victorian house has spacious piazzas on two sides and an inviting library/game room in addition to the four guest rooms. Built in 1907 as the second home of a prominent Hampton attorney, the Beaufort Inn, Port Republic Street (843-521-9000), has operated as a lodging since the 1930s. Completely rebuilt and expanded, the inn offers eleven guest rooms (named after local plantations) in the main house and two in the carriage house, all with private baths, telephone, television, and stocked refrigerators and some with fireplaces, whirlpool tubs, private porches, and/or wet bars. It is the only inn in Beaufort that offers an elevator. A fabulous three-story foyer is wrapped by balconies all the way up. A full gourmet breakfast is included with your stay, as is afternoon tea by reservation.

Go south on US 21 to St. Helena Island. During the Civil War, when the Union occupied the sea islands, the Penn Center School, Martin Luther King Drive (843-838-2432), the first school for freed slaves in the United States, was established on St. Helena Island by Quakers Laura Towne and Ellen Murray. Called the Port Royal Experiment, it was very successful in educating blacks in industrial arts, homemaking, and agricultural education and continues to operate as a conference center. Martin Luther King Jr. and his aides planned the march on Washington while they were on a retreat at the center. Listed on the National Register of Historic Places, the school's York Bailey Museum, Land's End Road (843-838-2432), houses original photographs, art work, artifacts, farm tools, and blacksmith tools, as well as rare oral histories that illustrate the historical and cultural aspects of blacks living on the sea islands in the 1800s. Slaves built the Brick Church, Land's End Road (843-838-3033), in 1855 for their masters, but within five years the builders were the primary members. The Penn School used the church after the Civil War as a classroom.

Continue south on US 21 to Hunting Island, home of Hunting Island State Park, US 21 (843-838-2011), a five-thousand-acre park with three miles of coastline offering one of the finest natural public beaches on the East Coast. Climb the 181 steps to the top of the 1875 Hunting Island Lighthouse for a spectacular view of the coast and marshes. The cast-iron lighthouse was designed for relocation if that became necessary. That foresight turned out to be very propitious—by 1889 the sea had cut away the northern end of the island, and the lighthouse had to be moved 1.25 miles to its present position.

From Hunting Island, you can continue to Fripp Island. An ancient hunting ground of the Yemassee Indians, the land of Fripp Island was acquired in colonial times by Captain Johannes Fripp, a hero in battles against the Spanish. Because the resort island has controlled access, walking or getting around by bicycle or golf-cart are the most popular methods of transportation. Its most famous resident today is author Pat Conroy, author of *The Great Santini* and *The Prince of Tides*.

Retrace US 21 to Beaufort and take State 802 to Parris Island. Parris Island is best known as the home of the U.S. Marine Corps Recruit Depot. The Marines have been a presence on the island for more than one hundred years. (See the section on Parris Island in the Introduction.) It was first visited by French Huguenots in 1562, then settled by the Spanish, who built Fort San Felipe and formed the 1566 village of Santa Elena, which served as the Spanish capital in America for a brief period. After the Indians destroyed the village in 1576, the Spanish rebuilt the village and constructed a larger fort they called San Marcos. They remained on Parris Island until 1587. English colonists came to the island next, and in 1735 relatives of Alexander Parris, who by then owned the island, settled there. By 1820 there were six plantations, all producing sea-island cotton. The plantation era, however, came to an abrupt halt in November 1861 when Federal forces took Port Royal. After the Civil War, the plantations were broken up into small farms and given to ex-slaves. Many of these farms are still owned by their descendants.

In 1885 construction began on a navy yard, and in 1891 drydock facilities were added and a Marine barracks established. In 1911, however, the navy yard was closed and for a brief time the island served as a prison. The property was given to the Marine Corps in 1915 for use as a recruit depot and the Corps has been there ever since.

During the first years of its existence the depot trained more than 46,000 recruits for duty in World War I. With the outbreak of World War II, Parris Island trained 204,000 Marines, with as many as 20,000 on the island at one time. Female Marines arrived in 1943 as reservists to take over administrative duties. In 1949 women became a permanent part of the Marine Corps with Parris Island as their only training site. Over the years more than one million Marines have graduated from Parris Island. Twenty thousand men and two thousand women complete their training there each year.

Travelers are encouraged to explore the island and parts of the base. Parris Island's main gate is located on State 802. To enter the base, ask the sentry to direct you to the Paul H. Douglas Visitors Center, Building #283 on Boulevard de France (843-525-3650), where you can schedule a bus tour or obtain a copy of *The Parris Island Driving Tour Book*. As you leave the visitors center, you'll pass the headquarters area where you can see and photograph the World War I statue *Iron Mike* and the columned entrance to the commanding general's building. Next, you'll drive through the Historic District, circa 1880 to 1890, where you'll see the dry dock, gazebo, and other historic buildings such as Quarters One, home of Parris Island commanders since 1883. From the marina near the Officer's Club, it is claimed that you'll see the best view in Beaufort County. Near the clubhouse at the golf course are the Spanish and French Monuments including the Ribaut Monument, which commemorates the French Huguenots, and the site of the Spanish forts and village.

You may see some marksmen in training at the rifle range or pugil-stick training (precision baton drilling) and recruits running the demanding Confidence Course at Leatherneck Square. A "must-see" stop is at the Recruit Chapel, where beautiful stained-glass windows are dedicated to the memory of Marines who served in the 1st, 2nd, 3rd, 5th, and 6th Marine Divisions. Other windows are donated by various Marine organizations.

If you're visiting the base on a Friday, you'll want to see the Friday Graduation Parade at the Peatross Parade Deck, named in honor of Major General Oscar F. Peatross, operations officer for the 28th Marines during the Iwo Jima campaigns and later commanding general at Parris Island. A reproduction of the famous *Iwo Jima* monument in Washington, D.C., stands next to the parade ground. Scheduled for most Fridays throughout the year, graduation is preceded by a Morning Colors ceremony on the steps of the commanding general's building at 8:00 A.M. Graduation follows at 9:00 A.M. with graduating companies in seasonal uniform. The ceremony features the Parris Island Band, pass-in review, achievement awards, and visiting dignitaries.

Finally, you'll reach the Parris Island Museum (843-525-2951), located in the War Memorial Building where displays detail the history and development of Parris Island, the Port Royal area, the Marine Corps, and recruit training. The museum is listed in the top twenty visitor attractions in South Carolina, so be prepared to spend adequate time there. In addition to the previously mentioned displays, the museum maintains a study collection and research facilities to aid scholars in studying regional military and Marine Corps history.

From Parris Island, take State 802 west to State 170 and turn west. When you get to US 278, turn east and stay on that route to Hilton Head Island. Largest of South Carolina's sea islands and one of the most popular resort islands on the East Coast, Hilton Head had an inauspicious beginning. In fact, in the 1600s discoverer William Hilton had to advertise for settlers in the London newspapers. Hilton Head wasn't even connected to the mainland until 1956 when the bridge was built.

Today, the peak tourist season brings fifty-five thousand visitors to the forty-two-square-mile island. The planned resort offers twelve miles of beach, nearly thirty public or semi-private championship golf courses, three hundred tennis courts—more than any other resort in America—marinas, nature preserves, upscale and outlet shopping, restaurants, and night-spots to the limited-access communities of Palmetto Dunes, Port Royal, Sea Pines, and Shipyard Plantations.

Learn more about Native-American life on fifteenth-century Hilton Head and see changing exhibits at the Coastal Discovery Museum, 100 William Hilton Highway (843-689-6767). Visitors can tour twenty-four ponds and the research building to see methods of raising seafood commercially at the James M. Waddell, Jr., Mariculture Research & Development Center, Sawmill Creek Road (843-837-3795). A driving tour includes the 1786 Zion Chapel of Ease Cemetery, US 278 and State 245; the 1800-to-1820 Baynard Plantation Ruins at Sea Pines Plantation; the 1815 Cotton Hope Plantation Ruins, Squire Pope Road; 1862 Fort Mitchell, Hilton Head Plantation; and the circa 1450 B.C. Indian Shell Ring, Sea Pines Forest Preserve.

From several Hilton Head marinas, you can gain boat access to Daufuskie Island, the setting for Pat Conroy's novel *The Water Is Wide*, which relates his experience about teaching disadvantaged children and which was made into the movie *Conrack*. A rural, remote, self-sufficient island inhabited by the descendants of former slaves, the island is characterized by small farms interspersed with the remains of antebellum structures and several luxury resorts. The entire island, known as the Daufuskie Island Historic District, is on the National Register of Historic Places. Among the sights are the 1874 Haig Point Lighthouse, 1770 Melrose Plantation, 1791 Daufuskie Island Cemetery, 1893 Union Baptist Church, and Bloody Point, where two significant battles took place. In the early

1700s, this southern tip of Daufuskie Island was used as a lookout by settlers. In 1715 two boats of Carolina scouts, led by John Palmer, surprised a group of Yemassee Indians camped on the point, and the Daufuskie Fight resulted in thirty Yemassee killed. But the name Bloody Point wasn't given to the area until 1828, when a party of Indians surprised a group of South Carolinians under Captain Barnabas Gilbert. All the settlers were killed except Gilbert, who was captured and taken to St. Augustine. A deed from 1891 shows that a plantation called Bloody Point existed on the spot.

Return to Hilton Head and retrace US 278 to State 46, where you will turn west to Bluffton. Named for its position set high on a bluff overlooking the May River estuary, Bluffton is a charming village noted for the polo matches that are held at Rose Hill Plantation, US 278 (843-757-4945), every other Sunday in the spring and fall.

Retrace State 46 to US 278 West and take 170 to State 462. Where the two roads intersect is the hamlet of Old House, named after Old House Plantation, owned by Thomas Heyward Sr. who was one of South Carolina's signers of the Declaration of Independence, as well as a statesman, a member of the South Carolina bar, a circuit-court judge, and founder and first president of the Agricultural Society of South Carolina. When he was named as a delegate to the Continental Congress in 1776, he was not yet thirty years old. A half-mile allée of live oaks near the junction of old US 278, now SC 336, leads to the Thomas Heyward Jr. Tomb in an isolated country cemetery overlooking the serene marshes and across the creek from White Hall Plantation where he lived. A bust of Heyward and a historical marker honor the patriot.

Continue west on SC 336 to Ridgeland. Once known as Gopher Hill, the town is the seat of Jasper County. The Pratt Memorial Library, 123-A Wilson Street (843-726-7744), houses rare books on the history of the Lowcountry as well as Indian artifacts, portraits, and maps. The Pauline Pratt Webel Museum, next door at 123-B Wilson Street (same phone), contains more ancient Indian artifacts, including pottery and arrowheads, historical materials, weapons, and relics relating to the Revolutionary War and the Civil War. Adults and children alike will be fascinated by the six dioramas pertaining to various stages in rice culture: a freshwater swamp, land clearing, preparing for planting, planting, and two plantation homesites. Painstakingly handcrafted, the dioramas contain miniature figures, landscaping, and buildings by James Richardson Jr., a contractor who was also instrumental in renovating the museum building, and backgrounds by Jacob E. Smart, a former president of the historical society. Learn interesting stories about the small towns in the county such as Switzerland, Old House, Coosawhatchie, and Pocotaligo. For example, Confederate General Robert E. Lee's famous horse Traveler was from Coosawhatchie. When Lee had a headquarters there, he admired the horse; the owner wanted to give it to him, but Lee insisted on paying for the steed.

Authentic Lowcountry cuisine, handmade crafts, and other events are the centerpieces of the annual Gopher Hill Festival, held each September.

Continue west on US 278 to Hampton, named for Civil War General and later South Carolina Governor Wade Hampton III. Begin your exploration at the Hampton Museum and Visitors Center, 99 Elm Street East (803-943-5318), where you can see Native-American relics, military artifacts, a children's room, medical equipment, communication tools, and exhibits of the various ethnic cultures of the Lowcountry.

A 115-year-old jail houses the Hampton County Museum, 702 First Street (803-943-3387). Downstairs, the cell blocks have been retained, and each houses a category of memorabilia. Cell Block #1, called the Country Store, houses county artifacts that might have been "store bought." Cell Block #2 is devoted to natural history, with wood cut from South Carolina trees, petrified wood, geologic specimens, snake skins, and mounted animals. Cell Block #3 is the children's room and is filled with antique toys that visiting children are actually encouraged to use. The other side of the downstairs was the living quarters of the jailer and his family and is now filled with military artifacts from all of America's wars.

Hampton County is the largest producer of watermelons in the state, and Hampton, along with its sister town of Varnville, is the host of the annual Hampton County Watermelon Festival (803-943-3784), held the last full week of June. South Carolina's longest continuing festival, it dates back to 1939 and attracts more than sixty thousand visitors. A week-long event filled with arts and crafts and food booths, it ends with a fun-filled Saturday that includes a parade, a watermelon-eating contest, a seed-spitting contest, the crowning of Miss Coastal Empire, and the Melon Ball.

Leave Hampton by traveling south on State 363 and turn south on US 321 to Estill. Until the late 1800s the only forms of transportation in the southwestern part of the state were the horse and buggy and the Savannah River. Then James Estill of Savannah brought the railroad through, and the town that sprang up along its route took his name. Lucille Godbold, the first woman in the South Carolina Hall of Fame, was from Estill. This quiet backwater saw the entry of tens of thousands of Sherman's troops into South Carolina from Georgia at Two Sisters Ferry along the historic Old Orangeburg Road, near Robertville, south of Estill. For a tour of this area including the Old Orangeburg Road with a native guide, contact Lawton O'Cain Tours (803-625-3240). To see the road, take US 321 south from Estill to Robertville and turn right at the

Robertville Baptist Church. Travel straight ahead when the pavement ends and straight again at the Y. Just a few yards farther, you can see what looks like an old logging road off to the left. If you hike along it for about two miles, you'll come to the river.

In this tranquil atmosphere it's hard to envision corps after corps of blue-clad troops, each more than five miles long, struggling up the hill with their equipment. The beginning of 1865 was the wettest winter on record and to cross the cresting river, the Union troops first had to build a nine-hundred-foot-long pontoon bridge. They also had to deal with land and water mines the Confederates had planted at Two Sisters Ferry. Sherman was so angry about what he called unfair and inhumane "infernal machines" that he vowed to destroy South Carolina. He later said that the South Carolina campaign was ten times more significant to the outcome of the war than the March to the Sea across Georgia. Once on the South Carolina side, the Union troops encountered only token resistance because the local troops were fighting in Virginia, but they did experience extremely muddy conditions and flooded swamps and had to construct a corduroy road. It took eight horses to pull one gun up the hill.

As the troops marched through Robertville, which was a thriving town, they destroyed it, leaving "not a stick." The Robertville of today is just a small crossroads with a church and a couple of houses and stores. The 1845 church is originally from the former town of Gillisonville. The residents of that town, warned that Union troops were coming, dismantled the church, numbered the boards, and hid them in the woods. When the church was rebuilt, it was relocated to Robertville. In the churchyard is the grave of Henry Martyn Robert, author of the world-famous *Robert's Rules of Order*.

The troops camped in Brighton, County 20 and County 19, on the Augusta Stagecoach Road and destroyed the village when they departed. The only remnant is the 1834 Brighton

Oaks Grocery, a still-operating general store. Confederate General Joe Wheeler's troops finally arrived to put up some resistance at Horsepen Branch, County 19, where the swampy areas on both sides of the road made it difficult for the Union troops to outflank the Confederates. The Confederates had to fall back, however, and there was a skirmish at Lawtonville, State 3, where the only things that remain of the town are the lovely cemetery and the masonry staircase and baptistry of one of the oldest Baptist churches in South Carolina.

This area is dotted with the mysterious Carolina Bays—shallow depressions that are one hundred feet to three miles long. Confederate soldiers put walnuts in the water that collected in the bays to sicken the Union horses who drank from them.

Stay at the John Lawton House B&B, 159 Third Street (803-625-3240), the turn-of-the-century town home of John Lawton, Jr. He was the son of "Steamboat John" Lawton Sr., owner of several steam-driven side-wheelers that plied the Savannah River from Augusta to Savannah, stopping at all the bluffs along the way. Although the family lived on nearby Jericho Plantation in Old Lawtonville, the drive into town each day by horse and buggy for his two little daughters to attend school was too strenuous, so the townhouse was built. A sixth-generation family member to live in the house, Ms. Lawton Clark O'Cain, is a fountain of knowledge about the surrounding area, as well as a gracious hostess in the southern tradition. Let her give you a glass of wine or one of her famous old-fashioneds and a homemade snack while she regales you with more information about the Old Orangeburg Road and about all the small towns, plantations, and cemeteries in the area. You won't have any trouble determining which side of "The Recent Unpleasantness" she favored.

Take State 3 south from Estill to US 601, turn north and go past Varnville to where State 363 merges with State 63, and continue north into Walterboro. In 1685 King Charles II granted Sir John Colleton a portion of land known as the Province of Carolina. Centuries and circumstances have greatly altered that land grant, but 1,050 square miles remain as Colleton County, a rural area that has depended over the years on rice, agriculture, and timbering. The inland terrain of the county is level to rolling, with abundant marshes along the Ashepoo, Combahee, and Edisto Rivers. Lush forests cover large portions of the county and provide homes for abundant wildlife. Edisto Beach, along the Atlantic Coast, offers recreation and bounteous seafood.

Walterboro is the county's seat of government and only large town. By 1800 Walterboro had been established as a summer retreat in the pinelands for Lowcountry planters seeking to escape with their families from the heat, humidity, and diseases along the coast. The village was named for Paul and Jacob Walter. They built the first house in the area called Hickory Valley, a commons considered as public property. In 1784, before the Civil War, the valley was used for military drills and public meetings; during Reconstruction, it was the site of political meetings and addresses. An 1879 cyclone destroyed many of the residences, but a concentration of them, spanning the period of 1821 to 1929, survive around Witsell and Webb Streets.

Walterboro became the county seat of Colleton District in 1817, and the town was officially incorporated in 1826. In 1828 thirty-three years before the southern states began to secede from the Union, Walterboro was the site of the first nullification meeting in South Carolina. By 1832 a handsome courthouse, designed by Robert Mills, as well as a jail, three churches, a market house, and both male and female academies existed. After the Civil War, many displaced planters from along the Ashepoo, Edisto, and Combahee Rivers had settled in Walterboro. Their combined business skills helped the area recover quickly during Reconstruction. By the mid-1890s the city had the largest railway station on the line between Charleston and Savannah, Georgia.

Today the charming town boasts many fine examples of nineteenth-century architecture. Pick up the brochure *Tour Guide of Historic Walterboro, South Carolina* from the Chamber of Commerce (843-549-9595), located in the Old Colleton County Jail, 213 Jefferies Boulevard, and take a driving/walking tour. Don't leave the old jail just yet, though. Built in 1855 to resemble a miniature fortified castle in the Gothic-revival style with a crenelated parapet and lancet windows, the building also serves as the Colleton Museum (843-549-2303), where you can see a collection of artifacts from the county's history and cultural heritage as well as changing art exhibits.

Another significant building listed on the National Register of Historic Places is the Colleton County Court House, Jefferies Boulevard and Hampton Street. Designed by Robert Mills and completed in 1832, the courthouse boasts walls that are three bricks (twenty-eight inches) thick. The front of the structure is set off by two curving stairways that lead up to the second-floor projecting portico that rests on a curved foundation. In 1828 the first public nullification meeting openly resisting tariff laws and calling for the immediate secession of the state legislature was led from the steps of the courthouse by Robert Barnwell Rhett, known as the "Father of Secession."

Fondly known locally as the "Little Library," the tiny white Federal-style wood-frame Walterboro Library Society Building, Wichman and Fishburn Streets, was built in 1820 and was the focal point for setting the boundaries of "three-quarters mile in every direction" when the town was incorporated. The common in front of the Little Library is often the site of special events such as the Hanging of the Greens in December. Directly across the street is St. Jude's Episcopal Church. Built in 1881 to replace an earlier structure, the striking white church is constructed in the frame carpenter-Gothic style of the Victorian period. You can drive by the Robert Barnwell Rhett House, Walter Street, known as the Nullification House because of Rhett's role in the movement. Forty-two other sites are described in the driving-tour brochure.

The official South Carolina Artisans Center, 334 Wichman Street (843-549-0011), located in a stately Victorian home in the Hickory Valley Historic District, is a retail outlet for the works of juried South Carolina artists. Peruse the items of folk art and fine crafts including handcrafted baskets, pottery, weavings, jewelry, stained glass, furniture, and sculpture to find unique keepsakes and whimsical gifts. Open daily, the center features working craftspeople demonstrating their skills, as well as periodic educational programs and special events. This is the place to find one-of-a-kind South Carolina handmade treasures.

The headquarters of the Edisto River Canoe and Kayak Trail (803-549-5591), a fifty-six-mile black-water river course, is at Colleton State Park, north of Walterboro, US 15 (803-538-8206). Along the trail, five boat landings make public access easy. Guided trips are also available. An ancient waterway commercially important to the Native Americans and in colonial times as well, the Edisto is reported to be the world's longest free-flowing black-water river. Accommodations are found in cabins beside the marsh, or you can camp along the ocean.

Visit the ruins of Pon Pon Chapel, one mile off State 64, which was one of two chapels of ease established by an act of the general assembly in 1725 to serve St. Bartholomew's Parish. The original chapel was constructed in 1726, but burned by Indians in 1754. A brick chapel replaced the original, but it was heavily damaged by fire during the Revolutionary War in 1782. Even though the church was rebuilt in the early 1820s, locally it has ever after been known as the Burnt Church. Enough of the original structure remains to distinguish its gracious features.

Go east on State 64, turn right on County 458, and proceed to Bonnie Doone Plantation. Formerly transferred as a land grant to William Hopton from England in 1822, the fifteen-thousand-acre plantation was a major rice producer. The mansion house was burned by Sherman's troops in 1865 and lay in ruins for more than sixty-five years. A new brick Georgian-style mansion was built in 1931, and a formal camellia garden was designed and planted next to the house. The name Bonnie Doone came from an adjacent piece of property that was added to the plantation. Bonnie Doone's ballroom was included in Mrs. Helen Comstock's book, *The One Hundred Most Beautiful Rooms in America*. A small cemetery with tiny headstones honoring family dogs lies nearby. Today the remaining 131 acres and the mansion serve as a camp and conference center operated by the Charleston Baptist Association. Located at the headwaters of the Ashepoo River in Colleton County, the secluded and tranquil site is characterized by a long avenue of century-old oaks, abandoned rice fields, woods, and marshlands. In addition to church activities, elderhostel classes are held at the center with accommodations in the main house, cottage, or cabins, and it is the site of weddings and private parties and is an ideal spot for a picnic. For more information, call 843-723-4571.

Go south on I-95 to Hardeeville, just across the Georgia/South Carolina line. The Hardeeville exit is the busiest interchange on I-95 in South Carolina and proclaims itself both the "Inn Village," because it offers more than one thousand motel rooms, and also the "Fireworks Capital of the World." *Old Number 7*, a 1910 steam engine residing permanently on a narrow-gauge track next to Town Hall on Main Street, is a rare mini-locomotive. Once the workhorse of Argent Lumber Company, it was actively used until 1957. It was ideal for short hauling trips from forested areas to the lumber mill. The locomotive had a top speed of 35 mph when hauling empty cars or 15 mph when full. During the third weekend each September, Hardeeville hosts the annual Catfish Festival (843-784-6776 or 843-784-3606), an event of food booths, arts and crafts, a

Old Number 7 *is located next to Town Hall on Main Street in Hardeeville.*

parade, a street dance, the Boat Poker Run, kiddie rides, and boat races on the Savannah River.

Most noted for its trendy beach resorts, the Lowcountry nonetheless offers a rich history with accompanying sites, alluring small towns, and countless outdoor recreational opportunities. If you want to explore beyond the bounds of the Lowcountry, historic Charleston and the tourism regions called Santee Cooper Country and Thoroughbred Country are conveniently located nearby.

For More Information

Lowcountry and Resort Islands Tourism Commission, P.O. Box 615, Yemassee, 29945. 843-717-3090 or 800-528-6870.

Edisto Chamber of Commerce, P.O. Box 206, Edisto Beach 29438. 843-869-3867.

Greater Beaufort Chamber of Commerce, P.O. Box 910, Beaufort 29901. 843-524-3163.

Hampton County Chamber of Commerce, P.O. Box 122, Courthouse Annex, Hampton 29924. 803-943-3784.

Hardeeville Chamber of Commerce, P.O. Box 307, Hardeeville 29927. 843-784-3606.

Hilton Head Island Chamber of Commerce, P.O. Box 5647, Hilton Head Island 29938. 843-785-3673 or 800-523-3373.

Jasper County Chamber of Commerce, P.O. Box 1267, Ridgeland 29936. 843-726-8126.

Walterboro-Colleton Chamber of Commerce, P.O. Box 426, Walterboro 29488. 843-549-9595.

5

Olde English District

A glance at any map of this region might make you think that you've picked up an English map by mistake. Predominant city names include Camden, York, Lancaster, Chester, and Chesterfield. But no, you haven't been mysteriously transported across the Atlantic. You're simply experiencing the deep English legacy and ties that imbue this corner of South Carolina.

In fact, the majority of the early settlers were English, Scottish, and Irish who had come over from Europe and settled in Pennsylvania, naming their towns after the home places they had left behind. When they moved on to new frontiers in South Carolina's uplands, they took those same place names with them. Many of these settlers maintained strong bonds with England and considered themselves Tories.

Just as with the fierce rivalries of England's Red Rose of Lancaster and White Rose of York, when the Revolutionary War broke out, loyalties were divided with as many settlers aligned with one side as the other. Although we tend to think of the Civil War as the only time in American history when brothers fought against brothers, in reality many of the troops fighting with the British were colonists. After the war, however, they learned to share the region's plentiful natural resources.

That sense of Englishness has remained strong. Many of the attributes that are considered so deeply southern—love of land and family, a devotion to horses and horse racing, courtly manners, and a reverence for antiquity—evolved from English values.

Long before the European settlers came, however, this area was inhabited by Catawba Indians. With a name that means "People of the River," these Native Americans developed a working partnership with the dangerous streams, which held no fear for them. In secret places along the rivers, they found clay, which they used for the fine art of their renowned pottery. The Catawbas are the only tribe maintaining a homeland in South Carolina.

Today the Olde English District is characterized by picture-pretty towns, peach orchards, textile mills, championship golf, trophy fishing, horse farms, and bed and breakfasts.

Begin your tour at Cheraw in the northeastern corner of the state at US 52 and State 9. More than fifty antebellum homes and churches, as well as numerous Victorian structures filling 213 acres, comprise the Cheraw Historic District, earning it the appellation "The prettiest town in Dixie." Named for the Cheraw Indians who reached the height of their power in 1650, the village was a well-fortified settlement on the Great Pee Dee River. The Cheraw, who were farmers, were different from many Native American tribes in that they had a princess rather than a chief. Unfortunately, diseases brought by the white explorers and early traders decimated their population, and what was left of the Cheraw tribe joined the Catawba Confederacy. English, Scottish, French, and Irish settlers began moving into the area in 1730. The town itself began as a small trading post and water mill in 1740. From lands they were granted in 1766, Thomas and Eli Kershaw laid out the wide streets and the town green of the present community, which is the nucleus of the National Historic District. During the 1830s silk production was promoted with some success.

Cheraw is the head of navigation for the Great Pee Dee River. The hundred-mile-long river is the longest waterway in South Carolina to flow into the Atlantic Ocean. Cheraw became a busy steamboat port and commercial and banking center in the nineteenth century. Corn, tobacco, rice, and indigo were major crops, but even more significant was cotton. Very important to the citizens of Cheraw, the river made it possible for them to receive goods ordered from New York City in "less than a month," which must have seemed like the speed of light in those days. The story is told that one man received an order in only nine days, promoting him to exclaim, "I think we are about to commence a new era in business in this section." An interesting musical side note: composer Stephen Foster's famous song "Way Down upon the Suwanee River" was originally written to be "Way Down upon the Pee Dee River."

Prior to the Civil War Cheraw was the largest cotton market between Georgetown and Wilmington and contained the second-largest bank in the state. With the profits from King Cotton, many significant buildings were erected. At the same time a triple row of elm trees was planted around the green, one row on each side and a row down the median, to enhance the aesthetics of the downtown area. Some of those elms remain to shade the median today. Some say the reason Cheraw has so many trees is because of a law that required those who were charged with being publicly drunk and disorderly to dig an elm from the woods and transplant it within the city. Cheraw takes pride in its trees and was not only designated as the state's first National Arbor Day Tree City, but has also won the honor more times than any other city in South Carolina.

Cheraw saw action in both the Revolutionary and Civil Wars. During the Revolution Cheraw was the center of a wide area of unrest and was considered strategic by both sides.

Patriot hero General Nathaneal Greene had a camp across the river, and a church was used by both sides as a hospital. Secession feelings were rife in the mid-1800s. In fact, Cheraw claims that its first secession meeting occurred four days before that of Abbeville, which claims to have held the first meeting. The town became a haven for refugees and a storage place for valuables and military stores during the Civil War. In March of 1865, Union General William Tecumseh Sherman and sixty thousand of his troops and twenty thousand camp followers occupied Cheraw—the largest congregation of Union troops anywhere in South Carolina. The mayor surrendered the town without a fight, and the Federals chased Confederate troops across the wooden covered bridge over the Great Pee Dee River, which the Confederates burned to prevent the Union troops from pursuing them. The Union troops then had the time-consuming job of building a pontoon bridge across the river before they could advance. Although many buildings in the business district were destroyed in an accidental explosion during the occupation, no public buildings or dwellings were destroyed deliberately. It is thought that the sheer number of troops in Cheraw prevented it from being destroyed. Sherman was afraid his troops would hurt each other in the melee. In addition, the soldiers were in good humor because of all the plunder they had taken so easily.

Cheraw's most famous native son was John Birks "Dizzy" Gillespie, one of the world's greatest jazz trumpeters. He earned the nickname because of the mischievous scrapes he so often got into as a child. In fact, of his childhood, Gillespie said, "In Cheraw mischief, money making, and music captured all my attention." Dizzy hung around the movie theater so much, he was given a job keeping people from sneaking in, becoming, as he described it, a child bouncer. His pay was seeing the movie free. In junior high school Dizzy played in the band; he also played and danced for money at the Chicora Club, where he was the only black allowed. In later years the

King of Bebop began all his performances with "I'm from Cheraw, South Carolina." In his honor, the Cheraw Arts Commission has Gillespie's upturned trumpet as its logo. Another easily recognized former resident was Aunt Jemima (Ann Harrington), whose name and likeness were lent to the famous syrup.

Cheraw has one of the most delightful policies about touring its historic buildings that we've ever run across. The town doesn't have the staff to keep the structures open to visitors, but all you have to do is stop by the office of the Cheraw Visitors Bureau located at the Greater Cheraw Chamber of Commerce, 221 Market Street (843-537-5886), and they'll give you the keys so you can tour on your own. Sarah Spruill, director of the bureau, says they've never had any problems with this laid-back, visitor-friendly policy.

You'll want to begin your exploration of Cheraw with the Town Green, bisected by Market Street and bounded by Second, Seaboard, Short Market, and Wall Streets. The green is the site of several antebellum structures such as the 1858 Town Hall, the 1836 Market Hall, the 1830 Inglis-McIver Law Office, and the 1820–25 Cheraw Lyceum Museum, as well as a collection of charming turn-of-the-century commercial buildings. The green, landscaped and maintained by the Civic League Garden Club, provides open space for many receptions, art shows, flower shows, and other gatherings.

First, visit the tiny Greek Revival Cheraw Lyceum Museum, which was historically a meeting place for political and cultural affairs. Members met monthly for the purpose of collecting books for a town library. At one time the small red brick, one-room building was used as a courtroom for the chancery courts and as the town's first telegraph office. Prior to the Civil War, the building was used by Chancellor John A. Inglis, who was the chairman of the committee that drafted the Ordinance of Secession. During that war Confederate troops had used the building as a quartermaster's office and when Sherman's troops took the town, they used it for the same purpose. Today the museum presents a miniature visual history of Cheraw with displays and artifacts from prehistoric times through the Native American period, the Revolutionary War, the steamboat period, Secession and the Civil War, and into the present. A small exhibit honors Dizzy Gillespie.

Across Market Street, the Inglis-McIver Law Office is a small white frame Greek Revival structure also used by Inglis, as well as by Alexander McIver and his sons Henry, who became an associate justice of the Supreme Court, and Edward, a circuit court judge. Originally located on Front Street, it was one of the survivors of the 1865 explosion. Steepled Market Hall, Market Street, was once used as a public market and equity court. Four Doric columns support a second-story porch reached by a double stairway. Originally, the ground floor was a bricked, open market where produce was sold, and the second floor was used as offices. Later, the ground floor was enclosed to make another room.

The Masons organization paid for part of the construction of the Town Hall, Market Street, and used the upstairs, which is reached by an exterior double iron staircase, for their meetings. The upstairs was also used as an opera house. Although the structure appears to be constructed of stone blocks, it is actually built from weatherboards bevel cut to resemble stone and painted with a mixture of paint and sand to complete the stone illusion. Today the Town Hall still serves as city offices.

Also on the green is the former Merchant's Bank Building, now First Citizen's Bank. Built in 1835, not only was it the biggest bank in the state outside Charleston, but it was the last bank to honor Confederate currency. As was the custom of the day, the cashier and his family lived on the premises to protect the money. Just behind the green at the corner of Second and Wall is Miller Ingram's Pee Dee River Artifact Collection, 204 Market Street (843-537-6565). Ingram, an attorney who dives as a hobby, has retrieved a vast number of artifacts from the river bottom, particularly relics from the steamboat era and the Civil War period, and displays them at his office. Just step in and ask the receptionist to admit you to the collection. On the other side of the square, the old movie theater has been transformed into the Theater on the Green, a venue for live performances.

Next, using the *Guide to the Cheraw Historic District* map that you picked up at the visitors bureau, drive to Church Street to visit Old St. David's Church (no phone). Circa 1770–74, the chapel was the last Anglican church built in South Carolina under King George III and always had black members. During the Revolutionary War, the church was used as quarters by the South Carolina militia and later as a hospital by the English Seventy-First Highlanders, a regiment of Lord Cornwallis's army. Many of the English soldiers died there of smallpox, and the common foot soldiers are buried in a mass grave in the churchyard cemetery. The officers were buried individually in graves covered by brick mounds. (Remains of many soldiers from all of America's wars are buried here.) After the Revolution, the church was rarely used because of anti-British sentiment and it was disestablished. After several decades, both the Baptists and Presbyterians used it, but eventually the Episcopal Church reclaimed it. During the Civil War the church was used as a hospital by both sides and was slightly damaged by the 1865 explosion. In 1970 the church was given to the Chesterfield County Historic Preservation Commission for restoration to the period of 1826. The simple interior is characterized by box pews, a centrally located pulpit, and a slave gallery. A Confederate Monument in the churchyard is purported to be the oldest in existence. In fact, the original inscription did not mention Confederate soldiers directly because Union troops still occupied the area. Also buried and honored here is Captain Mose Rogers, the first to make a steamboat crossing of the Atlantic in the USS *Savannah* in 1817.

Using the same brochure, make a leisurely driving tour of Cheraw's seventy-five historic sites. Adjacent to St. David's is Riverside Park on Yankee Hill on the banks of the Great Pee Dee. It is located on the site of the former steamboat landing and at one time was the location of a covered bridge. Today you can enjoy a boat ramp and picnicking facilities. The Cheraw Spring Festival held at the park each April includes tours of many of the town's loveliest homes, along with dances, arts and crafts, a quilt show, 5K and 10K races, food, and other entertainment, the highlight of which is a Civil War encampment and reenactment.

Ride along Third Street, a treasure trove of architectural gems that are private residences. Among the many historic houses is the Teacherage, 230 Third Street. Reputed to be the oldest dwelling in Cheraw, the original section was built prior to 1790; an ell was added in the 1840s. The six magnolias were planted during the Civil War—one for each son who was serving the Confederacy. Early in this century several teachers boarded in the house, earning it its nickname. Across the street at 235 Third Street is the Lafayette House, where a public reception was held for General Lafayette during his 1825 visit to the United States.

In the Powe Town neighborhood, the house at 143 McIver Street was used by General Sherman as his personal headquarters, and the residence at 135 McIver was used by General Howard. The St. Peter's Catholic Church, 602 Market Street (843-537-7351), which bears burns and saber marks from the Civil War, contains the furnishings of the Duke of Westphalia's private chapel.

Outside of town, Lake Jupiter provides a beautiful, tranquil backdrop for the 6,928-yard championship golf course at Cheraw State Park, US 52S (843-537-2215 or 800-868-9630); it is the oldest and largest of South Carolina's state parks. Bent-grass greens challenge the best golfer, but multiple tees make the course a good one for average golfers as well. In addition to golf and water sports, Cheraw State Park offers bridle trails. Naturalists will be interested in knowing that the park is the only place south of Pennsylvania where the shrub Hudsonia grows. Money was raised to purchase the initial acreage with nickels and dimes the schoolchildren of Cheraw collected and saved during the depths of the Depression.

You might want to spend some time in the Sand Hills State Forest, US 1S (843-335-8401), forty-six thousand acres of deep sands deposited by a prehistoric sea. Through forest management, the once-barren sand hills now support a large inventory of timber and a variety of game and nongame species of wildlife, including the rare red-cockaded woodpecker and the Pine Barren tree frog. In addition, the forest supports Pixie Moss, a small menotypic species of the Galax family which is characterized by a delicate pink bloom and a fernlike appearance.

If you want to stay overnight in the Cheraw area, you can choose between two historic properties. 501 Kershaw, 501 Kershaw Street (843-537-7733), is a completely restored 1850 antebellum, two-story colonial-style home. The spacious guest room features a fireplace and antique furnishing. In addition, the owners, Kay and Larry Spears, have purchased a cottage around the corner in which they also offer bed-and-breakfast accommodations. Called the Spears Guest House, appropriately enough, it features four guest rooms with private baths, as well as a common living room, dining room, and fully equipped kitchen, making it ideal for a family, small group, or an extended-stay visitor. 505 Market, 505 Market Street (843-537-9649), is located in a two-story residence dating from 1850. Broad steps lead up to a twelve-foot-deep front porch graced with rockers. Inside, the house features eight fireplaces, twelve-foot ceilings, and original pine flooring. Guest rooms have gas-log fireplaces and are decorated with period furnishings.

Take State 9 west from Cheraw through Chesterfield and Pageland. This route has the largest concentration of small flea markets we've ever seen. During the summer, they are active every weekend; the remainder of the year it's catch-as-catch-can—you'll often find them open in good weather. At Pageland you'll notice that the terrain changes and becomes more rolling. About four miles west of Pageland, turn south on US 601 to Kershaw, site of one of the largest granite flat rocks east of the Mississippi. Flat Creek Heritage Preserve and Forty Acre Rock, Conservancy Road off US 601 (803-734-3893), a National Natural Landmark, sits at the transition between the piedmont and the upper-coastal plain, is intermingled with the sandhills of South Carolina, and is the most diverse protected area in the piedmont. Among the habitats found there are granite flatrocks, a diabase dike, waterfall, waterslide, cave, beaver pond, piedmont cove forest, piedmont flood plain, chestnut and oak forest, and upland pine/hardwood forest. The forty-acre rock, which is actually fourteen acres, was a magma intrusion into a less weather-resistant rock eons ago and is the thickest flatrock east of the Mississippi. A well-marked, three-mile nature trail allows visitors to glimpse a large variety of wildflowers and plants, including a dozen rare and endangered species. A number of plants occur exclusively on granite outcrops. The pool-sprite plant is found only during a brief period when late-winter precipitation maintains water in small shallow pools at the top of the rock.

Take US 521 northwest to Lancaster. Named by settlers from Lancaster, Pennsylvania, the town was the site of the last witchcraft trial in America in 1816. Lancaster contains a stately courthouse and is also noted for its murals. The backs of many Main Street buildings contain murals of early residents, and the Wall of Fame across from the courthouse depicts famous area citizens: Andrew Jackson, James Marion Simms (a noted turn-of-the-century gynecologist), Elliott White Springs (a textile industrialist), Nina Mae McKinney (a 1920s actress), and Charles Duke (the Apollo astronaut).

The town's impressive Lancaster County Courthouse and Jail were designed by noted architect Robert Mills in the 1820s. One of the most outstanding features of this working courthouse, 104 Main Street, is a magnificent Palladian window, considered by many to be the most perfect example of the style in America. Three hundred thousand handmade bricks were used in the construction of the slave-built structure. Considered to be in the most original condition of all Mills's courthouses, this one features his trademark vaulted hall ceiling and arched doors. During a restoration several years ago, drawings—now preserved—by Civil War prisoners were discovered on the walls of the Grand Jury Room. Steel tie rods or earthquake rods were added in the 1880s when an earthquake in Charleston was felt in Lancaster. The story is told that a fiddler was playing for a dance held in the courtroom and when he felt the tremor, he threw down and broke his fiddle and never played again. The slave balcony has been removed, but the courtroom still contains the original judge's bench.

The 1828 jail, 208 West Gay Street, now government offices, is the only known example of medieval design by Mills. The two-story structure allowed the run-of-the-mill prisoners to be separated from the worst ones who were housed upstairs. As was the custom of the time, the jailer and his family lived on the premises and raised vegetables and chickens to feed the prisoners. Ten prisoners died in a fire in 1978, and the structure was never used as a jail after that. For information about seeing the courthouse or jail, you can contact the clerk of the court at 803-285-1581 or the Lancaster County Administration at 803-285-1565.

Catty-corner across the street from the jail is the City Hall, housed in an antebellum house. It was occupied by Union troops during the Civil War, although family members were allowed to remain in residence. It is reported that one of the daughters was ordered to play the piano for the officers' entertainment, but in defiance she would only play Confederate tunes. Family and troops watched from the porch as the roof of the jail was burned.

Although the Lancaster Presbyterian Church, 307 West Gay Street (no phone), is in a sad state of disrepair and awaiting funds for restoration, it is architecturally interesting in that it is the oldest brick building in Lancaster County, circa 1862. Sherman's troops stabled their horses inside the church and fed them from the pews. Union troops also stole the silver communion service. Many prominent citizens are buried in the churchyard. If you are interested in seeing the interior of the church, inquire at the Chamber of Commerce, 604 North Main Street (803-283-4105).

Browse and lunch at Southern Rose Tea Room and Gift Shoppe, 300 North White Street (803-286-7673), located in an 1885 house that remained in the same family for a hundred years. Recently renovated, it now contains a charming tea room, a framing shop, and a wide variety of gift and gourmet food items. Southern Rose is particularly noted for its homemade fudge. Luncheon choices range from salads to entrees, sandwiches, or quiche accompanied by soup or a salad, fresh fruit, and a homemade muffin, as well as Columbian coffees, wines, and sinful desserts. The chicken salad is so renowned that ladies drive to Lancaster from Charlotte and Columbia to buy it by the bucket. The menu as well as the decor are changed with the season.

"Old Hickory," America's seventh president, was born in South Carolina in a region known as the Waxhaws, which straddles the South Carolina/North Carolina state line. Jackson spent his boyhood years in this rugged pioneer area which once belonged to the Waxhaw Indians. His first warfare experience was at the age of thirteen at the Battle of Hanging Rock, where General Thomas Sumter achieved his greatest Revolutionary War victory over a Tory army. A statue of a young *Andrew Jackson, Boy of the Waxhaws* by Anna Hyatt Huntington, who created Brookgreen Gardens, honors the former president at Andrew Jackson State Park, US 521 (803-285-3344), a 360-acre park that interprets the period from 1750 to 1850. A museum and one-room school in the park offer reminders of the nineteenth-century Carolina back-country pioneer era. The museum displays Jackson papers, Indian arrowheads and artifacts from 8000 B.C. to A.D. 1600, bedroom and kitchen furnishings, as well as tools and implements such as a spinning wheel and loom. A small lock of Jackson's hair is the only item on display that belonged to the former president. In addition, the park offers camping, picnicking, a nature trail, year-round interpretive programs, and an amphitheater.

In 1754 Thomas Land built a trading post on the Catawba River at a ford used by both the Catawba and Cherokee Indians. Naturally enough, it became known as Thomas Land's Ford. The centerpiece of the Landsford Canal State Park, off US 21 (803-789-5800), is the Landsford Canal, the last of ten early-nineteenth-century South Carolina river canals and the only one with all its major features intact. Landsford Canal was the uppermost of the canals built on the Catawba-Wateree river system between 1820 and 1835. Although the river is placid above and below this spot, in a distance of only two miles the river drops thirty-two feet. Although a canoe can negotiate the rapids, the sixty-foot-long boats used to transport goods, such as the cotton grown in the surrounding area, could not. In 1820 a two-mile canal around the shoals was begun using Scotch-Irish laborers and took three years to complete.

Interpretive exhibits, including a model of a lift lock describing the canal system's history and technology, are housed in the only lockkeeper's house remaining in the state. A 1.5-mile trail follows the route of the canal and allows visitors to see portions of it, including the original culverts, a guard lock, and a three-compartment lift lock, as well as a bridge that was used by Sherman's troops to cross the canal.

The rocky shoals around which the canal was built are home to the world's largest concentration of rare rocky shoals spider lilies, which bloom in only a few isolated places in South Carolina, Georgia, and Alabama. The shoals provide a protected area for this showy member of the amaryllis family, whose Latin name, *Hymenocallis occidentalis*, translates to "beautiful membranous crown from the west." It is also believed that the oxygen-enriched swirling waters enable the plants to thrive. The flowers, known as the Queens of the Catawba River, are three to four inches across and grow atop a stalk that protrudes one to three feet out of the water. Peak blooming occurs from the end of May to early June, but a secondary blooming extends the viewing time through June.

No matter what the season, Landsford Canal State Park is a lovely spot to visit. From the parking area, the lightly wooded ground slopes gently down to the river's edge at the beginning of the shoals, a favorite feeding spot for many wading birds. Located along several major flyways, the park is popular with bird watchers, who come to observe, among others, bald eagles feeding in the early morning hours. A primitive 1790s log cabin has been moved to this area and is used for group functions. Scattered throughout the picnic area at the water's edge are carvings of people and animals by Smiley Small. When a tree falls or has to be cut down, rather than removing the stumps, park officials leave it and Smiley comes on weekends to do his carving, much to the delight of park visitors who can spend hours watching him and listening to his tales. If you get an opportunity, have red-haired park superintendent Joe Anderson tell a few tales of his own—particularly the ones about the local Blarney stone and the one about the twelve-year-old boy who charged folks to see the best view in South Carolina.

Take State 5 to Catawba. The heritage and culture of the Catawba Indians are preserved at the Catawba Cultural Preservation Center on the Catawba Indian Reservation, 1536 Tom Steven Road (803-328-2427), where pottery-making demonstrations and classes are held regularly. In addition to their distinctive pottery, the gift shop offers Native American books and crafts. Guided tours and special programs are available by appointment. The premier event each year is the Yap Ye Iswa Festival (The Day of the Catawbas), held each November, which explores the lifestyles and history of the Catawbas. Exhibits include pottery making, beadwork, basket making, hide tanning, and blow-gun construction, as well as storytelling, an herb table, and Native American cuisine.

Continue north on State 5, then US 21 to Rock Hill. Rock Hill is named for a cut made through white flinty rock during construction of the Columbia to Charlotte railroad. Nestled in the foothills of the piedmont, Rock Hill is the largest city in York County. Four captivating thirteen-foot female statues representing the cornerstones of life and prosperity and two sixty-foot Egyptian Revival columns surrounded by terraced gardens create The Gateway into Rock Hill.

Six acres of sculpted terraces, lily ponds, stately oaks, and flamboyantly blooming shrubs and thousands of bulbs and flower beds slope toward a serene reflecting pool and fountain at Glencairn Garden, Charlotte Avenue and Crest Street. The award-winning garden displays nature's finest colors, textures, shapes, and fragrances and is the site of the Come and See Me Festival, held each April. For information about the gardens or the festival, call the York County Convention and Visitors Bureau at 800-866-5200.

The Rock Hill Telephone Company Museum, 117 Elk Avenue (803-324-4030), offers a hands-on tour through a hundred years of communication. Place a call on a turn-of-the-century phone, be an operator on a 1940s switchboard, see how an electro-mechanical switch works as you place a call, and examine other telephones and tools that span a century.

Pick up a guide to Historic Rock Hill from the Visitors Center, 201 East Main Street (800-866-5200), located in the old 1931 post office. While you're there, peruse the *How We Got Here from There* transportation exhibit. Displays include a dugout canoe, covered wagon, locomotive, buggy, and an Anderson automobile.

Baseball fans will enjoy *Mighty Casey*, a fourteen-foot bronze sculpture of the legendary ballplayer from Ernest Lawrence Thayer's narrative poem *Casey at the Bat*.

Stay at the East Main Guest House, 600 East Main Street (803-366-1161), the beautifully restored and decorated turn-of-the-century craftsman-style home of Melba and Jerry Peterson, where you can choose from three guest rooms, all with cable TV and telephone, some with a gas-log fireplace and whirlpool tub. An upstairs sitting/game room contains a TV, phone, game table, and games. Other bed-and-breakfast accommodations can be found at the Book & the Spindle, 626 Oakland Avenue (803-328-1913), a 1913 brick Georgian home offering two rooms and two suites overlooking Winthrop University, and the Park Avenue Inn, 347 Park Avenue (803-325-1764), a 1916 home with four guest rooms.

Hampton House Restaurant, 204 Johnston Street (803-329-5958), located in the heart of historic Rock Hill, occupies one of the oldest and finest homes in town. Constructed in 1874–75 for sisters, Misses Sallie and Mary Elizabeth Gibson, Hampton House was Rock Hill's first big, truly fine house. It features a wide wrap-around porch and an entrance hall with a freestanding spiral staircase. Inside, the rooms are decorated in startlingly modern motifs.

Take I-77 north and turn east on State 160 to Fort Mill. Located in eastern York County, Fort Mill is the home of Springs Industries, one of the nation's largest textile manufacturers. One of the last meetings of the full Confederate cabinet met at the White Homestead nearby. Four monuments commemorating participants in the Civil War fill Confederate Park, Main Street. One is dedicated to Confederate soldiers, one to women of the Confederacy, one to faithful black slaves, and the last to the Catawba Indians who served in the Confederate Army.

The Radisson Grand Resort, 9700 Regent Parkway off Carowinds Boulevard (800-374-1234), formerly New Heritage USA, is a resort and theme park with a water park, horseback riding, boating, tennis, and roller skating. In December every corner of the park is awash with colored lights during the Festival of Lights.

Located to the west of I-77 is Lake Wylie. The lake is not only a beautiful lakeside community on the South Carolina/North Carolina border, but it is also the home of one of the state's technological marvels. Learn about nuclear energy through high-tech video games and films at Energy Quest, off State 274 at the Catawba Nuclear Station on Lake Wylie (800-777-0006), a Duke Power information center. Use hands-on computer video terminals to explore how electricity is made; watch nuclear plant operators training and being tested in a simulated control room at the National Academy for Nuclear Training; and enjoy presentations on energy, radiation, basic electricity, and Catawba's environmental leadership. Adult tours of the power plant are available with advance reservations. You should take the time to watch *Home Town*, an excellent movie about Rock Hill and its residents. A nature trail leads to picnicking facilities and an outdoor classroom. Plant food is provided to attract quail and geese, bluebird houses make the small birds welcome, and an area is planted in vegetation that entices butterflies—all attempts by Duke Power to coexist in harmony with nature. Special events throughout the year include Science Saturdays and Girls Encampments, when girls are shown the opportunities that are available to them in the science field. Call for a schedule of these special events.

Unlock the magic and mystery of herbs at the Riddle Mill Organic Farm, 1098 Riddle Mill Road (803-831-2506), thirty-five acres of fields, forests, and streams. Wander through the gardens and greenhouses which produce four hundred varieties of herbs and edible flowers and buy natural products such as homemade soaps, jewelry, clothing, vinegars, and more at the farm store. Periodic special events include herbal tea walks and herbal workshops.

The biggest amusement park in the state, Paramount's Carowinds, off I-77 on the South Carolina/North Carolina border, features exciting rides such as the Vortex, the only stand-up roller coaster east of the Mississippi, the mega-coaster Thunder Road, Carolina Cyclone, Days of Thunder, and Riptide Reef, as well as a water theme park and topnotch entertainment.

In mid-December gaily lighted and decorated boats parade past the brightly lit shoreline and under illuminated Buster Boyd Bridge during Lights on the Lake. For more information, call the Lake Wylie Chamber of Commerce (803-831-2827).

Retrace I-77 south to State 161 or State 5 and turn west to York. Although its first known inhabitants were the Catawba Indians, with the influx of Scotch-Irish settlers, it's not surprising that the city was named after York, Pennsylvania, as many of the new residents came from there. Later they were joined by English planters who moved inland from the coast. During the Revolutionary War, the area was the only part of South Carolina that refused to surrender to British forces. Today the "White Rose City" boasts Historic York, one of the largest National Register historic districts in the country with 340 acres and more than 180 structures and landmarks. Guidebooks for self-guided tours are available from the Chamber of Commerce, 23 East Liberty Street (803-684-2590).

The unlikely, the improbable, and the impossible are right at home at the Museum of York County, Mount Gallant and Museum Roads (803-329-2121). Among the outstanding natural history exhibits are more than two hundred artfully mounted animals, not only depicting the wildlife on seven continents, but comprising the world's largest collection of hooved African mammals. The personal collection of one man, Maurice Stans, they were donated by him to the museum. Positioned in simulated naturalistic habitats, most of the animals are behind glass, but a few are out where their presence is quite startling. You can stroke a panther and stand under the neck and head of the giraffe to get an idea of how tall the gangly animals really are. Connected to the African exhibit is a display of artifacts and arts of that continent. In addition to the African animals, there is an impressive display of North American animals representing the rocky crags and shadowy lairs of bears, wolves, mountain lions, and mountain goats. A fascinating exhibit shows how a taxidermist mounts animals and how the dioramas in which they are displayed are created.

A Native American exhibit includes tribal dress, artifacts, and examples of the renowned and highly prized Catawba pottery. This unique pottery is created only from clay found in this area and is shaped by hand from coils, not on a wheel. After the coils have been molded into the utensil the potter intends, the entire vessel is smoothed with a rock and then fired in an open fire, which is why the finished product shows variations in color.

Other attractions at the museum include the Settlemyre Planetarium; the Alternative Gallery; the Hall of Electricity; the Hall of Yesteryear; a snake exhibit; and three art galleries including contemporary art featured in the Springs Gallery, the famed illustrations of Vernon Grant—creator of Kellogg's Snap Crackle Pop—in the Vernon Grant Gallery, and the works of Carolina artists in the Local Accents Gallery. A shady nature trail draws visitors into a uniquely southern outdoor habitat. During the year, changing exhibits in science, history, natural history, and the arts are showcased.

Changing cultural exhibits and historical research materials chronicling York County prior to 1930 attract visitors to the Historical Center of York County, 212 East Jefferson Street (803-684-7262), housed in a restored 1920s schoolhouse, which also serves as a performing arts theater.

In 1780 a ragtag group of mountaineers slogged south from Tennessee and North Carolina to engage an overconfident Loyalist Tory force on a craggy promontory called King's Mountain. The battle, which was a complete victory for the colonials, was the site of Cornwallis's first step toward ultimate defeat and is considered to have turned the tide of the American Revolution. Cornwallis was forced to pull back into North Carolina and Virginia, allowing the Continental Army time to bring in fresh regulars and commanders. Visit the interpretive center at Kings Mountain National Military Park, off State 161 (864-936-7921), to see a film describing the incident and examine artifacts and life-size dioramas depicting the battle and pioneer life in the area. Then stroll up the 1.5-mile trail to the battle site. The park is the culmination of the Overmountain Victory National Historic Trail, which follows the 220-mile route the mountain men took from Abingdon, Virginia. Each October the Overmountain Victory Trail Association assembles for the Kings Mountain Encampment and Muster and the Overmountain Men at Kings Mountain National Military Park reenactment. Activities typical of military camp life include military demonstrations and camp activities. In May, you can step back in time to another recreation of eighteenth-century military life at the Catawba Militia Encampment.

Next, visit the Living Farm frontier homestead at Kings Mountain State Park (803-222-3209), immediately adjacent to the national park. The farm, which re-creates Upcountry life in the 1850s, includes the mid-1800s home place and typical farm outbuildings as well as a blacksmith/carpenter shop, a sorghum mill and cooker, and a cotton gin. Costumed interpreters describe the structures and furnishings, and farm animals and gardens contribute to an air of reality. Try to arrange a visit during the mid-September Pioneer Days and Muzzle Loaders Conclave, when the park is filled with music, arts and crafts, pioneer games, a quilt exhibit, and the sounds of the black-powder sharpshooters competition. Other demonstrations include blacksmithing, weaving, pottery making, woodcarving, natural dyeing, outdoor cooking, and soapmaking. In addition, the more than six-thousand-acre park offers camping, swimming, fishing, boat rentals, miniature golf, twenty miles of bridle trails, and sixteen miles of nature and hiking trails.

Particularly appealing to families are the educational farm tours at Windy Hill Orchard and Cider Mill, 1860 State 5 (803-684-0690), where you can go on a hayride, make a scarecrow, hear stories from Johnny Appleseed, and participate in making apples into cider. The facility is open from mid-August to December 21.

Take US 321 south to McConnells, a tiny country community spread over two square miles of pasture land dotted with old home places and groves of trees. Although it's hard to imagine, an area nearby was once the bustling town of Brattonsville. You can transport yourself to the century of 1750 to 1850 by visiting Historic Brattonsville, off State 322 ten miles west of Rock Hill (803-684-2327), a living-history village. The site was the home of the prominent Bratton family and was the location of the Revolutionary Battle of Huck's Defeat, an important victory over local Loyalists and their British support unit. Travel through a progression of lifestyles from the American Revolution to the plantation era to the mid-nineteenth century by exploring more than two dozen historic structures illustrating contrasting lifestyles in a diverse economy. Using a self-guided audio tour, you can begin with pre-Revolutionary War backwoodsman and McConnell log cabins, then examine the exquisitely restored 1780 Colonel Bratton plantation house, the 1823 Homestead House, slave cabins, a brick kitchen house, a nineteenth-century doctor's office, and other examples of historic architecture and arts. Farm animals, crops, gardens, and orchards contribute to the ambience of a working farm. Varieties of animals typical to the mid-nineteenth century are raised as part of the Historic Brattonsville's Heritage Farm Program, which includes the preservation of seed stock and agricultural techniques unique to the region. During monthly living-history programs and special events, watch costumed reenactors demonstrate skills of daily living such as sheepshearing, carding wool, spinning, planting and harvesting, or tending livestock. The gift shop purveys regional handcrafted items, reproductions, and decorative arts. During the autumn Red Hills Heritage Festival, watch old-time skills demonstrations, listen to the storytelling sessions, purchase crafts, and enjoy the food and music. The highlight of the Christmas Candlelight Open House is the tour of four historic homes lovingly decorated with eighteenth- and nineteenth-century ornaments and filled with the sights, smells, and sounds of bygone Christmases. The July Battle of Huck's Defeat Reenactment is imbued with Revolutionary fervor. Historic Brattonsville is open from March through November.

Go south on US 321, turn west on State 322, and then south on State 49 to Union. Organized around 1785, the town was named after the Union Church, which was jointly attended by both Episcopalian and Presbyterian congregations. Four South Carolina governors hailed from Union. The Downtown Union National Historic District, Main Street, is an outstanding collection of architecturally diverse public and commercial buildings. The East Main Street and South Street historic districts feature some of the finest homes in the county showcasing residences that range from cottages to mansions of up to eight thousand square feet.

A veritable melange of Civil War artifacts, farm tools, and local memorabilia are displayed helter-skelter at the Union County Museum, located upstairs in the American Federal Building on Main Street (864-427-9235 or 864-427-2029). Pride of the museum is the Secession Table on which the Secession Ordinance was drafted. Other Civil War memorabilia include military coats of General William H. Wallace and General States Rights Gist [his real name], flags of the local Johnson Rifles and Pea Ridge Volunteers, weapons, and ammunition. An Archives Room filled with family histories is available for genealogical research. The museum is open afternoons on the first weekend of the month or by appointment.

Built between 1828 and 1832, Rose Hill Plantation State Park, Sardis Road (864-427-5966), was the home of Governor William Henry Gist, who led South Carolina into secession from the Union. During its heyday, the Federal-style residence, surrounded on three sides by a rose garden and boxwood gardens, was the focal point of an eight-thousand-acre cotton plantation. Although the house was originally constructed of brick with a wooden split-shingle roof, during the 1850s Gist covered the brick with stucco scored to give the appearance of stone construction and replaced the roof with tin. Two-story porches were added in both the front and back. Inside, an unusual architectural feature is the upstairs ballroom with twin fireplaces so that the room could be divided with wooden partitions into two bedrooms. As was typical of plantation life of the period, a teacher lived on the property to instruct the children. The third floor of the mansion was used as a schoolroom and the teacher's bedroom.

Gist died at Rose Hill in 1874 and his wife in 1889, after which the estate was divided among the Gist grandchildren. The house fell into disrepair and was once used as a barn by a tenant farmer. During World War II, the Army Air Corps considered using the house for bombing practice, but it was saved by a concerned citizen and the ladies of the Daughters of the American Revolution.

Today, the mansion and forty-four-acre grounds combine to form the centerpiece of a state park. Among the 1860 period furnishings are many original to the house, including the Gist family Bible and hymn book and several of Mrs. Gist's dresses. The waistlines of these dresses are incredibly small, and considering the fact that she had twelve children, they're truly amazing. A brick kitchen house and a small house that served as a slave house and sharecropper's residence remain. Currently, that structure contains exhibits on the lifestyle of the Gist period. During the Christmas Open House, the mansion is bedecked with period decorations, and costumed hostesses offer demonstrations of open-hearth cooking, music, and entertainment.

If you're looking for an appropriate place to stay while in the Union area, you'll have a hard time choosing between the antebellum splendor of the in-town Inn at Merridun, 100 Merridun Place (864-427-7052), or the country atmosphere of the JUXA Plantation, 117 Wilson Road (864-427-8688). Built in 1855, the Greek Revival Inn at Merridun was named for the three families who lived there in the nineteenth century: Merriman, Rice, and Duncan. Originally Georgian in style, remodeling in the late 1800s resulted in the current style. The seventy-nine-hundred-square-foot mansion sports twenty-four hundred square feet of marble verandas. The large central hall culminates in a stunning curved staircase. Other significant architectural aspects include frescoed ceilings in the music room and dining room, mosaic tiles and turn-of-the-century stenciling and faux graining in the foyer, and gorgeous raised designs on the fireplace tiles. Also on the nine-acre property are a brick wing that used to house the servants' kitchen, a well, laundry house, servants' quarters, smoke house, and carriage barn still containing the Duncan's carriage. You can choose from five distinctively decorated guest rooms, each with a private bath. Hosts Peggy and Jim Waller will pamper you with plantation iced tea, freshly baked cookies, fresh flowers, evening desserts and beverages, and a full gourmet breakfast. The Inn at Merridun sponsors many special events such as mystery weekends, wine tastings, and Sunday brunches, and sells the works of Union artists Nancy Basket and Naida Shields. JUXA Plantation was built in the early 1800s by a Scottish family who had fled their native land after participating in a failed plot to kill the king. They changed their name from MacGregor to Gregory and prospered growing cotton and corn. Unfortunately, the drought years of 1844–48 devastated the family economy and many members moved to Mississippi to start over. The house passed through many owners, one of which, a Mr. May, named the plantation after an imaginary playmate of his. Today the Bresse family operates the house as a bed and breakfast, antique and gift shop, and the Magnolia Tea Room.

Retrace State 49 to State 9 and turn east to Chester. You'll appreciate the winding streets and unique blend of architectural styles in the Chester Historic District, which was used as the setting for the TV miniseries *Chiefs* fifteen years ago.

See Indian artifacts, an extensive gun collection, historic documents, Revolutionary and Civil War relics, and other memorabilia at the Chester County Historical Society Museum, McAiley Street (803-385-2330), housed in the 1914 jail behind the county courthouse.

On Fridays and Saturdays you can taste the red, white, and blush wines produced by the Cruse Vineyards and Winery, Woods Road off State 72 (803-377-3944), from classic and French hybrid grapes. This small family operation includes every step in the winemaking process from growing and harvesting the grapes, to crushing, fermentation, bottling, labeling, and packing in the climate-controlled basement of their pleasant ranch house. With equipment obtained in Italy and Switzerland, the Cruses produce fifteen hundred to twenty-five hundred gallons of wine annually. On Friday and Saturday afternoons you can stop by for a tour and tasting.

Stay at the 1832 Wade-Becicham House, 3385 Great Falls Highway (803-285-1105), a plantation home in a rural setting enhanced with an old store, barn, and farm animals.

From Chester, take US 321 south to Winnsboro. Winnsboro, often referred to as the "Charleston of the Upcountry," abounds with architecturally significant homes and buildings. Settled in the mid-1700s and named for the Revolutionary War hero Colonel Richard Winn, the town is the seat of Fairfield

County. It was the site of the Mt. Zion Institute, founded in 1777, and the location of British headquarters under Lord Cornwallis in 1780. During the Civil War, Winnsboro supplied twelve companies to the Confederate army. The town is also noted for its granite industry, and you'll see many residences and commercial buildings constructed or embellished with granite.

More than fifty structures in Winnsboro exceed one hundred years old. Making it particularly conducive to walking tours, Winnsboro's central core is listed on the National Register of Historic Places. Pick up a brochure for the walking tour of fifty-one sites from the Fairfield County Chamber of Commerce in the Town Clock Building, North Congress and Washington Streets (803-635-4242). The Winnsboro Town Clock is thought to be the oldest continuously operating clock in America. In 1833 the General Assembly authorized the town council to erect a market house in the center of town which was to be no wider than thirty feet. The clock was added to the narrow building in 1837. Since it arrived from France, the clock has kept its perfect cadence through war and peace, feast and famine, births and deaths.

Robert Mills, the first noted American architect, designed the Fairfield County Courthouse, Congress and Washington Streets, in 1823. His signature classical design has been altered with the addition of columns and circular stairs. The story is told that during the Civil War valuable county records were saved when the sheriff hid them in bags which he tied around the waists and under the skirts of his wife and daughters.

Winnsboro's Town Hall, North Congress Street (803-635-4943), located in the Obear-Williford House, was built in the mid-nineteenth century as a residence and was later used as a school. During the Civil War, many refugee citizens of Charleston were hidden here by the Obear family. On February 19, 1865, when Union troops were burning and looting Winnsboro, they broke into the house but departed quickly because one of the children was sick with what they thought was scarlet fever. Thespian Hall, East Washington Street, built in 1833, once served double duty as a railway passenger depot downstairs and a concert/dance hall upstairs. After a stint beginning in 1844 as the offices of the county's weekly newspaper, the hall now houses the News and Herald Tavern, a restaurant and bar (803-635-1331), that serves dinner on Friday and Saturday nights.

Artifacts and exhibits pertinent to local history are showcased at the Fairfield County Museum, South Congress Street (803-635-9811). Located in a Federal-style three-story townhouse built in the 1830s as a private residence, the building served for many years as a school for girls, then later as a boardinghouse, public school, and hotel. Similar in style to a Charleston house, the structure boasts superior brickwork, large granite blocks at the base of the building, and a cornice decorated with hand-finished wooden brackets at the roofline. Interior architectural details include original heart-pine floors and hand-carved woodwork, mantels, and cornices. The main floor is maintained as a historic house with antique furnishings in period rooms. Among the exhibits on the other floors are nineteenth-century clothing, quilts, Victorian accessories, toys, Indian and military artifacts, tools, kitchen and sewing implements, and banking and commerce displays. One of the most popular exhibits is the collection of First Lady dolls that is complete through Mamie Eisenhower. The museum also maintains a genealogy research room. Community and school art exhibits are held in the spring. In December the museum hosts a gala nineteenth-century Christmas Open House.

The congregation of the Ebenezer A. P. Presbyterian Church, US 321 ten miles west of town, hand-molded the bricks to build their church in 1788. During the Civil War, Union soldiers stripped the church of its pews and flooring to build a bridge over the nearby Little River. A written apology for the act is visible on the church's inside wall. Make arrangements at the Fairfield County Museum to see the church.

Congress Street is the commercial center of downtown and the place you'll find shops and eateries. Yummies, 128 North Congress Street (803-635-9779), serves sandwiches, soups, salads, and gourmet coffees, teas, and hot chocolates. While you're there, browse through the antiques for sale. Newton's Apple Bookstore, 110-A North Congress Street (803-635-3282), contains not only books, but greeting cards, toys, gift and specialty food items, and handmade afghans.

Stay at Songbird Manor, Zion Street (803-635-6963), a bed and breakfast in a grand 1912 home. Not only was the first owner so wealthy that he constructed the mansion with smooth pressed-brick imported from England, but he installed the first indoor bathroom in town. Among the outstanding interior features are chestnut pocket doors, beautiful plaster ceiling moldings, coffered ceilings, and imported scenic fireplace tiles. Three of the guest baths boast original clawfoot tubs. Bed-and-breakfast accommodations can be found at the Carriage House at Boycelynn, 509 South Congress Street (803-635-9714).

Take State 34 west and follow the signs to Blair. A tiny hamlet at the culmination of a dead-end country road, Blair is worth searching out. Country Store Antiques, Main Street (803-635-2788), located in an ancient general store/filling station, houses a treasury of merchandise, antiques, Edgefield pottery, and junk. The store retains the original counters, display cases, and rolling ladders. Pull up a chair to the working pot-bellied stove to warm your hands while you have some good conversation with the owners or spend hours poking around the store, which seems to go on and on forever. Every time you think you've looked into all the rooms, you find another. If you're hungry while you're browsing, sample and purchase some of the delicious hoop cheese the store carries.

Return to Winnsboro and turn south on US 321. At State 34 turn east to Rockton. On a railroad siding on the Rockton,

Rion, and Western Railroad is the South Carolina Railroad Museum, which displays several historic railroad cars, including *Number* 44, a ten-wheeler steam locomotive, as well as railroad artifacts and equipment. Visitors are welcome to explore the cars and take a short train ride on the third Saturday of the month from May through October. For more information, call 803-635-4242 or 800-968-5909.

Continue east on State 34 to Ridgeway. Originally known as New Town, Ridgeway got its current name when the Charlotte and South Carolina Railway decided not to build the railroad on the Camden route, but instead to use the ridge that bisects the county between the Broad and Wateree Rivers. The town was settled in the late 1700s by Scotch-Irish Presbyterian pioneers who came from Virginia. Later, Charlestonians fled to the uplands to escape a malaria epidemic. Begin your tour at the visitors center on Railroad Street (803-337-2213), where you can pick up a brochure for a self-guided walking tour. Among the historic sites is Century House, a private residence, which was used as a headquarters by Confederate General Pierre G. T. Beauregard after he evacuated Columbia.

Continue east on State 34 to US 1 and turn east to Camden. Established in 1732 as a trading post, Camden is the oldest inland South Carolina city. A large influx of Irish Quakers arrived in the early 1750s, followed over the next ten years by Scotch-Irish settlers. In 1758 Joseph Kershaw arrived to establish a store for a Charleston mercantile firm. Eventually, he started a sawmill, gristmill, and flour mill. It was only in 1768 that the town was named Camden in honor of Charles Pratt, Lord Camden. As the community prospered, so did its leading citizens. Kershaw, for example, constructed a large mansion.

As strong feelings for independence from Britain grew, few supporters of the king could be found in Camden, and the town was selected as the site for a powder magazine for the state of South Carolina. After Charleston fell to the British in 1780, Lord Cornwallis established several outposts in the interior of the state, Camden being one of them. Despite the fact that the local citizens fortified the powder magazine with a moat and an earthen wall, they could not withstand the British, and Cornwallis entered the town and established his headquarters in Kershaw's house. An attempt by the American Continentals and militia to retake the town failed in the Battle of Camden after which the British fortified the town even more heavily with a stockade and six redoubts. Although the British were successful in the Battles of Hobkirk Hill, their losses were so great, they were forced to evacuate, thus breaking the British hold on South Carolina. Today Camden is known not only for beautiful homes but even more so for the fine horses bred and trained there. In addition to the two well-known steeplechase races run in Camden, the county hosts numerous equine shows and races, polo games, and fox hunting.

Get a guidebook, audiotape, and map for a self-guided walking tour of historic Camden from the Kershaw County Chamber of Commerce, 724 Broad Street (800-968-4037). Featuring more than sixty historic sites, the National Register Historic District showcases Camden's 250-year architectural history with styles that range from cottages to antebellum mansions to the Victorian winter residences established at the turn of the century. Kirkwood, Chestnut, Union, Greene, and Lyttleton Streets showcase particularly outstanding homes. The architecture in the central business district is primarily Victorian commercial to modern, not because of the Civil War, but because so many structures were lost to fires over the years.

In order to understand the development of Camden, begin your tour with a visit to Historic Camden Revolutionary War Site, US 521N (803-432-9841), a Revolutionary War–era park connected with the National Park Service. The British army spent a dismal winter here when Camden was the chief supply center for the southern colonies and fourteen battles were fought in the vicinity. Referring to a 1781 map, the original town's locations are being systematically excavated. In the meantime, one historic house has been reconstructed and several other structures have been moved to the site. Walking or driving tours of the ninety-two-acre park permit you to glimpse the life of a colonial village. Begin with the tour headquarters and gift shop located in the Cunningham House, circa 1840, where you can purchase a large variety of local crafts and period reproductions. Then see restored fort sites, a powder magazine, two circa-1800 log cabins, and eighteenth- and nineteenth-century homes. Adjacent to the house is a replica of an early nineteenth-century blacksmith shed where smiths and other craftsmen often demonstrate their skills. McCaa House, circa 1825, served as a doctor's office and later as a tavern, which it is currently being restored to represent. The one large, light-filled room in Craven House, circa 1789, was probably used as an accountant's office. Window frames, closet doors, wainscoting, and the chimney wall with raised paneling are all original. Samples of the original green paint and pickled wood are displayed under plexiglass. Of much simpler construction is the 1800 log Bradley House, typical of early county structures with a large main room topped by a sleeping loft. Two interesting details set this house apart—very fine dovetailing of the logs and flat sandstones used in the chimney. The twelve-inch floorboards are original. After admiring the architectural attributes of the house, examine the exhibits depicting the area from Native American times through early colonial days to the early Revolutionary period. Another log home is the 1812 Drakeford House. Although the exterior shows little care in workmanship, the interior is more refined than that of the Bradley House. This house also contains displays including a model of the Kershaw-Cornwallis

House, which Lord Cornwallis used as his headquarters, and exhibits concerning Camden's role in the Revolution and the development of historic Camden. See a slide show detailing the town's history and examine a model of the original eighty-building village. The grand Kershaw-Cornwallis House served as headquarters, not only for Cornwallis, but also for Lord Rawdon, Banastre "Bloody" Tarleton, and other British officers. During the 1800s the house was used as an orphanage, a school, and a Confederate warehouse. During the Union occupation in 1865 the house was burned to the ground. The current house is an exact replica on the outside, but the interior layout is similar to Charleston houses of the period and is furnished with appropriate antiques. A formal garden is planted with vegetation found in a typical eighteenth-century South Carolina garden. Adjacent to the house, the Southeast Redoubt has been reconstructed. Note the earthen wall and dry moat outside, as well as the typical British pattern of firing steps and bastions inside. To the right of the Cunningham House is the reconstructed foundation of the powder magazine, the only military structure built by the Americans in pre-Revolutionary Camden. Forty-eight-inch-thick walls and supporting buttresses and pillars are typical of the colonial era. Follow the Nature Trail to a small pond and along a creek that supported Joseph Kershaw's mills. Special annual events include the November Revolutionary War Field Days with local crafts, living-history demonstrations, regimental drills, and other festivities.

Camden's love affair with horses dates back to 1802 when the first races were run. Since then, residents and visitors—both human and equine—have taken advantage of Camden's mild climate and near-perfect training conditions to establish a flourishing industry. Springdale Race Course and Training Center, 200 Knights Hill Road (803-432-6513), boasts five tracks, a variety of steeplechase courses, and more than three hundred stalls. Preakness winner Temperance Hill, England's Grand National winner Battleship, and four-time Eclipse winner Flatterer were all trained at Springdale. The racecourse is also the site of two of the most prestigious race meetings in the country. An annual rite of spring, the Carolina Cup, a day of steeplechasing and flat racing held in early April, is South Carolina's largest sporting/social event drawing more than forty thousand spectators. The racing season's grand finale is the world-renowned November Marion DuPont Scott Colonial Cup, the nation's richest steeplechase race. The event culminates in the choice of the distinguished Eclipse Award winner for the year. For information on either of the races, call 803-432-6513. Whenever horses are in residence, visitors are welcome to observe early-morning workouts.

A fine collection of bronzes and sculptures shares space with a library of steeplechase memorabilia and rotating art displays at the Fine Arts Center of Kershaw County, Lyttleton and York Streets (803-425-7676). The center is also the hub of live theater, concerts, plays, musicals, exhibits, a children's choir, and more.

History exhibits and Kershaw County memorabilia are displayed at the Camden Archives and Museum, 1314 Broad Street (803-425-6050), housed in a former Carnegie library building, circa 1915. Exhibits interpret early Indians of South Carolina, the Revolutionary and Civil Wars, colorful personalities from Camden and Kershaw County, and the diverse architectural heritage of the town's three national register districts. Among the treasures is the clockworks from Camden's original town clock, circa 1825. It is among the oldest operating municipal clockworks in the country. Two other treasures are a rare Early American medical chest from 1815 and a Civil War–company headquarters flag used by a local cavalry unit. The archive is recognized throughout South Carolina and the Southeast for its fine genealogical research section.

Serving as the office of the Kershaw County Historical Society, the Bonds Conway House, 811 Fair Street (803-425-1123), was built around 1810 by the first black in Camden to purchase his freedom. An ongoing effort is being made to furnish the house in the manner of a nineteenth-century cottage. The Kershaw County Chamber of Commerce is housed in the Price House, 722 Broad Street (803-432-2525). Built in 1830, it is a superb example of Federal architecture. Purchased in 1920 by Susan Price, an African-American, the structure has served as a house, store, and gathering place. King Haigler, known as "The Patron Saint of Camden," was a Catawba Indian who befriended early settlers. He is commemorated in the form of a life-size weather vane atop the 1886 Opera House Tower, 950 Broad Street.

Gracious Camden has a bevy of beautiful places to stay. The Greenleaf Inn, 1308–1310 North Broad Street (803-425-1806 or 800-437-5874), comprises the 1805 Reynolds House and the 1890 McLean House and includes the highly regarded Tavern on the Greenleaf gourmet restaurant. Built in 1810, the Aberdeen B&B, 1409 Broad Street (803-432-2524), is located in the oldest house in Camden. Other bed-and-breakfast accommodations include Candlelight Inn, 1904 Broad Street (803-427-1057), Camden Bed and Breakfast, 127 Union Street (803-432-2366), and the Carriage House, 1413 Lyttleton Street (803-432-2430).

In addition to the gourmet cuisine served at the Tavern on the Greenleaf, Camden boasts numerous excellent places to eat. Named for the mother and grandmother of two of the partners, Lucy's, 1043 Broad Street (803-432-9096), occupies a former men's store. Two mannequins in the front windows represent Lucy and her suitor, Jeffrey. They are arranged and dressed for vignettes that change with the season and tell an ongoing story à la the Taster's Choice commercials. Inside, artfully arranged on the magnificent bar from the Willard Hotel in Washington, D.C., is an array of Lucy's hats. The interior of the store was gutted to reveal the original tin ceiling and to expose the brick walls and hardwood floors. Accent pieces include five sets of shutters from Charleston, Coromandel panels, and a wrought-iron-and-wood gate. Both lunch and dinner are served. If you just want to pick up something on which to munch on the road, go early in the day to the Mulberry Market Bake Shop, 536 East DeKalb Street (803-424-8401), so you won't be disappointed. The shop's croissants, pastries, breads, sweet rolls, coffee cakes, cookies, and puff pastries are so popular, they sell out early. Many residents of Camden, as well as visitors to the area, choose to drive to Boykin for a casual meal at the general store or a formal meal at the Mill Pond Restaurant.

Take US 521 south to State 261 and turn south to Boykin Mill Pond Community, without a doubt, one of the most charming communities in South Carolina, where you can take a journey to yesteryear. Established around 1755, the community had a grist and flour mill, cotton gin, sawmill, church, and tavern. Unfortunately, the town was destroyed during the Civil War. The pond and surviving properties are owned by sixth-generation members of the same family. Watch whole grains being freshly ground into grits and cornmeal at the restored water-powered grist mill as it has been for more than two hundred years. Observe Susan Simpson as she fashions brooms by hand on century-old equipment at the Broom Place (803-425-0933), located in a restored 1760 slave house. Examine and purchase the grits and cornmeal ground at the mill as well as fresh farm products, general merchandise, gifts, gourmet foods, cake-in-a-jar, Jimmy's Whole Hog Sausage, and other tantalizing articles crammed into the floor-to-ceiling shelves at the rustic Boykin Mill General Store (803-424-4731 or 800-968-4037), where you can enjoy a southern-style breakfast or lunch either indoors or outside on the screened-in porch. One tiny corner of the store is a working post office with an antique stamp window and post-office boxes. The historic 1827 Greek Revival Swift Creek Baptist Church is open by appointment. Nearby is the Civil War site of the Battle of Boykin's Mill where local Confederate troops were defeated in the last South Carolina battle by an overwhelming number of Union troops. Among those killed were the last Federal officer killed in the war and Burwell Boykin, a fifteen-year-old volunteer with the South Carolina Home Guard. A monument was erected by the Fifty-Fourth Massachusetts Infantry, a black regiment, during the 130th anniversary reenactment.

Most important of all, arrange to be in Boykin in the afternoon so that you can have dinner at the Mill Pond Restaurant (803-424-0261), overlooking the pond for which the village is named. Housed in three connected nineteenth-century buildings—one of which used to be a post office—the restaurant is noted for its American regional cuisine. The highlight of the year in Boykin is the lighthearted Christmas parade in early December.

Cheraw is the centerpiece of a trail known as the Old Cheraws that you might want to follow as a short separate trip all its own. This trail visits sites in both the Olde English District and Pee Dee Country. From I-95 take State 9 west to Clio, driving through some of the finest farmland in the state. The heart of the Carolinas' Cotton Belt, the roads are lined with cotton and tobacco fields. Although Clio was founded in the early nineteenth century, its golden age was at the turn of the century, when the town is reported to have had more millionaires per capita than any other place in the country. The cotton barons built many palaces, of which several remain. Pick up a guide to the historic district at Calhoun's Store, built in 1905 and very much like it was in 1925. Continue west on State 9 to Bennettsville, founded in 1819. Marlboro County, of which it is the county seat, was so rich that it is said that farmland was sold by the pound, not by the acre. Admire the present imposing courthouse that was built in 1881, as well as the mural of early Bennettsville by Tom Goforth. The Marlboro County Historical Museum, 119 South Marlboro Street (803-479-5624), is the home of a display of early Marlboro County history including Indian relics, early farm implements, and the County Medical Museum. Tours of the Jennings-Brown House (1826–27) and the Bennettsville Female Academy (1833) begin here. Drive around the neighborhoods of beautiful antebellum and Victorian homes or enjoy Lake Paul Wallace. You can pick up a guide to the historic district at the museum or the Marlboro County Chamber of Commerce. Proceed west on State 9 to Cheraw.

From Cheraw turn south on US 52 to Society Hill, which was settled by Welsh Baptists in 1736. The town takes its name from the St. David's Society, which was formed in 1777 to establish a free public academy—one of the first free public schools in the nation. Society Hill was a cultural and intellectual center well into the nineteenth century. Among the surviving eighteenth- and nineteenth-century buildings are Trinity Church, circa 1834; the Old Library, circa 1822; Coker-Rogers Store, circa 1860; and the Sompayrac Store, circa 1813. You can get a guide to the historic district from the Cheraw Chamber of Commerce or the Society Hill Town Hall on US 52 North. Continue south on US 52 to Darlington, which is known for its tobacco auctions as well as for stock car racing. After picking up a guide to the historic district from the Darlington County Chamber of Commerce, 120 Orange Street, your next stop should be the fabulous mural of early Darlington Square painted on the side of one of the modern square's buildings. Displays about early county history as well as genealogical information can be found in the Darlington County Historic Commission Building, which was once the county jail. Then drive around the St. John's Heritage District, a neighborhood of fabulous antebellum and Victorian homes.

For a complete change of pace, stop by the Darlington Raceway, home of the Southern 500 and the NMPA Stock Car Hall of Fame/Joe Weatherly Museum. Take a five-mile walk along the boardwalk through moss-draped swamp lands at sixty-acre Williamson Park, Spring Street.

For More Information

Olde English District Tourism Commission, 107 Main Street, Chester 29706. 800-968-5909.

Chester County Chamber of Commerce, P.O. Box 489, Chester 29706. 803-581-4142.

Fairfield County Chamber of Commerce, Congress Street, Winnsboro 29180. 803-635-4242

Kershaw County Chamber of Commerce, 724 South Broad Street, Camden 29020. 800-968-4037.

Lancaster County Chamber of Commerce, 604 Main Street, Lancaster 29721. 803-283-4105.

Rock Hill Area Chamber of Commerce, 115 Dave Lyle Boulevard, Rock Hill 29731. 803-324-7500.

Union County Chamber of Commerce, P.O. Box 368, Union 29379. 864-427-9039.

Greater York Chamber of Commerce, P.O. Box 97, York 29745. 803-684-2590.

York County Convention and Visitors Bureau, 201 East Main Street, Rock Hill 29631. 800-866-5200.

Greater Cheraw Chamber of Commerce. 221 Market Street, Cheraw 29520. 843-537-7681.

Cheraw Visitors Bureau, 221 Market Street, Cheraw 29520. 843-537-8425.

Chesterfield Chamber of Commerce, P.O. Box 230, Chesterfield 29709. 843-623-2343.

Greater Clover Chamber of Commerce, P.O. Box 162, Clover 29710. 803-222-3312.

Fort Mill Area Chamber of Commerce, P.O. Box 1357, Fort Mill 29715. 803-547-5900.

Lake Wylie Chamber of Commerce, P.O. Box 5233, SC 49, Lake Wylie 29710. 803-831-2827.

Tega Cay Chamber of Commerce, Four Tega Cay Drive, Tega Cay 29715. 803-548-2444.

Pageland Chamber of Commerce, P.O. Box 56, Pageland 29728. 843-672-6400.

Kershaw Chamber of Commerce, P.O. Box 441, Kershaw 29067. 803-475-3778.

6

Old 96 District

Old 96 has to be one of the most intriguing place names we've run across in our travels. How, we wondered, did this name originate? Well, it seems that the district got its unique appellation from a British fort that was ninety-six miles south of the Lower Cherokee capital of Keowee in the foothills of the Blue Ridge Mountains. Naming places according to the distance they are from a certain point seems to have been a tradition in the area. You'll also run across Six Mile (a town), Twelve Mile Creek, and Six and Twenty Mile Creek. Today, the name Old 96 has been appropriated for an entire district that includes several counties and the towns of Abbeville, Edgefield, Greenwood, Laurens, McCormick, and Troy, as well as open country, deep woodlands, and a series of lakes. In fact, three lakes formed by damming the Savannah River are collectively known as South Carolina's "Freshwater Coast" and create the border between the state and neighboring Georgia.

The Old Ninety-Six fort evolved into an eighteenth-century frontier settlement populated with soldiers, Indian traders, and other adventurers and was the site of South Carolina's first Revolutionary War battle. The Confederacy itself is said to have begun and ended in the area. This district has spawned such prominent figures as Revolutionary War strategist General Andrew Pickens, statesman John C. Calhoun, black educator Benjamin Mays, and ancestors of twentieth-century tycoons William Randolph Hearst and Thomas Boone Pickens. Famous independent-thinking politicians include rip-roaring agrarian "Pitchfork" Ben Tillman and current senator Strom Thurmond. The Savannah River Scenic Highway winds more than one hundred miles along the river and the three lakes. Visitors to this sportsman's paradise will also find warm hospitality, spring peach blossoms, ripe summer peaches, and glorious flower gardens.

Begin your tour of the Old 96 District at Edgefield, located at the intersection of US 25 and State 23. Edgefield County has produced an astounding group of politicians—ten governors and five lieutenant governors and more Civil War generals than any other county—but it is most widely recognized for its distinctive olive-green or brown alkaline-glazed pottery. Some of the finest stoneware in the South, it is considered to be one of the most uniquely American art forms. Plentiful fine clays encouraged a boom in pottery-making from 1810 to the Civil War. The first pots made in the area were at Pottersville, north of present-day Edgefield. The Golden Age of pottery-making was considered to have been from 1840 to 1863. Three potteries produced one hundred thousand gallons of pots in 1850 alone.

Among the most proficient and inventive potters were African-Americans whose handicrafts had to be useful rather than simply decorative. Therefore, the pieces were likely to be kitchen and smokehouse utensils used for storage and preservation—jugs, jars, pitchers, crocks, and the like. They are most often decorated with loops and swags, but some of the more intricate designs depict slaves, ladies in hoop skirts, men on horseback, birds, snakes, flowers, or greenery.

The most famous of these early potters was Dave the Potter, a slave who learned to read and write while working for the newspaper of his owner, Abner Landrum. Dave's pots were distinguished by their unusually large size, their uncommon breadth at the shoulder, and the fact that Dave signed and dated them and often included a poem describing the purpose of the work.

Another characteristic form of pottery made by the Edgefield potters was the face vessel. They are in several sizes of water jugs, cups, and pitchers. A collection of rare Edgefield pottery is displayed at the Old Edgefield Pottery, 230 Simkins Street (803-637-2060), where you can watch potter Stephen Ferrel at work and purchase current pieces made in the Edgefield tradition.

Magnolia Dale, 320 Norris Street (803-637-2233), an 1830s residence, operates as the headquarters of the Edgefield County Historical Society and as a museum house. The estate is located on land that was part of a royal land grant in 1762, the earliest grant in what is now the town of Edgefield. One of the later owners was James Hammond Tillman, nephew of South Carolina's political czar "Pitchfork" Ben Tillman. Jim Tillman, also active in politics, went on to become lieutenant governor of the state. Among the period furnishings and decorative arts displayed in the house are many portraits of influential Edgefield citizens past and present. Several intricate models by artist Arthur Tompkins depict Magnolia Dale, Oakley Park, and other significant buildings in miniature. One room is dedicated to the political career of longtime senator Strom Thurmond, who has served under eleven presidents, and contains several items of his furniture, as well as family photographs, books, awards, and campaign memorabilia. Pay special attention to the floor, which looks as if it is covered with an area rug woven with scenes pertaining to Thurmond's career. In actuality, the design is painted on the floor.

Although the serene grace and grandeur of Oakley Park, 300 Columbia Road (803-637-4027 or 803-637-6128), shine through, the house has a tumultuous past. Built in 1835, it was the post–Civil War home of fiery Confederate General Martin Witherspoon Gary. Not only was he called the "Bald Eagle of the Confederacy" because of his bald head and piercing stare, but he is also considered the father of the Red Shirt movement. This movement began in response to years of tyrannical rule during Reconstruction of carpetbaggers and scalawags. In order to oust the Reconstruction government, which included several black legislators, and to elect someone more sympathetic to the southern aristocracy, General Gary, General M. C. Butler, and General Wade Hampton III formed a group to terrorize blacks into not voting. Members of the group wore red shirts so they could be easily identified. From the balcony of Oakley Park, General Gary and Andrew Pickens's daughter Douschka, called South Carolina's Joan of Arc, rallied fifteen hundred Red Shirts and marched into the village. Their reign of terror resulted in Hampton's election as governor in 1876, breaking forever the power of the Reconstructionists. An original red shirt and a carpetbag are among the relics displayed.

Another momentous event took place on the grounds at the well house you see near the rear of the residence. Before marching off to the Mexican War, Company D of the Palmetto Regiment received its handsome blue silk flag from Susan Pickens, a gift from the women of Edgefield. Of the 130 men who went to war, only 30 returned. The names of the soldiers are engraved on the well house. The original owner, Daniel Bird, chose the highest spot in town as a location for his grand mansion from which he could gaze down an avenue of oaks lining the carriageway and along the main street of town to the Robert Mills courthouse at the far end. Greek Revival in design, the house is wrapped by nine towering pillars. A large central hall stretches between the front and rear verandas. Off the hall are reception rooms and a dining room enhanced by carved mantels, gilt cornices, handsome draperies, prism chandeliers, and plaster ceiling medallions. Bedrooms are furnished in pieces that belonged to the Gary family. A Relic Room contains many pieces of Civil War and early Edgefield memorabilia. The house is open Wednesday through Friday or by appointment. A Confederate encampment is held on the grounds each April and November; at those times, lantern tours of the house are given during which costumed living-history interpreters present vignettes of life at Oakley Park.

Choosing an area that is renowned for its fishing and hunting opportunities, the National Wild Turkey Federation has established the Wild Turkey Center, US 25 (803-637-3106), where you can learn about the game bird and its conservation through an array of wild turkey artifacts.

Edgefield offers historical accommodations at Cedar Grove Plantation, State 283 (803-637-3056), a bed and breakfast located outside of town. Built in 1790, it is one of the oldest plantation homes in the Upcountry. The house retains many of its original features including hand-carved mantels and moldings, a barrel-vaulted entry-hall ceiling, and hand-painted French wallpaper in the parlor. Adjacent to the house is an original outbuilding that served as a kitchen and slave quarters. One guest room and a two-room suite are offered. Reputedly, the guest room is shared with a ghost. In addition, the property features a swimming pool and herb and flower gardens.

Proceed west on State 23 to Lake Thurmond. The second largest lake in the Southeast, Lake Thurmond is forty-two miles long and twenty-six miles wide and boasts seventy thousand acres and a twelve-hundred-mile shoreline where you can enjoy the numerous recreational opportunities. Turn north on US 221 to the Thurmond Lake Visitors Center, at Thurmond

Dam (864-333-2476), where you can examine regional and historical artifacts, study the aquatic life in the aquarium, and try the hands-on exhibits. You can drive to the base of the dam where plant tours are given.

Continue north on US 221 to Parksville, then turn onto State 33/138 to Price's Mill. McCormick County is justly proud of the picturesque, circa-1890, water-powered grist mill on the banks of Stevens Creek. Still in operation grinding grits and cornmeal, the mill is open by appointment. The current miller, Johnny Tolbert, will explain how the operation works. Admire the perfectly crafted hand-carved solid oak gears underneath the mill. Call the McCormick County Chamber of Commerce, 864-465-2835, to make arrangements.

Return to US 221 and continue north to Plum Branch. Not surprisingly, this small village is named for a nearby stream where the banks were covered with plum trees. It became a stagecoach and ferry stop between Edgefield and Augusta and had an active brickyard. Bracknell's Store was built in 1902 and became the largest mercantile establishment between Augusta and Greenville—claiming to serve its customers from the cradle to the grave. Its owner, John W. Bracknell, also served as president of the local bank and at the age of eighteen was the youngest bank president in the country.

Plum Branch has recently added a nice restaurant, Bracknell's Farm House Restaurant, on the corner of Calhoun and Jefferson Streets (864-443-2000). Operated by longtime local merchants Eula and Bill Bracknell, the restaurant specializes in Bill's Gourmet Southern Bar-B-Que Hash and Eula's divine chicken salad. Located in a historic home, the restaurant is open Thursday through Saturday for lunch and dinner.

Continue north on US 221 to McCormick. Cyrus H. McCormick, the inventor of the reaper and founder of International

Harvester, donated the land for the town named after him although he never set foot there. The area, however, had a long past before that. Paleo-Indians followed by the Westos, Yuchis, and Cherokees hunted the lands covered with pine, oak, and cedar. In 1540 Hernando DeSoto passed through the area searching for gold—not realizing that the ground beneath his feet held a vast lode of the yellow ore. In the mid-1700s the region was settled by the Scotch-Irish, French Huguenots, German Palatines, and African-Americans, whose values and diverse cultural heritages are reflected in today's citizenry. One of the first settlements was on Long Cane Creek, the boundary of the Cherokee Nation. Settlers straying across that border caused an Indian massacre in which John C. Calhoun's grandmother and fifty others were killed. Twenty-two of them are buried in a common grave marked by two large crude stones.

The first overt act of the Revolutionary War in South Carolina occurred at Fort Charlotte near Mt. Carmel in 1775. After the war a plantation economy developed with tobacco the first cash crop, replaced later by cotton. The yield of these crops was transported down the Savannah River on small, shallow Petersburg boats.

Prior to the Civil War, McCormick resident James Petigru, a descendant of the French Huguenots, was the only South Carolina statesman to vote against secession saying, "South Carolina is too small to be a republic and too large to be an insane asylum."

One of the most astounding historical events was William "Billy" Dorn's discovery of gold in 1852. Although he was considered a fool by many, his initial investment of $1,200 yielded him more than $900,000 in just seven years. In 1871 McCormick purchased Dorn's gold mine as well as the surrounding area, purchased stock in two railroads (which he persuaded to come to the town), and donated the land for the community. This was constructed over the labyrinth of five miles of mine tunnels—hence the saying "We're sitting on a gold mine." When fifty-six-year-old Dorn married sixteen-year-old Martha Rutledge in the grandest social event in Greenville, guests were disappointed by the apparently inexpensive gift of gloves Dorn presented to the minister. Each finger of the gloves, however, held five hundred dollars' worth of gold. Dorn is reputed to have used his wealth to outfit an entire troop of the Confederate army. "Fool" Billy had the last laugh—gold is still being mined in McCormick County.

With the arrival of the railroad in the 1880s, McCormick and the surrounding area flourished as eight passenger trains a day came through. During the 1930s when the cotton economy was devastated by the boll weevil, landowners sold their holdings to the government for Sumter National Forest. As a result, the county boasts an incredible amount of forest land—in excess of ninety-four percent of the county's land area. It is the greatest amount in the state, and forty-seven percent of the county is owned by the state or Federal government. Although McCormick County is the state's smallest, it has the most land area per person.

While searching for the resolution to the flooding in Augusta during the 1940s, the U.S. Corps of Engineers dammed the Savannah River to form Clark Hill Lake, now known as Lake Thurmond, which also provides hydroelectric power and recreation. During World War II a large manganese mine supplied the ore to aid the war effort.

The primary reason McCormick was listed in *The 100 Best Small Art Towns in America* is the McCormick Arts Council at the Kenturah (MACK), a dynamic organization that provides diverse cultural and artistic opportunities such as exhibits and performing arts. Located in the heart of the business district, the Kenturah, 115 South Main Street (864-465-3216), was built in 1910 as a hotel that housed visitors who arrived in town by train. Drummers, or traveling salesmen, set up their samples in the ballroom for public show. Constructed with walls three bricks thick and with sturdy heart-pine floors, the building went on to be a boardinghouse and then apartments before it was abandoned. Structurally sound, it was renovated through the efforts of volunteers. In addition to the periodic dramatic and musical performances at the Kenturah, the facility showcases year-round changing art exhibits and has a gallery/gift shop selling the works of local artists as well as unusual gift items. In addition to art studios, the facility maintains an apartment for visiting artists. Located in the rear of the Kenturah is the pleasant, shaded McCormick Amphitheater, from which music often wafts down the quiet streets. You can pick up a brochure for a driving tour of the town and county from the MACK, the Chamber of Commerce, or the *McCormick Messenger* office.

In the booming railroad days, McCormick supported another hotel, the 1882 McCormick Temperance Hotel, which also provided safe lodging for railroad passengers and a convenient place for drummers to display their wares. In 1905 Mrs. J. M. Marsh bought the hotel, and her children, including her seven-year-old daughter Fannie Kate, assisted in the operation of the establishment. After her mother died, an adult Fannie Kate assumed full responsibility of the hotel and continued to run it in the family tradition. To local folks, the hotel became affectionately known as "Fannie Kate's," so it was only appropriate that the current incarnation of the hotel should retain that name. Conveniently located next door to the MACK, the building has been meticulously restored as Fannie Kate's Country Inn and Restaurant, 127 South Main Street (864-465-0061), which houses a bed and breakfast and a restaurant open for breakfast, lunch, and dinner, with both indoor and outdoor dining.

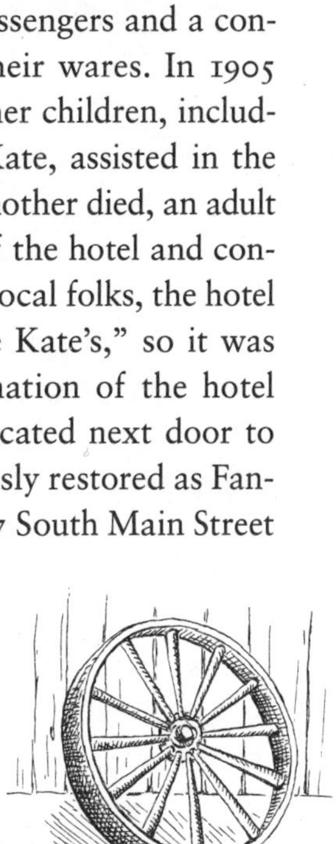

McCormick's commercial district has been restored to its turn-of-the-century appearance and among the adaptive uses of the historic buildings, the 1910 railroad depot has been converted to house two antique shops. Stop by Strom's Drug Store, 124 South Main Street (864-465-2011), for an old-fashioned cherry Coke or an ice cream sundae at the store's old marble-topped soda fountain.

Celebrate McCormick's golden heritage by attending the June Gold Rush Days Festival where you can not only pan for gold, but also enjoy the arts and crafts, beauty pageant, parade, tennis and softball tournaments, pancake breakfast, food, and other entertainment, all culminating with the Brasstown Ball. Call 864-391-3557 for more information.

Stop by the Willow Patch on US 378 (864-465-3178) to shop for one of its highly prized folk-art birdhouses, bent-willow furniture, antiques, and gifts. Through the spring and summer, the emporium is open Thursday through Saturday.

Leave McCormick traveling north on State 81, then turn northeast on State 10 to Troy. The town of Troy was the site of the 1760 Long Cane Indian Massacre. In October you can hear the sounds of cannons and muskets as Patriots and Tories do battle at the Troy Reenactment of the Battle of Long Cane, which occurred after the bloodshed between the Cherokee and settlers at Ninety Six. Several groups of patriots were camped in the Long Creek area in 1780 when the British decided to attack the Americans before they could muster any more recruits. Although the patriots were defeated, the Long Cane Militia went on to defeat the British at the Battle of Cowpens, a major turning point in the Revolutionary War. With the coming of the railroad in the nineteenth century, the town of Troy developed a park in the open, but shaded, area along the tracks, and this park became the destination of many excursion trains from as far away as Augusta because "no other place in the [rail]road has so pretty a park as Troy." During the early 1900s tennis courts, picnic areas, and a bandstand were added to the park. A tour of Troy includes twenty-six historic sites, residences, commercial buildings, and other significant points of interest.

Retrace State 10 to State 81 and turn north, continuing to Willington. On the shores of Lake Thurmond, Hickory Knob State Resort Park, US 221 (864-391-2450), sports an eighty-room lodge, a restaurant, lakefront cottages, a nature trail, campsites, an eighteen-hole championship golf course, a pro shop, tennis courts, a swimming pool, a skeet range, an archery range, boat slips and ramps, and a tackle shop. On the grounds is the historic two-hundred-year-old French Huguenot Guillebeau House, the only remaining documented structure built by the French Huguenots. Still visible etched into the logs are the Roman numerals that were put there for the purpose of fitting the parts of the rustic cabin together correctly. Celebrate a 1770 holiday during a Pioneer Christmas at the Guillebeau House.

On the death of Dr. John de la Howe, a prominent French pioneer, his estate went to the creation of a manual-training school, now known as the John de la Howe School, State 81 (864-391-2131). It is South Carolina's only state-supported children's home, the state's oldest institution, and the oldest manual-training institution in America. Among the unusual instructions in Howe's will were directions for students to gather beech leaves before the first frost and dry them for use in their mattresses because leaves were healthier than feathers. Constructed by the Works Progress Administration (WPA) on the grounds of the school, the rustic stone barn operates as a Saturday country market selling plants, furniture, and arts and crafts. Held on the school grounds in June is the Daisy Festival, an old-time country fair with nostalgic games and milking contests celebrating Dairy Month. The John de la Howe Museum Tract, on which the school is located, contains some of the state's oldest trees—the tract has been protected since the 1700s. There are few other forests in South Carolina as undisturbed as this one. One of its most famous trees was lost when it was struck by lightning in 1985. Known as the King of the Shortleaf Pine, it was 140 feet tall with an almost 10-foot circumference and a crown spread of 49 feet.

Continue north on State 81 to Mount Carmel, where McAllister and Sons (864-391-2121) has existed as a family business since 1888. Operating variously as a store, bank, drug store, hardware store, and a "place to keep mules," today, operated by the fourth generation of McAllisters, it offers an intriguing mixture of furniture, antiques, and farm equipment, served up with a generous helping of local history.

Retrace State 81 to State 28 and turn north to Abbeville, which holds a unique place in Confederate history. It is called the "Birthplace of the Confederacy" because an original document advocating South Carolina's secession from the Union made its debut there after the quiet of November 22, 1860, was shattered by a small group of fiery protesters who gathered in the town square. The assembly mushroomed into a crowd of two thousand, and when the square filled to overflowing, the conclave moved to an empty knoll nearby—later known as Secession Hill. This gathering is generally considered to be the first secession meeting in South Carolina.

Four years later, on May 2, 1865, a more troubled group gathered outside the home of Armistead Burt when the citizenry learned that President Jefferson Davis and some members of his War Council were meeting there after their escape from Richmond. The result of the council was final submission to the Union, thus earning Abbeville the additional sobriquet "Deathbed of the Confederacy." After that meeting, it is believed that Confederate Secretary of the Treasury Judah Benjamin threw the Confederate Seal into the Hominy Pot Whirlpool in the Savannah River near Mt. Carmel. The mystery remains as to what happened to the Confederate gold the officials were known to be carrying when they left Abbeville.

It had disappeared by the time Davis was captured in Georgia the following week, and reports are that the gold was transported across the Savannah River three times.

Famed American statesman John C. Calhoun launched his public career in Abbeville. Other famous residents include nineteenth-century black leader Bishop Henry McNeal Turner, one of the founders of the African Methodist Church, and Thomas D. Howie, a World War II hero known as the major of Saint-Lô. The artist Wilbur George Kurtz, who worked as an illustrator for newspapers and magazines here, was the creator of murals for the 1939 New York World's Fair and a technical advisor to both *Gone with the Wind* and *Song of the South*.

Abbeville's major claim to fame, however, is its fine Opera House, Court Square (864-459-2157), which presides over the town square like a dowager duchess. From the days of Reconstruction until well into the 1920s, traveling troops of actors, musicians, and vaudevillians passed through the bustling town performing one-night-stand productions on the square, in tents, or in any building with a large, empty space. The enthusiastic citizens conceived an idea to combine the need for a municipal office building with their desire for a permanent opera house. The resultant 1908 structure provides space for both—an attractive brick opera house with seating for 350 on the main floor, plus a balcony and four elegant boxes, as well as office space for the city government. The structure is considered to be an opera house rather than a theater because the stage space equals or exceeds the audience seating space. Backstage are three floors of dressing rooms with a window from each hallway opening onto the stage so performers can follow the action and not miss their cues. Four bricks thick without restraining rods, the one-hundred-foot-high back wall is the tallest freestanding brick wall in the western hemisphere. Between 1908 and 1930, the theater provided entertainment for all tastes—melodrama, minstrels, Shakespeare, and opera.

Over the years, entertainers such as Fanny Brice, Jimmy Durante, and Groucho Marx graced the stage. Beginning in 1910, silent moving pictures also came to the Opera House, but the advent of "talkies" spelled the decline of live entertainment. Fewer traveling shows passed through, and Abbeville's influence as a cultural center faded. The Opera House remained a movie theater until the 1950s when it joined many other grand movie houses forced to close, after which it slumbered like Rip Van Winkle for years.

Citizens and visitors missed legitimate theater and their opera house too much to allow its closing to become permanent. Under the leadership of George W. Settles, the Abbeville Community Theater was founded, dedicating itself to presenting live theater and revitalizing the Opera House. Completely restored to its turn-of-the-century appearance—with the exception of the addition of air-conditioning and comfortable rocking chair seats—the Opera House reopened in May 1968. The same hemp-rope-pulled rigging system for changing sets makes the Opera House the only remaining "hemp house" in South Carolina. Since the theater reopened, the increase in tourism to the region has permitted the theater organization to expand from solely a winter season to a community-theater winter season and a repertory-company summer season that together provide thirty-six weeks of live theater yearly. Free tours are available daily except during rehearsals.

Abbeville's downtown, graced by more than three hundred antebellum and postbellum homes, commercial buildings, and stately churches, is on the National Register of Historic Places. The neat-as-a-pin parklike town square is flanked by nineteenth-century buildings. The historic area is easily explored on your own, but guided walking and driving tours are available. Pick up a brochure at the Chamber of Commerce, 107 Court

Square (864-459-4600). While you're there, take time to see a collection of five historic paintings depicting life in Abbeville from 1756 through Reconstruction.

Visit the Burt-Stark House, North Main and Greenville Streets (864-459-4297), where Davis's council meeting took place. The Greek Revival mansion was built in the 1830s and is furnished in period antiques including two pieces of original furniture that remain: one, a desk used by Burt; the other, the bed in which Jefferson Davis slept after his ill-fated meeting.

Housed in an 1859 jail, the Abbeville County Museum, Poplar and Cherry Streets (864-459-2696), features memorabilia from the early days of the Abbeville district. Adjacent to the museum are two log cabins, an educational herb garden, and a stand of trees representing endangered species.

Trinity Episcopal Church, 101 Church Street (864-459-5186), built in 1859–60, is the oldest church in Abbeville. It is noted for its tracker organ and the stained-glass windows, which came from England and had to run the blockade of Charleston during the Civil War. The church's cemetery has graves dating back to 1859.

Abbeville native Dr. Samuel Poliakoff's collection of southwestern art is displayed at the Abbeville County Library, 203 North Main Street (864-459-4009). The collection is considered to be one of the best accumulations of contemporary Native American ceramics, bronzes, weavings, and paintings outside the southwestern United States. The McGowan-Barksdale House, 211 North Main Street (864-459-4148), a Gothic house under renovation, is the headquarters of the Abbeville County Historical Society.

If you love antiques and shopping, you'll love Abbeville. As with most towns, modern businesses have migrated to the suburbs, but the historic downtown is crammed with antique and craft shops, art galleries, trendy boutiques, and eateries. Rough House Billiards, Court Square (no phone), is an old-fashioned soda fountain/cafe/pool hall that looks like nothing has been changed—or dusted—for at least fifty years; however, they serve great hot dogs. The Uptown Exchange on the Square (864-459-2224) contains several antique and specialty shops and restaurants such as the Verandah Tea Room, which serves lunch daily and a dinner buffet on Fridays and Saturdays, and Just Desserts, which serves lunch and afternoon tea and sells desserts and gourmet coffees and teas.

Recognizing that Abbeville is one of the few places left that offers a simple rural life, within the past few years eighty Mennonite families have moved to the area. Enjoy the home cooking of one of several Mennonite restaurants in town. Yoder's Dutch Kitchen, State 72 (864-459-5556), one of the Top Ten Pennsylvania Dutch restaurants in the country, serves Mennonite country cooking for lunch Wednesday through Saturday and dinner Thursday through Saturday. The Dutch Oven, 112 North Main (864-459-5513), serves Mennonite country cooking and is especially popular for breakfast, although lunch and dinner are served as well.

It's no surprise that a town as historic as Abbeville offers several historic places to stay. Queen of the hostelries is the Belmont Inn, 106 East Pickens Street (864-459-9625), which is a perfect choice for theater-goers. Not only is the enchanting inn located just across the street from the Abbeville Opera House, but it offers theater/accommodation packages and light refreshments at intermission and after the show. The charm and elegance of the early twentieth century are reflected in the large—but cozy—rooms, high ceilings, fireplaces, and sweeping verandah. Originally called the Eureka, the hotel was built in 1903 and provided accommodations for railroad and textile executives as well as guests of the Opera House. It closed in 1972 and remained empty for more than ten years. Purchased and restored by Mr. and Mrs. Joseph C. Harden, it reopened as the Belmont in 1984, transformed into an intimate twenty-four-room hotel with an elegant lobby and a small sitting room that invite intimate conversations. Adding to the turn-of-the-century ambience, the inn is tastefully furnished in antiques and period reproductions. For drinks and snacks, visit the Curtain Call Lounge downstairs. A theater package includes accommodations, a welcome wine-and-cheese reception, dinner with wine, tickets to the show, after-the-show dessert, cocktails, and breakfast. The Heritage Room Restaurant at the Belmont Inn serves a complimentary continental breakfast to guests and is open for lunch and dinner as well.

Bed and breakfasts include Abbewood Bed and Breakfast, 509 North Main Street (864-459-5822); the Hitching Post, 503 North Main Street (864-459-2959); and the Vintage Inn, 909 North Main Street (864-459-4784).

Abbeville's two premier events are the May Abbeville Spring Festival (864-459-2211), centered on the square, which features live entertainment, a beauty pageant, antique and car show, home tours, Civil War encampment, food, and crafts, and the December Historic Christmas in Abbeville (864-459-4600), which includes home tours and holiday shopping in decorated shops.

Outside of town in the Sumter National Forest, Parsons Mountain Recreation Area, State 28 (864-229-2406), features a twenty-four-mile motorcycle trail and a twenty-six-mile bridle trail, as well as more traditional recreational opportunities such as hiking trails, swimming, camping, fishing, and picnicking.

From Abbeville, take State 72 east to Greenwood. Although the area was settled in 1802, it wasn't until 1824 that Judge John McGeehee named his plantation Greenwood for its beautiful rolling hills and green forest lands. Eventually, a town developed that took the Greenwood name.

At the Greenwood Museum, 106 Main Street (864-229-7093), located in a former 1930s furniture store, you can take a stroll down memory lane as you are transported back to the gaslight era at the turn of the century. Experience an old-time general store, a drug store, a one-room school, a parlor, a pioneer doctor's office, and a kitchen among the exhibits along the re-created street. In addition, the general museum has collections in cultural history, natural history, technology, and the arts with particular emphasis on Greenwood County and the surrounding region. Natural history is highlighted with collections of rocks and minerals, mounted specimens of American and African animal heads, and shells from the Atlantic and Gulf Coasts. The Gertrude Morse Collection contains materials from Africa. Textiles, transportation, and communication are interpreted in the Monsanto Exhibition Hall. The Gallery showcases the works of regional and national artists and is the site of traveling exhibitions.

You've probably planted the seeds or received a catalog from the venerable Park Seed Company, State 254 (800-845-3369), the largest family-owned mail-order seed company in the world. Visit the company's test garden, which is at its most flamboyantly colorful in June and July. Packages of vegetable and flower seeds are for sale at the gift shop.

From Greenwood, take State 34 to the town of Ninety Six. The present town boasts many turn-of-the-century homes and commercial establishments, as well as a railroad depot that has been converted to a community center. Inside the Town Hall, Railroad Avenue (864-543-2900), are paintings depicting the Revolutionary War battle that occurred nearby. Bed-and-breakfast accommodations are offered at the Kinard House, 227 West Main Street (864-543-4306).

Then take State 246 south of town to the Ninety Six National Historic Site (864-543-4068). The frontier settlement and Revolutionary War battle site began at the ninety-sixth milepost on the trail used by Indians and traders. A small store existed there as early as 1737 and by the mid-1700s colonists had found the area a desirable place to settle. During the early days of the settlement, troubles with the Indians were rife. In

1760 the Cherokees twice attacked Fort Ninety Six, which had been built for the settlers' protection. Romantic legend says that a Cherokee raid on the little settlement was foiled by the Indian maiden Cateechee who rode the ninety-six miles from her village on horseback to warn the settlers because she was in love with an English trader there. The settlers fled into the stockade and were spared, although some of their homes were burned.

The first land battle of the Revolutionary War in the South was fought at Ninety Six in 1775. Five hundred patriots built a crude fort from fence rails and bales of straw and fought off an attack from a much larger force of Tories. The battle ended with a formal truce. Realizing its strategic importance, the British fortified Ninety Six, built a stockade around the village, and at one corner constructed a star fort of massive earthen embankments. Inside the star fort, American loyalists under British Colonel John Cruger were able to hold out for twenty-eight days in May and June of 1781 against a siege by the American Continental Army under General Nathanael Greene. This was the longest siege of the entire war. During this time, the Americans, under the direction of Greene's aide Thaddeus Kosciuszko, a Polish military engineer, began a tunnel through which they planned to blow up the fort. An onslaught led by "Lighthorse Harry" Lee's legion fought its way into the west redoubt, but the Loyalists in the fort were able to drive them off. British reinforcements arrived, however, and the Americans were forced to withdraw. Although the Americans were tactical losers, they were strategic winners because the British soon abandoned the village.

Another legendary heroine is connected with the siege. Kate Fowler, a pioneer daughter who was in love with a British officer, smuggled the news into the star fort that reinforcements were on the way, encouraging the British to hold out.

After the Revolutionary War, the town of Ninety Six was rebuilt and flourished. An academy was established and the name of the town was changed to Cambridge. When it lost its courthouse to another town in 1800, Cambridge began a precipitous decline. Ninety Six was reinstituted as the name in 1852 when the railroad came and brought with it renewed prosperity.

Through two hundred years, the ruins of the star fort, the patriots' zigzag siege lines, and thirty-five feet of tunnel have survived in good condition. Archaeologists have unearthed traces of stockades built in 1760, as well as the foundations of the courthouse and jail built in 1770. Get insights into the area's history by touring the restorations and an archaeological dig at the one-thousand-acre national park. Begin at the visitors center where you can see a background film, then take the one-mile interpretive trail around the site, past sunken roadbeds worn down by decades of use, the star fort, a reconstructed rifle tower, a partially reconstructed stockade, and a furnished log cabin that interpret civilian and military life in the back country. Historical Heritage Festival Days are celebrated at the park each year with a reenactment by colonial units in authentic dress. Craft shows and other activities lend zest to the event.

Retrace State 246 to State 72 and turn east. At US 221, turn north to Laurens. The town and county were named for Revolutionary War statesman Henry Laurens, who was imprisoned in the Tower of London for his patriotism. Long an outspoken advocate of the rights of the American colonists, he was captured at sea while sailing to Holland and charged with high treason for his role in the Revolution. He remained a prisoner for more than a year before he was exchanged for Lord Cornwallis, who had surrendered to Washington at Yorktown. Later, the town was the home of Andrew Johnson, who operated a tailor shop there. When the village was founded in 1792, the entire courthouse square was purchased for two guineas (about twenty-one dollars). Laurens County is a showcase of historical sites with four historic districts, twenty-one historic sites, and two Revolutionary War battlefields.

An excellent example of Upcountry Federal architecture, the 1812 James Dunklin House, 544 West Main Street (864-984-4735, 864-682-9200, or 864-682-3026), is one of the oldest residences in the county. It was built on three hundred acres by Washington Williams as a wedding present for his daughter and her husband, James Watts. Although of simple design, the house boasted some finer features such as wainscoting, moldings, and carved mantels. You can find some names etched into the original panes of glass in the elegant parlor. Apparently it was the custom that when a girl became engaged, she would use the diamond in her ring to write out the name of her betrothed.

Over the years, the house passed into the Todd family and several others before being purchased in 1950 by James Dunklin, a longtime collector of southern antiques. Mr. Dunklin restored the house to its nineteenth-century character and furnished it with the finest pieces from his collection. The room over the back porch, for example, is furnished and dedicated to Erby Dunklin, one of the first doctors in Laurens. Of special note are his medical instruments, boots, medical bag, and journal.

Two of the bedrooms are furnished with pieces that belonged to two famous (or infamous) early residents. "Bloody Bill" Cunningham was a defector during the Revolutionary War. He led the Tories in the Hayes's Station Massacre where many patriots were killed. His massive bed is decorated with hand-carved tobacco leaves rather than the rice motifs that were so popular in the Lowcountry. His kinswoman, Ann Pamela Cunningham, wanted to restore the family's good name—a quest in which she was ultimately successful. Considered the "first lady of preservation" in this country, she organized the Mount Vernon Ladies Association of the Union to purchase and restore the home of the first president. Her bed is also a tobacco bed, although it is on a more dainty scale. Upon James Dunklin's death, the house and a trust fund for its upkeep were donated to the Laurens County Landmarks Foundation. A carriage house, smokehouse, and barn on the property were converted to homes and are private residences today.

Drive by the Duckett House, Downes Street, the historical home of Charles H. Duckett, at one time the only African-American in the Southeast to operate a retail lumber business.

History, culture, and outdoor activities attract visitors to the Old 96 District. National and state parks vie for your attention with cultural performances and activities in Abbeville and McCormick. Many historic homes are operated as house museums while others operate as bed and breakfasts. From the Old 96 District, you can explore the Upcountry, the Olde English District, Capital City/Lake Murray Country, and Thoroughbred Country.

For More Information

Old 96 District Tourism Commission, P.O. Box 448, Laurens 29360. 864-984-2233 or 800-849-9633.

Abbeville County Development Board, P.O. Box 533, Abbeville 29620. 864-459-2181.

Greater Abbeville Chamber of Commerce, 107 Court Square, Abbeville 29620. 864-459-4600.

Greenwood County Chamber of Commerce, P.O. Box 980, Greenwood 29648. 864-223-8431.

Laurens County Chamber of Commerce, P.O. Box 248, Laurens 29360. 864-833-2716.

McCormick County Chamber of Commerce, P.O. Box 938, McCormick 29835. 864-465-2835.

Ninety Six Chamber of Commerce, P.O. Box 8, Ninety Six 29666. 864-543-2900.

Old Edgefield District Courtesy Center, 104 Court House Square, Edgefield 29824. 803-637-4010.

7

Pee Dee Country

Few people outside this region of South Carolina know that the lyrics to Stephen Foster's "Way Down Upon the Suwanee River" were originally "Way Down Upon the Pee Dee River." One of the major river systems of the South, the Great Pee Dee is a hard-working stream that feeds a large agricultural region. Born as the Yadkin high on the Eastern Continental Divide, the river becomes the Pee Dee, is dammed for electric production and recreation, then cuts through timber and farmlands before emptying into Winyah Bay at Georgetown. The Little Pee Dee River has been designated a Natural Scenic River by the Department of the Interior.

The earliest inhabitants of the river region were Native Americans of the Pee Dee tribe who lived and hunted in the river's broad valley and gave their name to the stream. Once early explorers ventured into the area, they spread the word about the desirability of its plentiful natural resources. Soon both English gentry and French Huguenots settled there. Rice, indigo, and tobacco plantations flourished. Although the production of indigo has long been surpassed by other crops, a vestige of that culture remains throughout South Carolina today. (A blue paint was created from indigo with which inhabitants painted around doors and windows and sometimes porch ceilings to ward off evil spirits.)

The Pee Dee region, which includes Darlington, Dillon, Florence, Lee, Marion, Marlboro, and Williamsburg Counties, is an area filled with history and characterized by black-water swamps and pastoral scenery—lazy rivers, moss-bearded live oaks, the grace and grandeur of stately homes, and, most of all, by gracious hospitality. It is also the home of the heart-stopping thrills of the Darlington Superspeedway. Farming country, the region is noted for its tobacco (millions of pounds are sold at auctions in Mullins) and the miles and miles of cotton fields that form a snowy blanket in the fall.

Begin your tour of Pee Dee Country at Bennettsville, seat of Marlboro County, once one of the wealthiest counties in the state, where farmland was sold by the pound, not by the acre. Those gracious days are preserved by the stately courthouse and in the wealth of Greek Revival and Victorian homes. One of the foremost historic houses is the Jennings-Brown House, 121 South Marlboro Street (803-479-5624), a simple home built in 1826–27 by Dr. Edward W. Jones, one of the first physicians in Bennettsville. In 1852 Dr. J. Beaty Jennings bought the house and his family lived there for the next fifty-two years. In the waning days of the Civil War, during Dr. Jennings's tenure, Union troops captured Bennettsville, and Major General Frank P. Blair commandeered the house for his headquarters. The house was moved to its present location sitting far back from the street in 1904. The restoration depicts the house as it was in 1852 when the formerly detached kitchen was connected to the main house by a porch and a breezeway. A unique feature of this house is the painted and stenciled ceiling in the master bedroom. Each of the eight rooms is beautifully furnished with antiques appropriate to the period. Sharing the same grounds is the Marlboro County Historical Museum, 119 South Marlboro Street (803-479-5624). In the heart of Bennettsville is the Tom Goforth mural depicting the courthouse as it looked around 1910. (See Olde English District.)

You may be familiar with Blenheim Root Beer. What you may not know is that it is Bennettsville's claim to fame and originated as "doctored-up" Blenheim Springs mineral water, which was discovered in 1781. For generations, people came from nearby towns to drink the water, and Dr. C. R. May prescribed it for stomach ailments. It was he who devised the fiery ginger ale in 1903. You can see the site of Blenheim Mineral Spring on West High Street/State 381.

Take advantage of one of Bennettsville's most glorious mansions by staying at the 1886 Breeden House Inn, 404 East Main Street (803-479-3665), an imposing Greek Revival home that operates as a bed-and-breakfast inn with three guest rooms in the big house and four in the carriage house. The portico is supported by four two-story columns, but even more impressive are the twenty-nine columns supporting the wrap-around porch.

Take State 9 to I-95 and the town of Dillon, located near the North/South Carolina border. Dillon has two claims to fame: South of the Border and the Dillon Wedding Chapel. Although it may be the ultimate in tacky, South of the Border, located at US 501 and I-95 (800-922-6064), is a must-stop attraction for the lighthearted. In fact, the complex is the third-most-visited tourist attraction in South Carolina. You'll know you're almost there when you see Pedro, the gigantic towering 104-foot figure of a Hispanic male wearing a colorful sombrero with dangling pompoms. In addition to the food, gas, lodging, and amusements offered, you can pick up fireworks and souvenirs. In 1949 Alan Schafer built a simple eighteen-by-thirty-six-foot beer stand known as South of the Border Beer Depot, just on the South Carolina side of the state line. Because it adjoined several dry North Carolina counties, busi-

ness boomed. All in fun, Schafer exploited the double meaning of South of the Border to represent the United States/Mexican border. A few years later, Schafer added a ten-seat grill and changed the name to the South of the Border Drive-In. By 1954 he had added motel rooms, a swimming pool, two restaurants, a Mexico shop, and a gas station. He went to Mexico to establish import connections and met two men who wanted to come to America and become citizens. He helped get them admitted to this country and gave them jobs as bellboys. People called them Pedro and Pancho and eventually called both of them Pedro. When the giant figure of a Hispanic male was erected in the sixties, it seemed only natural to dub him Pedro. His underpinnings are sunk eighteen feet deep in solid clay, and he weighs seventy-seven tons and contains four miles of wiring. The largest neon sign east of the Mississippi, Pedro is tall enough for a car to drive beneath the arch created by his legs. South of the Border now covers 350 acres and includes a welcome center, motel, campground, eight restaurants, fourteen shops, bingo, three gas stations, an amusement area, and even boasts its own post office. It has been said that South of the Border is a little bit Mexican, a little bit southern, and a little bit kosher, but it's certainly good, clean fun.

Dillon has the distinction of being the "Wedding Capital of the East." More marriages are performed in Dillon—nearly seven thousand each year—than anywhere east of the Mississippi except New York City. So renowned are Dillon's quicky weddings that the town has been dubbed "Little Las Vegas." South Carolina does not require a blood test, and although a marriage license must be obtained through the probate judge, there is no waiting period. Because Dillon is located close to the army base at Fort Bragg, North Carolina, and Pope Air Force Base at Fayetteville, North Carolina, many couples cross the border to South Carolina to get married. With its brick facade and white columns and pediments, you'd never know that the Dillon Marriage Chapel, State 9 Business (893-774-2671), was once a skating rink. Inside the chapel, which has been featured in *Parade* magazine, USA *Today*, and on national television, waiting rooms are filled with couches and chairs, potted plants, and piped-in music. The actual ceremony takes place in a churchlike room with cushioned pews and white silk flowers.

The story of Dillon's founding involves a little home brew. It seems that in order to persuade Atlantic Coast Line officials to route their new railroad tracks through land that James W. Dillon had just purchased south of the North Carolina line, he plied them with libations and offered them a fifty percent interest in the land. He succeeded in striking a deal that led to the establishment of the town that took his name, as well as the sister villages of Latta and Lake View. Needless to say, Mr. Dillon, who came to America as a poor Irish immigrant, prospered.

Dillon House, 1304 Main Street (803-774-8496), built in 1890, was James Dillon's home. Now a house museum, it is filled with period furnishings and memorabilia from the town's past. Mr. Dillon lived there until his death in 1913, after which it was divided into apartments; it later fell into disrepair and suffered an almost disastrous fire. Dr. Suzanne Black was instrumental in saving the house from being demolished in the sixties, and as community support grew, land was donated on which the house was relocated, and countless citizens donated time or labor to restore the building. Many others donated furniture and memorabilia. Also located on the grounds is a very "modern" turn-of-the-century kitchen house with a Hasty Baker iron stove among its artifacts. The house is open on major holidays and by appointment.

Part of the state's coastal plains region, Dillon County is largely rural with gently rolling terrain broken by lush row crops, cypress swamps, and pine and hardwood forests. A good place to see a microcosm of the state's topography is at Little Pee Dee State Park, County 57 (803-774-8872), an 835-acre park on the Little Pee Dee River featuring a wide range of habitats from a small swamp characterized by bottom-land hardwoods to sandhills distinguished by pines and scrub oaks to one of the mysterious Carolina Bays.

Take US 501 south to Latta. Tobacco and the railroad gave Latta its start in 1887. Established as a major warehousing and distribution railhead by the now defunct Florence Railroad Company, the town grew quickly. Also in 1887 the Atlantic Coast Line Railroad built the Wilson Short Cut Line from Florence to Wilson, North Carolina, eliminating the necessity of traveling to Wilmington to reach many South Carolina points. The Short Cut acted as a magnet in bringing more families to the area. The name Latta honored Captain Robert Latta who was in charge of engineering for the railroad and who drew up the original town map of forty acres. By the end of World War I, mercantile establishments lined one of the widest main streets of any small town in America. Latta boasts two historic districts of large antebellum and Victorian houses. The Dillon County Historical Society is restoring an early Latta dentist's office for use as a museum—one room to represent an early 1900s dentist's office, the others dedicated to various aspects of Dillon County history.

Thought to be the oldest cotton press in existence, the Eighteenth Century Cotton Press, State 38E, was built in 1798 and was used to bale cotton. It was powered by an ox or mule rotating the beam to tighten the press. The cotton, hand-picked and hand-seeded, was stacked on the ground in a cotton sheet, and the animal pulled the board around and pressed it into a bale, a method used in the days before the cotton gin.

Superior bed-and-breakfast accommodations are offered at Abingdon Manor, 307 Church Street (803-752-5090), a grand Greek Revival mansion listed on the National Register of Historic Places. Four enormous guest rooms and a spacious two-room suite feature private baths, gas-log fireplaces, and sumptuous furnishings. The luxuriously appointed inn retains many original architectural details such as counter-weighted shutters, as well as ornate mantels and mirrors. A full gourmet breakfast is served in your room or in the formal dining room, by a crackling fire if the weather warrants it, and early evening refreshments are served in one of the elegant formal parlors. Guests can take advantage of the exercise equipment, bicycles, and outdoor Jacuzzi if they desire. Despite the luxury of the inn and its wealth of amenities, what makes it so outstanding is that owners Mike and Patty Griffey know how to pamper their guests—little things such as sending a bag of freshly baked cookies along on your day trip to explore the surrounding area.

Continue south on US 501 and follow the signs to Marion. Although it began life as an Indian trading post, Marion rapidly became a courthouse town. The town's well-preserved nineteenth-century buildings cause many beach-bound travelers to refer to it as "that pretty little town on the way to the beach." Standing like a sentinel in the square across from the Robert Mills courthouse is a statue of the Revolutionary War hero Francis Marion, the Swamp Fox, whose name was appropriated for the county and town (as well as for a college and a national park). The entire downtown has been declared a historic district and the historic Old Opera House, 109 West Godbold Street, built in 1892, is the home of the Marion Chamber of Commerce and the Playmakers theater group.

Located in the stately 1887 Marion Academy building, the Marion Museum, 101 Wilcox Avenue (803-423-8299), houses furnishings, Oriental and English rugs, and antiques. The original school bell and its rope pull are still in place. One of the old classrooms is set up as it might have been at the turn of the century. Another is dominated by a full-size nineteenth-century turpentine distillery backed by a mural of a pine forest, but also contains farm implements and an intricate diorama of a nineteenth-century farm. In the Sandlapper Room, you'll find a miscellany of items including the table and chairs used in the signing of the Ordinance of Secession.

Take US 76 east to Mullins, the site of one of the largest tobacco auctions in the world. Each year from July to September, the warehouses are piled high with millions of pounds of tobacco, and the chants of the auctioneers fill the air. Tobacco is celebrated during the Golden Leaf Festival. The attractive old railroad depot, now restored, houses the Mullins Chamber of Commerce.

Located in a rustic log cabin along the river, the Little Pee Dee Lodge, 2361 US 76 (803-464-8900), specializes in oysters. A staff person will come to your table to shuck them at your request. Be forewarned, however: even a half-order served as an appetizer will fill up two people to the point that you may not be able to finish your entree. The restaurant also features other seafood and steaks.

Located in a refurbished old hotel in the center of town, O'Hara's, 123 East Wine Street (803-464-7287), operates a bed and breakfast as well as a restaurant.

From Mullins, take State 41 south to Hemingway, where you will turn west on State 261 to Kingstree. When King George III gave out the land grants in 1730 to what became Williamsburg County, he retained the rights to all the white pine trees and specified that the tallest and straightest be marked with a red arrow and saved for use as masts on ships in the Royal Navy. These were known as the "King's Trees." Calvinists from Ireland started a small settlement near one of these trees on the banks of the Black River in the early 1730s and over time the name of the town

evolved into Kingstree. Cattle raising and the planting of hemp, flax, indigo, and corn were among the prosperous industries of the early township. Revolutionary War hero Francis Marion formed the nucleus of Marion's Brigade from Kingstree men. The Revolutionary War Battle of King's Tree occurred on August 27, 1780. The county suffered destruction and hard times during the Civil War although Kingstree itself was spared by the shrewd strategy of Colonel James Fowler Pressle, who led a small group of Confederates of the Home Guard in burning bridges over the Black River and patrolling the river to prevent Union crossings. In this century, famous people who have come from Williamsburg County include actor Robert Mitchum, singer Chubby Checker, and Dr. Joe Goldstein, winner of a Nobel Prize in medicine. Still, the commercial center is in a primarily agricultural area, and Kingstree's cotton gin produces the largest quantity of cotton in the state.

The most significant house in the county is Thorntree, State 527 (803-354-9616), believed to be the oldest house in Pee Dee Country. It was built in 1749 by James Witherspoon who had immigrated to the Carolinas in 1734 aboard the *Good Intent*, landing at Charles Towne with many relatives and friends. They settled in Williamsburgh Township, and Witherspoon was granted three hundred acres on the Black River. After his death, the house passed to his son Gavin. During the Revolutionary War, British General Banastre Tarleton, one hundred of his dragoons, and many Tories under Colonel Elias Ball camped on the plantation, but it is not known how Gavin felt about it. Upon Gavin's death, his heirs sold the plantation, and it changed hands many times before the Williamsburg County Historical Society acquired the house, moved it, and restored it. Furnishings represent the time period 1749 to 1826. Each year Thorntree sponsors a Taste of Williamsburg during Old-Fashioned Days as well as a Christmas Open House.

Kingstree's classic Williamsburg County Courthouse on Main Street, designed by Robert Mills, was completed and occupied in 1823 and is still operating. On the grounds is a Civil War statue commemorating the dead from that war. If you look at the statue closely, however, you'll realize that the soldier depicted is a Union soldier. Apparently the company that created this and many other war memorials got an order mixed up. This statue was to go to a town in New England, and the one they got was to come to Kingstree. Each town decided to keep the statue it got as a gesture of peace between North and South and because the story makes such good conversation.

Next door to the courthouse is the county complex building housed in an old carriage/car dealership. In addition to the county offices, the building contains an auditorium, affectionately called the Opera House, with wonderful old wooden theater seats where live productions are presented.

Along Mill Street is a fascinating mural depicting the townspeople greeting General Francis Marion as he returns to his blacksmith shop. The mural was created by eighty-two local artists.

The railroad has long played a vital role in Kingstree's history and still does today. You can set your watch by the Amtrak train that stops at the turn-of-the-century depot in the middle of town. In fact, it is reported that more passengers board and disembark in Kingstree than at any other place between New York and Miami. Eat dinner at the Station House Restaurant, 134 East Main Street (803-354-5042), located in the depot. If you want tourist information, the chamber of commerce utilizes the depot for its office as well.

A mixture of historic artifacts is displayed at the Williamsburg County Museum, Main and Academy Streets (803-354-7418 or 803-354-5428, both home phones of historical society members), located in the Old Exchange Bank. Among the items are a twenty-foot hand-hewn cypress dugout canoe, vintage clothing, and early medical instruments. The museum maintains copies of the *Old County Record* back to the early 1800s as well as genealogical records.

In addition to the Station House Restaurant, Kingstree also boasts Robert's, where you can order anything from chicken pot pie to specialty seafood and steaks, or Thomas Brown's Barbecue, which has provided food to Washington, D.C., functions. Shopping opportunities abound from the General Store where you can purchase anything from a straight pin to a harness, the Palmetto House where you can find antiques and rare books, and Cotton Tales, a children's shop.

Take US 52 north to Lake City. The town was established in 1732 as McCrea's Crossroads. Tobacco was introduced in the late 1800s, and a tobacco market was established in 1889. Today, Lake City's tobacco market is one of the largest in the state.

West of Lake City on State 341 is the Browntown Museum (803-558-2235), a classic old farmstead. An outgrowth of the Browntown Project sponsored by the Three Rivers Historical Society of Hemingway, Browntown preserves and interprets a typical small mid-1800s Lowcountry farm. The origin of Browntown was a plantation system developed by two brothers, Robert and William Brown, and their families, who eventually amassed more than eight thousand acres. This was not the romanticized plantation of *Gone with the Wind*, but rather a self-contained farm where the family lived and produced just about everything it needed for survival. The primitive Brown-Burrows House was built in 1845 by Robert's son John and was moved to this location from a site about two miles away. It first consisted of only two rooms on the first floor with one large open room above. Shed rooms, a covered walkway or "dogtrot," a kitchen, and a dining room were added later. The house, which is simply furnished, features a large recessed

The Browntown Museum in Lake City features a preserved farmhouse built in 1845.

front porch with banisters and freestanding columns. The most remarkable outbuilding is the heart-pine-and-oak cotton gin, which is still standing on its original massive supports. The symmetry of the hand-carved wheels and gears remains a fine example of the skill and ingenuity of early craftsmen. The first floor of the building is set ten feet above the ground, allowing space for the machinery and for mules or oxen to turn the gears. The upper floor housed the gin and cotton bins. The gears of the gin, capable of producing a bale of cotton a day, could also be offset to power a gristmill. Wooden pegs instead of nails were used in the construction of the corn crib and smokehouse. Among the other accouterments of a farm are the blacksmith shop, well, an outhouse, and syrup cooker. Restoration of all the buildings has been kept to a minimum, in order to preserve the area in as original a state as possible. The only new building is a large barn constructed to house and exhibit the farm equipment and artifacts donated to the museum. Among the hodgepodge of items is a collection of six dugout canoes, wagons, and the post office interior from Poston. Although the museum is open on Fridays through Sundays, the highlight of the year is the first Saturday in November when Old South Days is celebrated with traditional southern foods and crafts and skills demonstrations.

Continue west on State 341/403 to Lynchburg, where you can visit historic antebellum Tanglewood Plantation, 4000 US 341 (803-437-2222). Tanglewood originated as a land grant from King George III in the mid-1700s and was the birthplace and home of Ellison Durant "Cotton Ed" Smith, for many years one of the nation's most powerful senators. He was born in 1864 and when he died at age eighty, he had served in the U.S. Senate longer than anyone else. His brother Coke Smith, who served as the Methodist Bishop of Virginia, and his nephew John Andrew Rice, a Pulitzer Prize–winning author, were also born at Tanglewood. The current house, built in 1840, escaped Sherman's torch because the loyal slaves refused to leave and let it be burned. Among the original and reconstructed outbuildings are a kitchen building, a 1700s cypress-log smokehouse, a 1910 one-room schoolhouse, a tackhouse with gear dating to before the Civil War, a blacksmith shop, a sugarcane syrup mill, barns, and a slave cemetery. Today the plantation is the home of artists Dona and Jerry Locklair and their sons.

The Locklairs' work is noted for its realism and historically accurate depictions of life in the Old South. What is particularly interesting about their paintings is that each is a team effort merging both their talents. They maintain their studio and gallery on the grounds.

Take US 76 to Florence, the heart and trade center of the Pee Dee region and its only city. Florence began as a railroad town in the 1800s and today has a rich aviation heritage. Once the home of Pee Dee Indians and wealthy planters, Florence now boasts a mixture of small town charm and metropolitan flair. The city offers a colorful palette of cultural events from which to choose: ballet, symphony, theater, and a variety of museums.

Several significant events occurred in and around Florence during the Civil War. In 1862 a Confederate Navy Yard was built in Marion County, and three vessels were built there. Only one, the CSS *Pee Dee*, was commissioned as a naval vessel. It covered the crossing of the Great Pee Dee River at Cheraw and was blown up to prevent capture when Union forces descended on Cheraw. Beginning in the late summer of 1864, Florence became a prisoner-of-war camp. The Florence Stockade was constructed and fifteen thousand Union prisoners were shipped there by train.

Two thousand, seven hundred and thirty-eight prisoners died during their confinement and were buried on the nearby land of James H. Jarrott. The first burial took place in September 1864, and in 1865 President Lincoln established a National Cemetery, 803 East National Cemetery Road (803-669-8783), in Florence. Remains—most of them unidentified—from the Florence Stockade, as well as remains from Darlington, Cheraw, Marion, and Charleston were reinterred there. One of the five known interments was that of Florena Budwin, who disguised herself as a man and enlisted in the Union Army to be with her husband, a captain from Pennsylvania. Her husband was killed, and Florena was captured; her true identity was discovered at the stockade where she remained to help nurse the other prisoners. Florena became ill herself and died in January 1865. She is believed to be the first female service member buried in a national cemetery. The cemetery has been expanded several times and veterans representing all of America's wars and conflicts are buried there.

Relics and treasures from the Civil War are displayed at the War Between the States Museum, 107 South Guerry Street (803-662-1471). Portions of the CSS *Pee Dee* and related artifacts are among the displays, as are flags, Confederate money, bayonets, sabers, items used by common soldiers and civilians, rare books about the war, reunion souvenirs, and memorabilia from the United Daughters of the Confederacy, Sons of Confederate Veterans, and the Grand Army of the Republic, as well as many photographs of both Confederate and Union soldiers. The museum was founded in 1988 by members of the Pee Dee Rifles, Camp 1419, Sons of Confederate Veterans, and most of the artifacts were donated by them. The museum is housed in the boyhood home of founding member R. Frank McKain and was donated by his sister.

Learn more about Florence's heritage at the Florence Museum of Art, Science, and History and Timrod Park and Shrine, 558 Spruce Street (803-662-3351), which features art and regional history displays as well as exhibits of Oriental and primitive cultures. During World War I a group of patriotic ladies organized the Blue Bird Tea Room to raise funds to purchase a collection of Southwestern Indian ceramics. The acquisition, which wasn't completed until 1924, was the foundation upon which the current museum was built. Located in a 1939 art deco–style home, the museum's collection has expanded to include Asian pieces representing almost every Chinese dynasty, African artifacts, Greek and Roman archaeological finds, and American art. The History Hall contains items of historic interest to the Pee Dee area. On the grounds are a 1917 Vulcan steam locomotive and a tiny one-room schoolhouse where Henry Timrod, poet laureate of the Confederacy, once taught.

Modeled after Millwood, General Wade Hampton's Columbia plantation home, The Columns, 5111 East Old Marion Highway (803-669-6730), is the quintessential antebellum southern mansion. Reached by way of a long drive lined with pecan and sycamore trees, the house, built between 1854 and 1857 on Mars Bluff, is an outstanding example of Greek Revival architecture. All the materials used in the construction came from the estate owned by Dr. William Rogers Johnson, a prominent statesman who served in both the House and Senate and who attended the Secession Convention. Bricks were made on the grounds and used to form the twenty-two giant freestanding Doric columns, which were then covered with stucco. These columns support an overhanging hipped roof to form a deep porch on three sides of the house. Logs used in the interior and exterior were cut on the property and hauled by oxcart to a sawmill in Cheraw. Then the lumber was floated back to the property via the Pee Dee River. Local artisans hand-hewed the roof support beams and created original plaster moldings, fine wainscoting, and heart-pine floors. If visitors get a feeling of déjà vu when arriving at the house, it may be because they have seen its twin, Devereaux, in Natchez, Mississippi. Today, The Columns is the center of a working plantation and offers bed-and-breakfast accommodations.

Located on US 52N, just a mile from I-95 at the northwest edge of Florence, the Pee Dee State Farmers Market (803-665-5154) offers a vast variety of fruits and vegetables not readily available in conventional markets as well as thousands of bedding and gardening plants in many varieties. Operated by the Marketing Division of the South Carolina Department of Agriculture, the market operates year round, although the best selection is available June through September. A visit to the Farmers Market is a friendly, affordable, leisurely experience.

Take US 52 west to Darlington. The first settlers arrived in 1758. There was a disagreement between the two most influential men in the county about where the courthouse should be located. As a compromise, they agreed to ride horseback toward each other, starting from their respective communities, and the courthouse would be built where they met. They converged at a crossroads on the plantation of John King near Swift Creek. King donated the lot on which the courthouse would be built, and in an early example of shrewd land speculation, he subdivided all the surrounding land into small marketable lots. The village that developed was called Darlington Court House until 1890 when it became simply Darlington. Despite this quiet beginning, Darlington is a name instantly recognizable around the world.

The roar of the engine and the thunder of the cheering crowd characterize the "granddaddy of them all"—the Darlington Raceway, State 34 (803-393-4041). Home of the Dodge International Race of Champions, the Mark III Vans Zoo, and the NASCAR TranSouth 500 stock-car race in the spring and the Gatorade 200 and the historic Mountain Dew Southern 500, NASCAR's oldest superspeedway race, on Labor Day weekend, the track attracts champion drivers and a massive tide of fans. The Southern 500 is the biggest one-day tourist attraction in South Carolina.

Carved from a cotton field on the edge of town, the raceway opened in 1950 as stock-car racing's first superspeedway. The 1.366-mile track has a relatively narrow racing groove and disproportionately banked east and west turns, making it the most demanding oval in NASCAR, the most unpredictable and toughest in NASCAR racing, and earning it the name "the track too tough to tame."

Next door to the Darlington Raceway is the Joe Weatherly Stock Car Museum/National Motorsports Press Association's

Stock Car Hall of Fame (803-393-4041), the repository of the largest collection of stock racing cars in the world, including those of such famed drivers as Buddy Baker, Bill Elliott, David Pearson, Richard Petty, and Fireball Roberts. In addition, the museum houses engines and other coveted historical pieces connected with NASCAR racing. You can feel the thrill of speeding around the raceway at more than one hundred mph in a racing simulator. Each year the National Motorsports Press Association votes on the best driver of the year; each of the winners is honored with a state-of-the-art exhibit displaying personal memorabilia, audio and video showcasing his or her career, and a pencil sketch by local artist Jeanne Barnes. Darlington Raceway souvenirs and merchandise connected with various race-car drivers are available in the museum's gift shop.

In early December Santa's Workshop at the Raceway returns to the Darlington Raceway Garage Area. Thousands of bright lights make the track glow, while inside, the excitement of Christmas is depicted in an extravaganza of individual vignettes filled with angels, ornaments, race cars, dolls, elves, snowmen, and Christmas characters of every kind. As part of the tour, everyone gets to do what the race-car drivers do—ride on the toughest track in NASCAR. In this case, however, it's a hay ride. Finally, children get to sit on Santa's lap and tell him what they want for Christmas while getting their picture taken. All the money raised goes to local charities. Call the raceway ticket office at 803-395-8499 for exact dates.

In recognition of what racing has meant to Darlington, the town has created the Winston Walk of Fame, Liberty Lane, located downtown off Pearl Street. The names of previous Darlington winners are written in concrete and accompanied by an impression of the driver's hand prints.

Don't neglect the rest of the lovely, quiet town of Darlington. One of the few South Carolina towns with a town square, Darlington's common has not only a modern (and not very attractive) courthouse and Victorian-era commercial buildings, but it features a mural of the town square as it was in the 1930s by the artist Blue Sky, who has painted several murals around the state. The square is the scene of many of the year's special events, such as horse shows and the cotton market.

Just off the square, the Historical Commission, repository of the county archives and genealogical records, is housed in a former jail, built in 1937 as a Works Progress Administration (WPA) project under President Franklin D. Roosevelt. The interior walls are adorned with rare old photographs of the area.

You can get a visitor's guide to Darlington from the Historical Commission and set off on a walking or driving exploration of the town. You'll want to spend some time admiring the imposing homes in the Oak and Spring Streets neighborhood and the St. John Street Historic District. At the end of St. John Street is St. John's Elementary School, the oldest elementary school in the state. This site has been the location of a school since 1818, beginning with the Darlington Academy. At the close of the Civil War, Federal occupation troops turned the school into a hospital and turned the academy green into a campground. The present building dates from 1902.

Go west on State 151 and follow the signs to Hartsville. In 1817 Thomas Edward Hart and his wife bought eight thousand acres of land along Black Creek and established their plantation on the cliffs above the river. Hart opened a country store and post office on his land and became the first postmaster. He also became Commissioner of Free Schools, a merchant, and a captain in the South Carolina militia. During the Depression of 1837–38, he went bankrupt and was forced to sell his plantation to his son-in-law Colonel T. C. Law. In 1845 John Lide Hart, one of Thomas's sons, purchased 491 acres back from his brother-in-law and established Hartsville

Plantation where downtown Hartsville now stands. He constructed his home at what is now East Home Avenue and established a carriage factory, steam-powered sawmill, gristmill, workers' homes, a store, post office, school, and church. In 1855 John Hart's carriage business failed, and he was forced to sell the business and his other holdings to Caleb Coker.

Coker in turn gave the holdings to his son, Major James Lide Coker. Major Coker and his sons established the Pedigreed Seed Company, an oil mill, a fertilizer plant, a department store, a bank, a silver company, a paper company, and the Southern Novelty Company, which became the Fortune 500 Sonoco Products Co. Coker also established the Welsh Neck High School, which became Coker College, and was instrumental in building a railroad spur to Hartsville. David R. Coker began his experiments in the fields, using the latest in scientific breeding of crops. His work was instrumental in the agricultural revolution in the South. By 1963, 65 percent of the cotton acreage in the Southeast, 80 percent of the oats, 75 percent of the flue-cured tobacco, 40 percent of the hybrid corn, and an increasing percentage of soybeans could be traced to seeds developed by Coker scientists.

To learn more about Hartsville and its heritage, begin your tour at the Hartsville Museum, 222 North Fifth Street (803-383-3005), located in the attractive 1930 post office building. Original interior features that have been retained include mahogany paneling, fanlights above the doors and windows, high ceilings, brass fixtures, and terrazzo, marble, and maple floors. Take special notice of the depression in the marble floor caused by the scores of citizens who stood in that spot to buy stamps over a sixty-year period. The original skylight has been restored and enhanced by panels that represent Hartsville's history: the cotton plant and long-leaf pine, representing industry, and the magnolia and Kalmia blossoms, representing natural beauty.

The museum's pride and joy is an original Locomobile Steam Car, designed by the Stanley Brothers of Stanley Steamer fame, in 1899. The Locomobile was America's best-selling car in 1900. This particular car, purchased for $600 by J. L. Coker Jr. as the first automobile brought to South Carolina, was bought in Massachusetts, shipped by boat to Virginia, and then driven over rough roads the rest of the way to Hartsville. The car was given by family descendants to the Charleston Museum, but that organization returned it to the Hartsville Museum, its rightful home.

In the Lawhon History Gallery you can learn about southeastern Indians with artifacts collected along the Pee Dee River, Carolina cotton, the African-American influence on the county, and lifestyles of the nineteenth century. You'll see green and brown experimental cotton among the agricultural artifacts and learn that cotton products are used in explosives, film, paint, oil, feed, and fertilizer as well as in cloth. Among the African-American artifacts are sweetgrass baskets—one of the oldest crafts in South Carolina. For a brief period from 1907 to 1908 Hartsville boasted the Eastern Carolina Silver Company, which created tea sets, pitchers, cups, trays, and other silver hollowware pieces enhanced with southern motifs, such as cotton blossoms, grapevines, and several southern flowers. Each was stamped with a palmetto tree and identified as made in Hartsville. Unfortunately, the skilled silversmiths who had been imported from Massachusetts to do the work became homesick and returned to the North. As they were not replaced, the business was discontinued after 150 pieces were created. Some of these pieces, on loan from private collections, are on display. A corner of the museum has been restored as a post office in honor of the building's original use.

On permanent display is the Centennial Quilt, made in 1991 to celebrate Hartsville's 100th birthday. The four corners duplicate the design in the museum's skylight, and each of the other squares depicts a historic Hartsville building. Other permanent and changing displays feature early domestic implements, clothing, and photographs.

When you've done justice to the displays at the museum, ask for a brochure describing Hartsville's two self-guided walking tours: the Founder's Pathway and the City Pathway. Each concentrates on a historic district and covers about 1.5 miles. Among the significant buildings on the tours are the John Hart Cottage, 108 East Home Avenue, thought to be the oldest house in town; the David R. Coker House, 213 East Home Avenue, home of the founder of the Pedigreed Seed Company; and the J. L. Coker & Company Building, 111 East Carolina Avenue, at one time the largest department store between Richmond and Atlanta.

John Lide Hart built the John L. Hart Cottage, 116 East Home Avenue (803-332-6401), in 1845 from pines felled on his plantation. Costumed docents provide guided tours on the first Sunday of the month from February through November.

Kalmia Gardens, 1624 West Carolina Avenue (803-383-8145), named for the *Kalmia latifola* (mountain laurel) that cascades down the cliff, embraces an almost complete sampling of the state's flora and fauna. Ancient deposits of sands and clays comprise the bedrock that was carved by Black Creek into a sixty-foot bluff. The thirty-acre arboretum maintained by Coker College is a microcosm of the state from the ocean to the mountains. Kalmia Gardens is located on the very same plantation that Thomas Hart began in 1817. Hart's house on the bluff was typical of farmhouses of the era—one room deep with a central hall upstairs and down. Each of the four original rooms contains paneled wainscoting and mantels carved by Hart. After the property was acquired by the Coker family, they added a sitting room, dining room, bedroom, and kitchen to create the house you see today.

More important, Miss May, wife of David R. Coker, decided to turn the neglected property into a scenic attraction.

Already known as Laurel Land because of the profusion of native mountain laurels, the property became known as Miss May's Folly because no one could believe that she could carve a public garden from a wilderness. She was indomitable, however, and with the help of gardeners and a mule, she created trails down the bluff and introduced azaleas, camellias, wisteria, tea olives, and other exotic plants. Old railroad ties were used to break the steepness of the trails. A pond was dug, fed by an artesian well. In 1935 the thirty-acre gardens were opened free of charge to the public. A set of beautiful wrought-iron gates was crafted to highlight Miss May's favorite flower, the camellia. In 1965 Miss May gave the gardens to Coker College in memory of her husband. The gardens were renamed, and a second set of wrought-iron gates was dedicated to Miss May's memory in 1992. Guided by walking trails, visitors can explore a black-water swamp, laurel thickets, pine-oak-holly uplands, a beech bluff, and the hidden pond.

South of Hartsville is the small village of Kellytown, site of the historic Jacob Kelly House, Kellytown Road, a typical nineteenth-century Federal-style country house. During the Civil War when Sherman's troops left Columbia, the Third Division under Major General John E. Smith foraged the countryside appropriating supplies and destroying property, and Smith headquartered for two days in the Kelly House. Kelly, who was eighty-five years old at the time, gathered up his money and valuables and a faithful slave took him to a small island in Segars Mill Pond for safety. It is reported that the soldiers tore open all the feather mattresses in the house looking for valuables and "feathers covered the front yard like snow." The house was not destroyed, nor were the mills at Kellytown—rather, they were operated overtime to provide meal for the Union soldiers.

Originally, Kelly built a one-room log structure in 1820. A portion of that cabin was enveloped by the parlor when the house was expanded, and traces of it can still be seen on the outside by the chimney. With modifications over the years, the existing floor plan consists of a dining room, central hall, parlor, upstairs hall, children's room, parent's room, and grandmother's room. More often called a Preacher's Room, the grandmother's room was added on, but had no entrance directly inside the house. That way, travelers—even complete strangers—could be given overnight shelter without having them in the house with the family. The hand-carved mantels, chair rails, wainscoting, and moldings are original to the house, and all the furniture is handcrafted. On the front porch is a southern joggling board. Although you may have heard the stories that these boards were simply the forerunners of the porch swing or that they were used by courting couples, you may not know that the plans for the joggling board were sent from Scotland to a Mrs. Huger in Sumter County because she suffered from rheumatism, and exercise by joggling was thought to help this condition.

A cookhouse filled with kitchen implements stands behind the main house. This kitchen is unusual because it has a sleeping loft, where servants slept to keep the fire going at night. A smokehouse and a privy, or "necessary" house, also provide insight into the lives of the early residents. The Jacob Kelly House is open the first Sunday of the month except January and February, and from time to time living historians present both day and lantern tours and battle reenactments. For information about the Jacob Kelly House, call the Greater Hartsville Chamber of Commerce at 803-332-6401.

Turn your attention from history to the present technological world at the Robinson Visitor's Center, at Carolina Power and Light Company's H. B. Robinson Electric Power Plant, State 23 (803-857-1238). The center houses interactive exhibits including a minicontrol center that allows you to try your hand at controlling a power plant, a giant calculator that lets you add up how much electricity is needed to run a home, and a watts cycle that tests muscle power by converting the body's calories to electricity.

Missouri Inn, 314 East Home Avenue (803-383-9553), a bed and breakfast, offers the graciousness of a southern home with the amenities of a small European luxury hotel. The clapboard, two-story house surrounded by four acres of landscaped grounds was built around 1900 and is operated by the grandson of the third owners, the Fitchetts. The inn got its name because Mrs. Fitchett was said to be as stubborn as a Missouri mule. Tastefully furnished with antiques, the inn has five guest rooms, three with fireplaces.

From Hartsville, take US 15 south to Bishopville in Lee County, where cotton rules. Each fall, snowy bolls blanket thousands of acres of farmland, and harvesting and ginning begin. Cotton made many a local resident extremely wealthy, and the grand homes of Bishopville are reminiscent of plantation days.

What more appropriate place to pay tribute to the contributions of cotton to South Carolina than in Bishopville? Step back to the era of King Cotton at the South Carolina Cotton Museum, 115 North Main Street (803-484-5145), which showcases the economic, social, and political impact of cotton not only in Lee County, but throughout South Carolina and the South. Original implements, photographs, products, artwork, crafts, and five-hundred-pound cotton bales are displayed in the old Copeland's grocery-store setting where you can get a Coke or Hot Blenheim Ginger Ale and enjoy a pack of Nabs. Browsing through the exhibits will give you an opportunity to feel, smell, and touch a way of life and find out about cultivation and production then and now. Visitors are guaranteed to be taken aback by the gigantic figure of the boll weevil that destroyed South Carolina's cotton economy in the 1930s and to be fascinated by the working model of the cotton screw press, the plantation spinning ginner (a combined gin, carding machine, and spinning wheel), the 1920s cotton mopper (used to kill the boll weevil before the advent of crop dusting), or the 1921 Ford pickup truck. In the simplest terms, a small sign tells the story of cotton: "First day white, next day red, third day dead. This little plant of short duration helps to feed and clothe the nation." See brown, ivory, red, and green experimental cotton which, it is claimed, will intensify in color as it is washed. Local products, souvenirs, reproductions of the Original Cotton Museum Lamp, and publications about local history are sold in the gift shop.

While in Bishopville, visit one man's odyssey with the creativity and challenges of growing topiary at Fryar's Topiary Garden, 165 Broad Acres Road (803-484-5581). Pearl Fryar began with just one topiary plant and was inspired to transform his yard into a three-acre wonderland of sculpted arches, spirals, and geometric designs. Fryar, who has appeared on the PBS program, "Victory Gardens," relies on organic gardening and experiments with all types of plants to create his exotic forms. He opens his garden to the public free of charge, although donations are accepted.

Bishopville is also the site of the annual Lee County Cotton Pickin' Festival, held the third weekend in November with arts and crafts, a parade, street dance, a cotton-pickin' contest, a 5K race, a bed race, historic-home tours, tours of the largest cotton gin east of the Mississippi and a textile yarn-spinning plant, and the crowning of not only the Queen of the Cotton Pageant, but also the crowning of Little Miss and Master Cotton. Call 803-484-5145 for more information.

For a glimpse of the county's natural beauty, visit Lee State Park, County 22 off I-20 (803-428-3833). A park full of trails, Lee State Park boasts a six-mile equestrian trail, a scenic driving trail that winds past two-hundred-year-old trees, and hiking trails that lead visitors to a river swamp.

Rich in history, the Pee Dee Region brims with significant sites that interpret the past, but the technological age is well represented as well. Other attractions range from the sublime to the ridiculous. From the Pee Dee Region, you can easily make forays into the Olde English District, Santee Cooper Country, and the Grand Strand.

For More Information

Pee Dee Tourism Commission, P.O. Box 3093, Florence 29502. 803-669-0950.

Darlington Chamber of Commerce, P.O. Box 274, Darlington 29532. 803-393-2641.

Dillon County Chamber of Commerce, P.O. Box 1304, Dillon 29536. 803-774-8551.

Florence Convention and Visitors Bureau, One Civic Center Plaza, Florence 29502. 803-664-0330.

Greater Hartsville Chamber of Commerce, P.O. Box 578, Hartsville 29551. 803-332-6401.

Greater Lake City Chamber of Commerce, P.O. Box 669, Lake City 29560. 803-394-8611.

Marion Chamber of Commerce, P.O. Box 35, Marion 29571. 803-423-3561.

Marlboro County Chamber of Commerce, P.O. Box 458, Bennettsville 29512. 803-479-3941.

Greater Williamsburg County Chamber of Commerce, 130 East Main Street, Kingstree 29556. 803-354-6431.

8

Santee Cooper Country

The Santee Cooper Country is born of two unlikely sister rivers—the Santee and the Cooper. The tumultuous Santee, which got its name from the Indian word for "river," gathers the fierce currents of a dozen mountain streams and then surges past high bluffs and cathedral-like woodlands on its way to the sea. In complete contrast, the quiet Cooper seeps from marshes and small streams and meanders slowly past once-proud plantations on its course to Charleston. In 1941 the Corps of Engineers linked the two rivers in a huge hydroelectric project that created lakes Marion and Moultrie, which are connected by a 6.5-mile diversion canal. One of the goals of the Santee Cooper project was to create a route for inland navigation from Columbia to Charleston. Today's boaters can utilize this clearly defined waterway through 122 miles with the help of the seventy-five-foot-high Santee Cooper Lock.

As a side benefit, the project created some of the world's finest and most varied fishing and multitudinous recreational opportunities. The combined lakes create a sports enthusiast's paradise. Especially renowned for fishing, the lakes are teeming with striped bass, large-mouth bass, crappie, bream, and catfish. In fact, the state's striped-bass record catch, weighing 55 pounds, and record blue catfish, weighing 109 pounds, were caught in the Santee Cooper Lakes. When the lakes were created in the 1930s, it was the first time in history that one river had been diverted into another to generate electricity. The two lakes, however, differ greatly in their topography. Most of Moultrie's basin was cleared before the water filled it, but Marion was filled before the timber was cleared. This submerged timber creates innumerable hideouts for marine life and makes the fishing superb.

Situated in the midland region of South Carolina east of the geographic heart of the state, the region's topography ranges from river swamp lands to an area known as the "High Hills of the Santee." In all, Santee Cooper Country offers 450 miles of shoreline and 171,000 acres of land covered by 6.5 million gallons of water.

Begin your tour of Santee Cooper Country at the town of Santee, located at I-95 and State 6. North of town is Santee State Park, 251 State Park Road (803-854-2408), which offers land-based and pier-based cabins, swimming, tennis, boat ramps, boat rentals, a tackle shop, camping facilities, nature trails, tours of a limestone cavern, and boat tours on Lake Marion. The park's Lake View Restaurant features family-style, "all-you-can-eat" buffets on Friday and Saturday nights and Sunday at midday.

Take State 6 north to Elloree. Established in 1886 (the name for the town was derived from an Indian word for "home I love"), Elloree became the smallest municipality to achieve Great Town status. In March the Elloree Trials, flat races for thoroughbred and quarter horses, is an annual event of national interest. For more information, call the Elloree Town Hall (803-897-2821).

Retrace State 6 through Santee and continue south to Eutawville. "Eutaw" is the Cherokee word for pine tree, and Native Americans called the area Eutaw Springs. On September 8, 1781, the Revolutionary War Battle of Eutaw Springs was the last major battle of that war fought in South Carolina. A monument at the Eutaw Springs Battlefield on US 6, overlooking Lake Marion, designates the historical spot as one of the bloodiest battles of the Revolution. (The town of Eutaw, Alabama, is named for the battle and the area.) In 1836, planters along the Santee River, seeking refuge for their families from summer humidity and mosquitoes, founded the nearby town of Eutaw Village, which eventually became Eutawville. Noted for its superb fishing, the town is the site of several major fishing tournaments. St. Julian Plantation, on US 6 (803-492-7556), offers pick-your-own strawberries and blackberries from April through June, peaches in July and August, and vegetables such as sweet corn, cantaloupes, beans, peas, okra, and tomatoes from March through August. Tiny Eutawville is noted for several excellent places to eat. Chef's Choice Steak House, State 6 and State 45 (803-492-3410), is noted for its steaks and seafood. You can cook your own over a charcoal pit or let the chef prepare it for you. Sweatman's Barbecue, State 453 (no phone), has been called the best in the South by *Southern Living*. On the shores of Lake Marion just outside of town is the Cypress Shores Marina, Restaurant, and Brass Bass Lounge, Cypress Shores Drive off State 6 (803-492-9594), a full-service marina offering a deep-water dock, slip rentals, boat rentals, a convenience store, professional guide service, waterfront camping, and cottage rentals. The restaurant offers everything from salads and sandwiches to seafood platters, steaks, ribs, and pastas, as well as good times anytime in the lounge.

As you continue south along State 6, Lake Marion gives way to Lake Moultrie. At the far southern end of the lake is Monck's Corner. Berkeley County played a strategic role in the Revolutionary War. The Francis Marion National Forest, US 17N (843-765-5222), the site of the battle between the forces of British General Banastre Tarleton and Francis Marion, offers an abundance of wildlife to visitors to the 245,000-acre park. Marion was born and is buried at his family's plantation, Belle Isle, off State 45 near Eadytown.

Flowing through Monck's Corner is the Tail Race Canal, from which the state's record catfish was taken. The lucky fisherman reported that it took him an hour to pull the fighting-mad 109-pound fish into his boat. Fishing, boating, waterskiing, and other water sports are popular diversions on the canal. On the banks, overlooking the canal through two walls of windows is The Dock Restaurant (843-761-8080). Many diners, in fact, come by boat to feast on the catfish specialties. Each year, the restaurant sponsors the Family Open Catfish Tournament.

One of South Carolina's newest state parks, Old Santee Canal State Park, 900 Stony Landing Road (843-899-5200), on the old Stony Landing Plantation along the banks of Biggin Creek, recognizes the contributions canals made to the development of the state. Get into the mind-set to learn about eighteenth-century canals as you enter the museum building through a life-size replica of a lock. Inside the museum, you can watch a movie on the history of canals in general and the Santee Canal in particular. Rivers were the first superhighways, but sometimes movement down them was impeded by falls or shoals, and the solution was to build canals and locks around them. The Santee Canal was the first in the country to connect two bodies of water—the Santee River and the Cooper River. This twenty-two-mile canal was started in 1793 with ten workers and completed in 1800 with one thousand workers. The economic effect of completing the canal was instantly realized. Previously, it had cost two dollars per bale to ship cotton to Charleston by road; the canal reduced that cost to fifty cents per bale. The Santee Canal was active for fifty years until the lakes Marion and Moultrie projects flooded most of the canal. Take a leisurely look at the display on lock-building, which includes a working model of how a lift lock works.

In addition to its emphasis on canals and locks, the park promotes the environment. The Please Touch table introduces visitors to the textures of various natural and wildlife items. A gigantic model of a live oak is the home for various mounted animals that are common to the area. You can see a movie about caves in a life-size replica of a limestone cave. Outdoors, a boardwalk and overlook allow visitors to observe nature. You can rent a canoe to further explore Biggin Creek. The photogenic raised-cottage-style plantation house is used for special functions.

Located at the entrance to the state park, but operated independently, is the Berkeley Museum, 950 Stony Landing Road (843-899-5101). The first thing that greets you upon entering the museum is the mounted world-record catfish caught in the Tail Race Canal. Various periods from Native Americans through the present are represented through impressive displays which are primarily composed of replicas. Among these displays are ones on agriculture, early-twentieth-century medicine, rural electrification, and the Francis Marion State Forest. On the front lawn sits a replica of the Confederate torpedo ram CSS *David*, affectionately known as the *Little David*. The Confederate torpedo ram made history when it delivered the first torpedo attack in history on the night of October 5, 1863. Its target, the Union ship *New Ironsides*, was so badly damaged it never saw action again. The original *Little David* was captured by Union forces.

Outside of town you can visit a monastery and a world-famous swamp garden. Enter Mepkin Abbey, State 402/River Road (843-761-8509), to see the chapel and gardens through a wide avenue of oaks and follow the signs to the reception center where you will ring a large bell on a pole for assistance.

The monks have taken a vow of silence, so only a few of them are permitted to speak to visitors. The brethren at Mepkin Abbey have the Rule of St. Benedict, which goes back fifteen hundred years, as their fundamental law. They observe a contemplative life and earn money by selling eggs and a special compost they call "tea." The beautiful property, located on the Cooper River, was once the rice plantation of patriot Henry Laurens, who was the president of the Continental Congress before the Revolutionary War and who was later imprisoned in the Tower of London as a traitor. Laurens used the method of cultivating rice fields by flooding along a tidal river. The technique was called the Mepkin Plan and was widely copied elsewhere. The plantation was burned by the British during the Revolutionary War and again by the Union during the Civil War. In this century the plantation was purchased by Henry Luce, publisher of *Time*, and his wife, congresswoman and diplomat Clare Boothe Luce, but, after the death of their daughter, they donated it to the Cistercian-Trappist monks of the Catholic Church for a retreat. Laurens, his family, and both Luces are buried on the property. Visitors to the elegantly simple contemporary chapel must also observe the vow of silence. The rolling terrain of the grounds is dotted with ancient live oaks, azaleas, camellias, and other flowering bushes. Terraces drop down to the river banks, an excellent place for quiet reflection.

South Carolina's climate is ideal for growing flowers year round. At Cypress Gardens, 3030 Cypress Gardens Road off US 52 between Charleston and Moncks Corner (843-553-0515), paths and water trails lead through a black-water swamp highlighted by a cypress forest and, in season, azaleas, camellias, and spring bulbs. You may recognize the swamp from the television miniseries *North and South* and the movie *Swamp Thing*. Where the gardens now stand was originally part of Dean Hall Plantation, one of the Cooper River's largest and most prosperous rice plantations. In contrast to the rice grown by the Mepkin Plan, rice at Dean Hall was originally grown using the inland method, where water from a reservoir—in this case the swamp—was used to flood the adjoining fields by a system of trunks (gates) and ditches. Later, the tidal or Mepkin method was used. Dean Hall fell into disrepair after the Civil War and in 1909 it was purchased by Benjamin R. Kittredge as a winter retreat for his homesick Lowcountry wife. In the 1920s Kittredge is said to have been particularly struck by a red maple reflected brilliantly in the glassy-smooth black water of the swamp, and he conceived the idea of planting a garden of other colorful flora that would be enhanced by mirroring in the swamp. In 1927 he began planting thousands of azaleas, camellias, dogwoods, tea olives, magnolias, and a host of bulbs. A crew of two hundred men constructed paths across the swamp, and Mr. Kittredge paid children a penny each for native Atamasco lily bulbs they dug up from the woods for transplanting. More exotic trees and shrubs were planted, and Mrs. Kittredge imported thousands of winter-blooming daphne, her favorite flowering shrub. The gates were opened to the public in 1932 and, since then, thousands upon thousands of visitors have enjoyed the swamp gardens.

Cypress Gardens reaches its peak in March and April, but a trip through the swamp is a treat in any season to see the countless wildlife species from the transparent ghost shrimp to tree frogs, alligators, ducks, wading birds, and bald eagles. Although you're not likely to see them, deer, raccoon, and bobcat leave tracks to testify to their nocturnal visits. The most traditional way to see the gardens is by flat-bottomed boat, but you can also stroll around the manicured garden paths or the rustic nature trails. A small working rice field was recently re-created so that visitors can once again see rice planted, tended, and harvested by centuries-old methods. The trees in the garden swamp are so incredibly thick that it is hard for your boat guide to maneuver between them, yet the gardens lost twelve thousand trees to Hurricane Hugo, and hurricane recovery is still in progress. Spend some time in the new butterfly house.

An appealing place to stay in the Monck's Corner area is Rice Hope Plantation Inn, 206 Rice Hope Drive off River Road/State 402 (843-761-4832), which sits among eleven acres of live oaks on a bluff overlooking the Cooper River near Mepkin Abbey. Rice is etched into the glass of the front door of the sprawling nine-thousand-square-foot antebellum house, which was expanded in the 1920s. Five guest rooms are decorated in antique and reproduction furnishings. Breakfast is served in the magnificent dining room with windows on three sides and French doors opening up toward the river. After enjoying your meal, you'll want to explore the grounds which drop to the river in a series of camellia-filled terraces. Among the many varieties of camellias is one gigantic bush more than two hundred years old. At the bottom of the terraces, the grounds open into a sweeping lawn and a dock from which you can enjoy the view of the river, watch eagles and wading birds, or try your hand at fishing. A tennis court is also located on the property, and bicycles are provided for guests. In fact, once guests arrive here, they never have to leave the property to ensure a restful stay.

From Monck's Corner, take US 17 ALT west to Summerville (see Charleston chapter) and turn northwest on US 78 to Branchville. Founded in 1734 by a Prussian immigrant, Branchville is one of the oldest towns in the state, but even more important, it is the site of one of the oldest railroad junctions in the world. The town celebrates its ties to the railroad industry each fall by hosting the Raylrode Daze Festivul.

Take US 21 north to Orangeburg. Native American inhabitants in what was to become Orangeburg County were joined by an Indian trader named George Sterling in 1704 and, soon after, by a few cattle-raising settlers. The district was named for William, Prince of Orange, but remained lightly populated until the General Assembly established eleven townships along the banks of the major rivers in 1730. Five years later, two hundred Swiss, German, and Dutch immigrants formed a community near the banks of the North Edisto River, choosing the site because of its fertile soil and abundant wildlife, as well as its river outlet to Charleston for agricultural and lumber products.

One of only twenty-six testing grounds in the country for the All-America Rose selection process, Edisto Memorial Gardens, US 301 (803-533-5870), also blankets the banks of the black-water Edisto River with masses of other southern favorites. The gardens occupy rifle pits where fewer than six hundred Confederate soldiers temporarily halted the advance of the Union army at the river. Unfortunately, on February 12, 1865, outflanked by a much larger force, the defenders were forced to retreat to Columbia. Although at the time of the Civil War, the area was marshy swamp overgrown with brush, local citizens began to clear five acres for the memorial garden in the 1920s. Azaleas were planted first, and over the next thirty years, in addition to adding acres more of gardens, a city playground was built, followed by a greenhouse, a nursery, and a memorial entrance fountain dedicated to soldiers who have died in America's wars. Today, the gardens cover 150 acres and showcase azaleas, camellias, roses, and other flowering trees and plants set among the giant oaks, ancient cypresses, and other native trees.

The city has a contractual agreement with All-America Rose Selections, Inc. to display past and current award-winning roses from their authorized test gardens. Always on display are four thousand rose bushes representing at least seventy-five labeled varieties. The test garden is dedicated to recognizing five of the most desirable hybrid-tea-rose introductions each year.

Among the other garden features are a floating fountain in the pond, two hundred Yoshino cherry trees, and a garden for the blind. If you want to visit during the peak seasons, choose mid-March to mid-April for blossoming azaleas, crab apple, dogwood, and wisteria; mid-April to early-November for roses; or late-November through March for camellias.

A major addition to the gardens, the Home Wetlands Park permits visitors to glimpse plants and animals found in the wetlands via a 2,600-foot boardwalk into a tupelo/cypress area located between the rose garden and the river. A self-guided nature trail through the gardens and along the river highlights native trees. The park also features a boat dock with a gazebo and an interpretive shelter with an educational counter imparting the role of wetlands in our environment. The most novel attraction at the gardens is a small antique water wheel reminiscent of Oriental rice-paddy irrigation wheels.

Housed in the enclosed old River Pavilion in the Edisto Memorial Gardens, the Orangeburg Arts Center, 649 Riverside Drive (803-536-4074), offers performances in the visual, performing, literary, and media arts. Exhibits in such media as pottery, needlework, and miniatures change monthly in the Lusty Gallery. With advance reservations, the center provides guided tours through the gardens.

Named to the Top Twenty Tourism Events in the Southeast by the Southeast Tourism Society, the South Carolina Festival of Roses is the premier annual event in the gardens. Held the last weekend in April among thousands of blooming roses, the event includes arts and crafts, a black-water river race, road races, sports tournaments, continuous entertainment, and the Princess of Roses Pageant. For more information about the festival, call the Chamber of Commerce at 803-534-6821.

During late November and throughout December, the gardens are festooned with thousands of twinkling lights creating dozens of Christmas displays for a Children's Garden Christmas. Call 803-533-6020 for more information.

The longest black-water river in the world, the Edisto River is lined with swamp hardwoods and cypress forming natural cathedrals over the north and south forks. On its way to the ocean, the river winds past two hundred miles of swamp forests where bird life and fish are abundant. Suitable for the novice, one of the most popular canoe trips begins at Shillings Bridge Road (County 74) and runs seven miles to Edisto Memorial Gardens. A 12.3-mile run between the gardens and County 39 provides a bigger challenge with unpredictable currents and plenty of deadfall. Since colonial times, the Edisto redbreast has been one of the most popular game fish, but anglers can also cast their lines for largemouth and striped bass, jackfish, pike, warmouth, catfish, and bream.

Founded in 1869, Clafin College in Orangeburg was South Carolina's oldest historically black college. In 1872 it was reorganized into the Agricultural and Mechanics Institute for Colored Students, which became South Carolina State University in 1992. Visit the university's I. P. Stanbuck Museum and Planetarium, US 601 (803-536-7174), where Sunday shows are projected on the forty-foot-high dome at the state's largest planetarium. In addition, the university has an art museum featuring all types of art including an outstanding collection of African-American works.

In addition to the Festival of Roses, Orangeburg hosts another popular event. Every January coon-hunting enthusiasts converge on the city for the Grand American Coon Hunt. Also named as one of the Top Twenty Tourism Events in the Southeast, the Grand American is the largest field trial for coon dogs in the country and serves as a qualifying event for the World Coon Hunt. Wild raccoons living in their natural habitat are hunted but not harmed. Coons are counted as "treed" when the judges confirm the dog's tracking ability. To learn more about the event, call the Chamber of Commerce at 803-534-6821.

From Orangeburg, take US 601 to St. Matthews. Located near the west bank of the Congaree River, this rich land was one of the first plantation realms above the Charleston tidewater. Calhoun County wasn't formed until 1908, but the history of the white settlers goes back nearly three hundred years, when trader George Sterling was given the first land grant in 1704. By the 1730s, a few English, Irish, and Huguenot families were joined by groups of Swiss and German settlers. The year 1780 saw one of the most colorful events in the region's history. Rebecca Motte's home was commandeered by British forces, although they let her remain in the house with them for a while. The British built a fort, called Fort Motte, around the house and later forced Rebecca to move into the overseer's cabin. She was able to leave the fort and join with American forces who set the roof of the house on fire, driving the British out, and thus recapturing the house. Some accounts say that Rebecca supplied the fire arrows; another account says that a soldier soaked rags in kerosene, lit them, and hurled them onto the roof. Regardless, both British and American troops pitched in to douse the fire and save the house. That night Rebecca, back in her own home, served dinner to troops from both sides.

The town of St. Matthews dates back to 1841 when the railroad reached what was then called Lewisville. The deep railroad cut through the middle of town was entirely dug out with picks and shovels.

Costumes, period furniture, Indian exhibits, and other displays tell the story of the area at the Calhoun County Museum, 303 Butler Street (803-874-3964), located in a renovated and expanded pecan factory. The mother of current director

Debbie Roland was the previous director, and Debbie grew up immersed in the museum and its contents, so she knows a fascinating story about every item in the museum. The lives of several prominent South Carolina citizens are recounted in the displays: Catherine Kinsler Kagler, whose portrait was cut by the sword thrusts of angry Union soldiers; Lawrence Keitt and Olin M. Dantzler, who were among the ten most-influential men in South Carolina in the mid-1800s; Emily Geiger, who was a Revolutionary War spy; Rebecca Motte, who helped recapture her house from the British; and William Ellison, a former slave who became a successful inventor and businessman. Other displays include fashions of yesteryear, the work of major South Carolina silversmiths, early plantation medicine, African influences, a children's corner circa 1880, and a nineteenth-century colonial kitchen. One room is set up to resemble a turn-of-the-century street with a general store, post office, bank, and vintage vehicles. Genealogical records dating back to the 1600s can be found in the Research Room and Archives, which may be used by appointment.

Continue north on US 601 to US 76 and turn east. At State 261 turn north to Statesburg. A flower recognized worldwide, the flamboyant red poinsettia was named for Joel Poinsett, a South Carolinian statesman who died in Statesburg in 1851. Poinsett had discovered the flower in Mexico and brought it back to Charleston to propagate. Over time, the poinsettia has become synonymous with Christmas. Poinsett's grave is found in the churchyard at the 1850 Gothic Revival Church of the Holy Cross, State 261 (803-494-8101). Also admire the intricate ornamental ironwork fences and gates around some of the plots. Constructed of rammed earth, the church boasts beautiful Bavarian stained glass windows, including a rose window on the altar wall and side windows that each feature a different style cross. The altar ceiling is covered with ornate plasterwork. Each burnished pew is capped on the aisle end with a fleur-de-lis. The walls are faux-finished to resemble white marble. One of only a few still operational in this country, the organ is by Henry Erben, a renowned nineteenth-century New York organ maker.

Across the street, set far back from the road and just barely visible, are three antebellum homes, which are private residences. One was the home of Mary Boykin Chestnut, the famed Civil War diarist, and another the home of William Ellison, the ex-slave turned business man. Retrace State 261 past US 76 and continue south to Poinsett State Park, State 261 (803-494-8177), where you can examine a rare and curious blend of Upcountry and Lowcountry plant life on one thousand acres at the edge of Wateree Swamp. Typical of the foothills are the hilly terrain, rich hardwood forest, and mountain laurel, but Spanish-moss festoons hanging from the trees give a Lowcountry flavor. The park road climbs through the high hills creating the feeling of a trip to the mountains. Facilities and activities at the park include cabins, camping sites, a nature center, year-round interpretive programs, swimming, nature and hiking trails, fishing, boat rentals, and picnicking spots.

Nearby, visit Thomas Sumter's grave site at the General Thomas Sumter Family Park and Cemetery, off State 261 (803-494-8177). Follow the signs from the intersection of US 76/378 and State 261. Now part of the state park system, the gravesite includes a small chapel and the crypt of Countess Natalie DeLage Sumter, the general's beloved daughter-in-law. It is the oldest Catholic chapel in the state outside Charleston.

Retrace State 261 to State 763 and turn east to Sumter. Both the city and county were named for Revolutionary War hero Thomas Sumter, whose nickname "Gamecock" was appropriated by the University of South Carolina as its mascot. Well known for his battle feats, he was also a frontiersman and served as a senator at the age of seventy-six.

Although Palm Sunday, April 9, 1865, is considered to mark the end of the Civil War because it was the day Lee surrendered to Grant at Appomattox Courthouse, Virginia, the armies in South Carolina didn't know that yet. Confederate forces were still engaged in desperate last-ditch struggles with Union forces. Huge numbers of locomotives and railroad cars loaded with Confederate supplies were trapped on the Wilmington and Manchester line near Sumter. Sherman was determined to destroy this valuable war material. Under the command of Union General Edward E. Potter, 2,500 men made up from seven regiments of white and black soldiers marched toward Sumter. As they advanced, they took what supplies they needed, burned the rest, and gathered up all the contraband slaves on their route—swelling their ranks by several thousand. Although there were no regular Confederate units in the area, Sumter citizens were determined to make a stand. Confederate Colonel George W. Lee, commander of Sumter's Twentieth South Carolina Militia, mobilized a small force, which was joined by several other units, as well as furloughed and convalescing soldiers, but the total force amounted to only 575 men and boys. They decided to make their stand at Dingle's Mill. The first two Union assaults were driven back, but the Federals finally flanked the Confederates and carried the day. Overwhelming odds had defeated the small band of Confederates, but their determined defense against a force more than five times their size, under heavy fire and direct assault, earned them a place in history. Following the battle, Potter's men occupied Sumter and destroyed railroad rolling stock and equipment and burned the jail, courthouse, warehouses, and other buildings. Shops and homes were ransacked and much personal property taken. Detachments fanned out from Sumter to destroy bridges, mills, and cotton.

The 30 locomotives and 250 cars of supplies, which were the objectives of the Union expedition, were eventually destroyed before word was received of General Joseph E. Johnston's surrender or Lee's. Dingle's Mill Memorial Park and monuments, just south of the intersection of US 521 and US 15, are maintained by the United Daughters of the Confederacy. Reenactments of the battle are held periodically.

Visitors to Sumter discover a wide array of choices: impressive historic sites, flourishing gardens, architectural landmarks, and agricultural and nature experiences. Throughout the year, swans glide gracefully through the lily pads on the dark, forty-five-acre swampy lake at Sumter's Swan Lake Iris Gardens, West Liberty Street Extension (803-773-3371), but it is in the late spring (mid-May through June) that visitors can walk through the 150 acres of landscaped grounds wreathed in splashes of color provided by thousands of Dutch and Japanese irises—one of the largest collections of irises in the country, with twenty-five varieties represented. In addition, depending on the season, camellias and azaleas bloom, as well as annuals, roses, nandina, holly, purple Japanese magnolias, southern magnolias, yellow jessamine, dogwoods, and crepe myrtles. Tall cypress trees dip their roots in the onyxlike waters, and beards of Spanish moss hang from the live oaks.

During the 1920s Sumter businessman Hamilton Carr Bland wanted to landscape his yard with exotic Japanese irises, but the flowers failed miserably. He was so disgusted, he directed his gardener to uproot the bulbs and dump them on the thirty acres of cypress swamp he had recently bought as a fishing retreat. The following spring the irises were blooming magnificently along the edge of the lake. With this accidental success, Bland began designing, planting, and developing a garden on the site, which he eventually donated to the city.

Colored by tannic acid leached into the water from the cypress trees, the inky waters of the lake form the understage for the iris which grow abundantly in the moist soil. When in bloom, small islands float in the lake like a colorful necklace. The crown jewels of the lake, however, are the magnificent swans, gathered from all over the world. The royalty of waterfowls, this collection includes all of the eight species of swans: trumpeters, royal white mutes, black-necked, black Australians, whoopers, Bewick, whistling, and Coscorobas. The gardens are claimed to be the only place in the world with all eight species. Bring your own bread and crackers to feed the swans or purchase food from vending machines located throughout the park. A special effort is made to breed the swans and increase their number: babies, called cygnets, stay in "swandominiums" until they are old enough to join the adults.

The gardens extend on both sides of West Liberty, with the iris garden, known as the Bland Garden, on one side, and the Heath Garden, 120 acres donated by A. T. Heath Sr. on the other side. A covered walkway accessible by elevator has been constructed so that visitors don't have to cross traffic to enjoy both gardens. During the year, special events at the gardens include the spring Iris Festival, the Fall Festival of the Arts, and December's Christmas Tree Lighting Festival, when a lighted cedar tree is floated out onto the lake and numerous lighted Christmas figures and designs are scattered throughout the park.

Fine period furnishings and other historic objects are housed in the circa 1845 Victorian Williams-Brice House, which serves as the Sumter County Museum and Archives, 122 North Washington Street (803-775-0908). Built in 1845 by Andrew Jackson Moses, who lived here with his wife and fourteen of their children, the house remained in the family until the 1920s. In 1922 the house was purchased by O. L. Williams, a wealthy industrialist whose daughter Martha Williams Brice lived in it until 1969. Surrounded by formal gardens, the house features crystal chandeliers, beveled glass, a mix of rococo revival and Empire furniture, and gracious southern charm. Among the displays are children's period furniture, toys, and dolls; the 1930s Watch Repair Shop and Country Store; the War Memorial Room; the Textile Gallery, which includes a variety of 1840–1940 clothing and quilts, as well as coverlets dating back to 1820; and exhibits that document the development of Sumter's agricultural and transportation systems. Featured throughout the museum is art by local and national artists, including Rembrandt Peale's portrait of Thomas Sumter. In the carriage house you can see an elegant carriage that belonged to South Carolina Governor Richard Manning. The archives room, staffed by the Sumter County Chapter of the South Carolina Genealogical Society, is a rich resource for research.

The antebellum home of the late Elizabeth White, Sumter's most renowned artist, showcases local, state, regional, and national art exhibits at the Sumter Gallery of Art, 421 North Main Street (803-775-0543). The gallery gift shop features unique art gifts made by members of the Sumter Artists Guild and other invited artists.

Sumter Opera House, 19–21 North Main Street (803-436-2500), is a palatial 1890s Richardson Romanesque stone architectural treasure crowned by a one-hundred-foot, four-faced clock tower with a working antique clock operated by weights. The building now houses City Hall and a six-hundred-seat auditorium where various cultural programs are held. Another jewel in Sumter's crown is the Patriot Hall, 135 Haynsworth Street (803-436-2260), the home of music, art, theater, and dance. One of the finest cultural centers in the Southeast, it boasts a 1,017-seat auditorium.

Shop for antique furniture at bargain prices, as well as lamps, prints and paintings, glass, china, clocks, collectibles, Christmas decorations, handmade crafts, one-of-a-kind items, and much more at Antique Row, 204–210 Broad Street (803-778-1890 or 800-773-4214), a collection of sensational shops in four turn-of-the-century Victorian homes providing fourteen thousand square feet of space.

The Hampton Park neighborhood overflows with palatial Queen Anne, Victorian, prairie-style, Greek Revival, Mediterranean villas, Cape Cod homes, and "mosquito" cottages, as well as handsome churches. Central to the neighborhood is Memorial Park, which was established with private contributions in memory of local citizens who fought and died in World War I. The park features a bandstand surrounded by colorfully landscaped walkways, benches, tennis courts, and picnic areas. Swan Lake Drive neighborhood, leading to Swan Lake Iris Gardens, is one of the most fashionable addresses in the city, although the houses are not of the vintage of those in Hampton Park.

Some of Sumter's rich store of historic houses are used as bed-and-breakfast accommodations. Magnolia House, 230 Church Street (803-775-6694 or 888-666-0296), is a Greek Revival home with five fireplaces, stained-glass windows, and inlaid oak floors. Each of the five guest rooms is decorated with antiques from a different era. Breakfast is served in the large formal dining room decorated with massive French antiques. Enjoy afternoon refreshments on one of the porches or in the formal rear courtyard. Bed and Breakfast of Sumter, 6 Park Avenue (803-773-2903 or 886-786-8372), is located in an 1896 prairie-style home overlooking Memorial Park. Guest rooms are warmly decorated with antiques. Your gourmet breakfast can be served on the veranda, in the dining room, or in your room. Located in an early 1890s house built by the present owner's great-uncle, the Calhoun Street Bed and Breakfast, 302 West Calhoun Street (803-775-7035 or 800-355-8119), offers four eclectically decorated guest rooms richly appointed with family antiques, as well as medieval, nineteenth-century, and contemporary art. Breakfast is a hearty meal served in the dining room or on the back porch overlooking the two old rose gardens.

You'll also need to drive a little way outside of town to eat at some of the Sumter area's most popular restaurants. Lilfred's, 11 Main Street, Rembert (803-432-7063), serves what is fondly known as "gourmet-by-the-side-of-the-road." Located in an unassuming building directly on the highway, the restaurant's interior is surprisingly elegant and the food superb. Farther out, in Boykin, is the Mill Pond Restaurant (see the Olde English District chapter). Santee Cooper Country adjoins every other tourist region in South Carolina with the exception of the Upcountry and the Old 96 District and is therefore ideally situated for travelers to extend their explorations into these areas.

For More Information

Santee Cooper Counties Promotion Commission, P.O. Drawer 40, Santee 29142. 803-854-2131 or 800-227-8510.

Berkeley County Chamber of Commerce, Nesbit House, Monck's Corner 29461. 800-882-0337.

Calhoun County Chamber of Commerce, P.O. Box 444, St. Matthews 29135. 803-874-3791.

Orangeburg County Chamber of Commerce, P.O. Drawer 328, Orangeburg 29116-0328. 800-242-3435.

Greater Sumter Convention and Visitors Bureau, P.O. Box 1449, Sumter 29151. 800-688-4748.

9

Thoroughbred Country

As the name implies, Thoroughbred Country is horse-and-rider heaven, but farmers and loggers came to the area first, drawn by the deep, loamy soil and long growing season, as well as by the towering native pines that provided ready-to-hand building materials and a dependable cash crop. Later, the year-round green pastures attracted the owners of standardbreds (pacers and trotters) and thoroughbreds, lured by the springlike winters and the leisurely pace of life. In addition, the region has pioneered in cotton and textiles, quarried granite, and mined kaolin—a clay exported to the china factories of Belgium, France, and England. The Savannah River Site is a federal facility for atomic products.

Begin your tour at Allendale, located at US 301 and US 278 in the southwestern corner of the state. Indian artifacts, war memorabilia, natural history displays, and changing arts and crafts exhibits are exhibited at the Allendale County Art Gallery and Museum, US 301N (803-584-2191). Located behind the museum is Miss Annie Arnold's Schoolhouse, an authentic one-room school used in Allendale around 1875.

Serving as both a community center and museum, the Allendale County African American Culture Center, East Flat Street (803-584-7400), located in the former Allendale Training School, offers educational, social, and cultural events related to African-American heritage.

From Allendale, go northeast on US 301 and turn east on State 64 toward Ehrhardt. Rivers Bridge State Park, State 64 (803-267-3675), features the remains of the breastworks constructed by Confederate troops in an attempt to halt the advance of Union troops in 1865. Union General William Tecumseh Sherman's troops clashed here with Confederates defending the Salkehatchie River. Vastly outnumbered, the Southerners held the crossing for two days before being forced out of their breastworks. This battle was one of only a few episodes of major resistance encountered by the Northern army on its march through the state. In 1876 the Confederates killed there were reburied in a common grave near the battlefield. The breastworks survive as a stark, silent monument to the battle at the only South Carolina park that commemorates the Civil War. The park also includes several monuments and a museum containing Civil War relics. Periodic encampments and reenactments depict the battle and interpret military life during that era.

Retrace State 64 past US 301 and continue to Barnwell. For more than 150 years, the town's rare vertical sundial, thought to be the only one of its kind remaining in America, has given the correct time of day to passers-by. The sundial is located on the grounds of the 1878 courthouse in Courthouse Square. Although it was erected two years before time was standardized, it keeps within two minutes of Eastern Standard Time. Captain Joseph D. Allen, a wealthy Barnwell resident and lover of monuments, had the sundial made in Charleston. He adorned his parents' graves with ornate monuments and made sure his nanny's grave and that of his dogs were well marked. It is ironic that after losing his wealth in the Civil War, Allen was buried in a grave not even marked with a headstone.

At the Barnwell County Museum, Marlboro and Hagood

Streets (803-259-1916), you can examine a collection of memorabilia pertaining to the history of Barnwell County.

Built in 1856 of cypress in the carpenter-Gothic style of the English parish church, the Church of the Holy Apostles, Hagood Street, was used as a stable for Union horses during General Sherman's march through the area. It was reported that soldiers used the valuable large stone baptismal font, believed to be from medieval times, as a watering trough. The congregation had the foresight to remove the stained-glass windows, which they buried for protection. After the war, the windows were replaced. Several noted South Carolinians are buried in the churchyard including a governor, senator, and congressman. Tours can be arranged through the Chamber of Commerce (803-259-7446).

Take State 3 toward Blackville. Since the beginning of recorded history, the artesian wells of the Healing Springs, found north of town, off State 3, have supplied legendary mineral waters to pilgrims seeking relief from a variety of ailments. Indians believed in the spring's natural healing powers and brought wounded Revolutionary soldiers here to drink. Locals still drink its waters.

Backtrack to Blackville and turn west on US 78 and then go to Montmorenci. South Carolina has only two wineries, and one of them is Montmorenci Vineyards, 2989 Charleston Highway (803-649-4870), which grows its own grapes, hand picks them, and gently presses and ferments them in small lots. You can visit the winery for a tour and tasting of some of their wines. If you'd like to spend the night in the area, Annie's Inn, US 78 (803-649-6836), offers bed-and-breakfast accommodations in an antebellum farmhouse.

Continue west on US 78 to Aiken. *"La beauté d'un cheval, c'est bonne pour l'âme d'un homme."* The beauty of a horse is good for the soul of man. This age-old adage has been the motto of Aiken, known as both the Queen of Winter Resorts and The Sports Center of the South, for more than a century. Many towns claim to be representative of horse country, but we know of no other town where roads and streets retain their sand surface so as not to injure the horses' feet. Every house seems to have a horse trailer parked outside instead of a recreational vehicle or boat. There are traffic signal change buttons located at a height where a mounted horseman or carriage driver can reach them without dismounting.

Within the city limits, Aiken boasts the two-thousand-acre Hitchcock Woods—the largest urban forest in the country—as well as a sand course for flat racing, a grass course for steeplechasing, a clay course for harness racing, and several polo fields. Horses are exercised in the woods, and groups meet there for carriage rides. Riding trails with names such as Devil's Backbone and Foxes' Den crisscross the preserve. Cathedral Aisle Trail is part of the original Hamburg-to-Charleston railroad and is a Rails-to-Trails path. Sand River is actually a strange sand pathway and geological oddity that winds through the whispering pines. The park is also popular with joggers and walkers. Automobiles, bicycles, and other vehicles are prohibited.

Even in its infancy Aiken was a health resort for lowlanders from the Carolina coast who recognized the town as a "place of retreat from the heat and malaria of unhealthier regions." The town was named for William Aiken, a magnate of the Charleston-Hamburg Railroad, then the longest rail line in the world. This train was affectionately called the "Best Friend" because the farmers felt the train was so serviceable in transporting their cotton to Charleston. Both the first U.S. mail car and the first passenger train passed through budding Aiken in the 1830s.

Aiken was a site of an 1865 free-for-all during the last days of the Civil War. General Sherman had sent a detachment of his Union soldiers to destroy the cotton mill at nearby Graniteville. Confederate forces, under General Joseph Wheeler, met them on the main street of Aiken. As the battle ensued, it straddled the railroad tracks. A locomotive pulling into town began blasting its whistle to clear the tracks, but the soldiers paid no attention. Fortunately, the engineer was able to stop the train and put it in reverse to flee the scene. The battle was one of the Union's rare defeats in South Carolina.

The town came into its greatest prominence in the late nineteenth century, however, when wealthy northerners discovered that the area was a perfect place to winter with their horses. Not only were the terrain, sandy roads, and mild climate ideal for fox hunting, but the area was also perfect for conditioning their horses for spring races up north. The winter colony that soon developed supported several grand hotels until the visitors built their own cottages—gargantuan mansions that ranged up to ninety rooms situated on vast grounds. A moneyed and sophisticated lot, they created an ambience of beauty, culture, and quiet opulence that remains today. Three Winter Colony historic districts boast an array of architectural styles, as well as beautiful parkways, shaded streets, and double avenues.

Although those glory days are over, Aiken continues to attract some of the nation's most promising horses, trainers, and horse enthusiasts, whether as visitors or permanent residents. As many as nine hundred polo, steeplechasing, trotting, and riding horses winter here. Polo matches and fox hunting are still very much part of the yearly calendar.

Visiting Aiken at any time is a treat, but a visit during one or more of the spring Triple Crown events is a special indulgence. The Triple Crown activities occur three weekends in a row, usually in March: the Aiken Trials, a flat race; the Aiken Hunt Meet, a steeplechase; and harness racing by pacers and trotters. Since 1942 the Aiken Trials has served as the public viewing of some of the most promising racing thoroughbreds in the world. Their annual training is culminated by bringing the young two- and three-year-olds out under full grandstand conditions and pitting them against each other in timed trials. The Hunt Meet is the first event in a year-long season of steeplechasing sanctioned by the National Steeplechase Hunt Association and includes a circuit of forty meets along the Atlantic seaboard. In harness (sulky) racing, horses are kept to a prescribed gait and not allowed to run free. The annual harness race in Aiken gives young two-year-old horses who have never raced before their very first exposure to crowds. What began as a few people getting together with tailgate picnics, the Triple Crown has evolved into three days of upscale equine celebration. These races are so popular, you should make your hotel reservations well in advance. Nationally recognized dressage, hunter, and jumper, and combined training shows are among Aiken's other major annual events, as is a cutting-horse show.

You can visit the Aiken Mile Track Training Center, 620 Banks Mill Road S.E. (803-642-7637), a seventy-seven-acre facility for standardbreds featuring three tracks, seven barns, one hundred forty-seven stalls, and living quarters for twenty-four grooms. A special landmark is the large oak in the center of the training track, beneath which is the grave marker of Blue Peter, the 1948 champion two-year-old thoroughbred. Through the success of its horses, the Aiken Mile Track has brought much fame to Aiken. Jimmy Larente, a trainer of pacers and trotters, won the world's championship in trotter and pacer competition with a two-year-old named Scully. Scully's accomplishment is a rare one because horses are usually trained to be either a trotter or a pacer, but Scully was both.

Polo became an integral feature of the winter season in Aiken in 1882, just six years after the sport was introduced in the United States. As the news spread, scores of enthusiastic players came to Aiken, and the town became the polo center of the South, some even claimed of the world. At one time, there were sixteen polo fields there. Thomas Hitchcock built the first of those polo fields, and it was later acquired by William C. Whitney. Polo matches are still played at Whitney Field (803-648-7874)—the site of the longest consecutive period of play on one field in the United States—on Sunday afternoons between September and November and between March and July.

The best way to get an overview of Aiken and pick up some juicy tidbits of local history is to take a town tour with Aiken Tours (803-641-1111). It is best to make a reservation, but not absolutely necessary. Tours meet in front of the Municipal Building in The Alley at 10:00 A.M. on Saturday mornings. The Alley is a quaint street filled with restaurants and shops located between Laurens and Newberry Streets. The ninety-minute tour showcases the historic Winter Colony neighborhoods, passes the three racetracks, points out Rye Patch estate and the exclusive Palmetto Golf Club, and makes a brief stop at Hopeland Gardens.

After the tour, return to the Aiken County Historical Museum, South Boundary and Newberry Streets (803-642-2015), housed in a huge rambling mansion that was begun prior to 1850 and completed in 1931, on the Banksia estate. What began as an unpretentious cottage on five acres developed into a mansion with thirty-two rooms, fifteen baths, and a full-size ballroom. The museum's collections are astounding—especially for a small town. Room after room after room are crammed to overflowing with local memorabilia representing almost every facet of life in eighteenth- and nineteenth-century South Carolina. In addition to a parlor and kitchen, another room is set up with the complete contents of a post office. Yet another, from the former town of Dunbarton, contains an old-fashioned drug store with a soda fountain. One room is devoted to the Polidor and Schreadley Miniature Circus collection—the largest and most-comprehensive collection in the country of miniature circus tents, parade wagons, animals, and more. Two structures have been moved to the grounds, both appropriately furnished—an 1890 one-room schoolhouse and the 1808 Ergle log cabin, thought to be the oldest standing structure in the county.

Hopeland Gardens, Whiskey Road and Dupree Place, the grounds of a former Winter Colony mansion, consists of fourteen landscaped acres behind a serpentine brick wall. The estate, which was the winter home of Mr. and Mrs. C. Oliver Iselin, was given by Mrs. Iselin, who lived to be 102 years old, to the city with the stipulation that the house be torn down to avoid high maintenance costs. The Iselins planted the Deodar cedars, live oaks, and magnolias that now form a canopy over the camellias, azaleas, dogwoods, and bulbs in the garden. They bordered the paths with cement copings and installed statuary and a fountain. After the house was demolished, Robert E. Marvin, a noted landscape architect, was retained to design a master plan for the property. He incorporated reflecting pools with fountains where the house had stood and added two lakes. A Touch and Scent Trail for the visually impaired features bronze plaques with both braille and regular letters describing the plants along the way. Called the doll house, but actually plenty big enough to house a small family, a small building constructed by the Iselins for their daughter is the headquarters of the Aiken Council of Garden Clubs and houses a horticultural library. Visit the Thoroughbred Hall of Fame (803-649-4357 or 803-642-7630) located in the old carriage house and stables on the grounds. For a horse to be inducted into the Hall of Fame, it must have been trained in Aiken and have won the Eclipse. Photos, racing silks, trophies, equine paintings and sculpture, and other memorabilia from these champions are displayed. Some polo memorabilia are exhibited, as well as a large collection of trophies from races won around the world by Aiken-born or trained horses. Outdoor concerts and theatrical productions are performed on the grounds during the summer months.

Next door, the Carriage Museum at Rye Patch, Whiskey and Berrie Roads (803-642-7630), is located on the former estate of the late Dorothy Knox Goodyear Rogers. Although the main house, built in 1905, is used only for special functions, you can examine the fine carriages, buggies, and surreys, see the stables, laundry house, and the clay tennis courts, which have been redesigned as a formal rose garden, and then have tea or a light lunch in the guest cottage, which has been converted to a restaurant.

If you have time, visit the galleries of the Aiken Center for the Arts, 122 Laurens Street (803-641-9094), then explore the quaint shops in The Alley and those on Laurens and Newberry Streets. For tasteful Aiken souvenirs, visit The Hope Chest, 130 Kings Grant Drive (803-648-6125), and the Screenprint Factory, 157 Laurens Street (803-649-7552). Plum Pudding, 101 Laurens Street (803-648-2744), is a large general store with a wide range of American and international items as well as a coffee and cappuccino bar.

The Battle of Aiken, a Civil War reenactment and encampment, is held in Couchton. Contact the Sons of the Confederate Veterans (803-649-4151) to learn more. The most unique event is the Lobster Race, held in May downtown in and around The Alley. This event consists of live lobster races at the World's First Official Thoroughbred Lobster Racing Track, as well as gourmet seafood, beach bands, kiddie rides, entertainment, and tons of sand for a real beach party. Contact Chuck Martin at 803-648-4981. Free summer Concerts at Hopeland Gardens are held on Monday nights. Contact Aiken City Parks and Recreation (803-642-7630). In September, Aiken's Makin' is a two-day arts-and-crafts festival with a food fair, street dance, and plenty of other entertainment. Contact the Chamber of Commerce (803-641-1111). The Blessing of the Hounds is an annual event that marks the beginning of the Aiken Hounds hunt season. Horses, riders, and hounds meet on Thanksgiving morning near the Memorial Gate in Hitchcock

Woods to be blessed. Contact the Chamber of Commerce (803-641-1111). The last steeplechase event in a year-long season sanctioned by the National Steeplechase and Hunt Association, the Steeplechase-Hunt Meet is held at Conger Field. Contact the Aiken Steeplechase Association (803-648-9641). During Christmas in Hopeland Gardens, the candlelit gardens are open Wednesday through Saturday nights for three weeks in December. Contact the Chamber of Commerce (803-641-1111).

Only one of the Winter colony hotels remains. The Willcox Inn, 100 Colleton Avenue (803-649-1377), built in 1898 after the period of the really large hotels that had once peppered Aiken, is an intimate thirty-room inn. It was established by Englishman Frederick S. Willcox, a former valet and caterer. Over the years it has seen its share of famous visitors—Franklin D. Roosevelt, Winston Churchill, John Barrymore, the Duke of Windsor, and Count Bernadotte of Sweden, to name a few. Legend has it that at one time the doormen would admit only gentlemen whose shoes were properly polished. Today the atmosphere is much more relaxed. Take advantage of the cozy lobby with several fireplaces; the intimate, clublike bar; or the elegant Pheasant Dining Room.

Located downtown in a former turn-of-the-century mercantile building is the Holley House and Inn, 235 Richland Avenue West (803-648-4265). The inn sports a more recently constructed addition and the Holley Inn Courtyard restaurant and lounge. At the White House Inn, 240 Newberry Street (803-649-2935), a bed and breakfast located in an old Aiken house, some of the guest rooms feature fireplaces.

Aiken boasts many delectable restaurants. Up Your Alley, 222 The Alley (803-649-2603), has the feel of a neighborhood pub. Exposed brick, oak antiques, and stained glass create a warm, friendly ambience. The lunch menu has an extensive list of salads, sandwiches, burgers, and Mexican dishes.

Malia's Restaurant, 120 Laurens Street, S.W. (803-643-3086), located in a historic storefront, is open for lunch daily and dinner on Friday and Saturday and features a changing blackboard international menu. No. 10 Downing Street, 241 Laurens Street (803-642-9062), located in an 1837 house, features four cozy dining rooms with fireplaces. In addition to international gourmet cuisine served for lunch and dinner Tuesday through Saturday, the restaurant features a bakery, gift shop, and attractive gardens. Reservations are recommended on weekends and holidays. Olive Oil's Restaurant, 232 Chesterfield Street (803-649-3726), located in a Victorian cottage, serves Italian cuisine in the casual dining room, on the porch, or on the patio seven days a week. The West Side Bowery, 151 Bee Lane (803-648-2900), is a historic pub and restaurant with patio dining on The Alley. Its extensive lunch and dinner menus feature primarily American and Italian cuisine.

From Aiken, go south on State 302 and turn west on US 278 to Beech Island. The Beech Island Historic District, located next to the Savannah River and not really an island at all, is one of the oldest settlements in South Carolina and was an important Indian trade center. Hernando DeSoto was reported to have crossed the area in 1539. Many Swiss settlers were lured to the area by pamphlets the government printed giving glorious descriptions of the land and rivers. Several times in 1775 and 1777 English naturalist William Bartram visited Silver Bluff and called it "a very celebrated place." In 1781 Lieutenant Colonel Henry ("Light Horse Harry") Lee took Fort Galphin and all its stores of powder, balls, small arms, liquor, salt, blankets, and other articles needed by the American forces to take Augusta from the British. In 1846 Governor James Hammond and eleven other farmers organized the Beech Island Agricultural Club for the diffusion of agricultural knowledge. The club still holds monthly meetings and is one of the oldest surviving societies in the state. Farming became profitable in the area and, as a consequence, large plantations developed.

One of those was Redcliffe Plantation, now the centerpiece of Redcliffe Plantation State Park, US 278 (803-827-1473). Redcliffe mansion was the huge 1850s plantation home of former Governor James Henry Hammond, one of the state's most controversial historical figures. Overlooking the Savannah River, the residence was last owned by John S. Billings, Hammond's great-grandson and a former editor of both *Time* and *Life*. The house is furnished with original family pieces and personal effects of the Hammond-Billings family. Every year in late May Beech Island hosts a Heritage Day Festival complete with colonial living-history demonstrations, Civil War reenactments, Indian culture, and arts and crafts.

After visiting Redcliffe Plantation State Park, go north on State 125, turn west on US 1, then north on US 25/State 121 to North Augusta. Although several small villages had existed in the area, it was not until 1890 that James Urquhart Jackson purchased fifty-six hundred acres of land and formed the North Augusta Land Company and divided the property into lots, streets, and parks. North Augusta is located on the South Carolina side of the Savannah River across from Augusta, Georgia. The twin cities were connected by a steel bridge in 1902. At the same time, a street car line was established to connect Augusta with Aiken and was the longest electric railway in the world. Also at the turn of the century, the twin cities became important winter resort destinations for wealthy northerners when Augusta, Georgia, was the southern terminus of some northern railroads. The sprawling Hampton Terrace Hotel, which burned in 1916, catered to such rich and famous guests as John D. Rockefeller, Marshall Field, Harvey Firestone, and President William Howard Taft. Others built their own winter cottages, actually immense homes. Unfortunately, when the railroads pushed into South Georgia and Florida, the wealthy abandoned North Augusta and its twin for more exotic locales. Many of the cottages remain, however.

Get the driving tour brochure *Historical Sites of North Augusta* from the North Augusta Chamber of Commerce, 235 Georgia Avenue (803-279-2323), so that you can be informed about several of the city's imposing mansions built at the turn of the century.

Two of the mansions, Rosemary Hall and Look-A-Way Hall, across the street from each other at the corners of Georgia and Carolina Avenues, were built by brothers Walter and James Jackson, the original developers and promoters of North Augusta. Both Greek Revival in style and surrounded by column-supported porticoes, they have been painstakingly restored and operate as luxurious European-style inns. Both can be reached by calling 803-278-6222.

Fact and fiction surround the historic home, now a restaurant, B. C. Davenport's, located at 301 Georgia Avenue (803-278-4462). The house was built by Joe Davenport, a printer who operated out of a small shop behind the house. He was apparently also a pharmacist who made and sold a product known as "Frog Pond Elixir," which was reputed to cure anything. In addition, he was the fire chief, although he never lived down the fact that he slept through the conflagration that destroyed the Hampton Terrace Hotel. Mrs. Davenport was the first woman ever elected to the City Council and a well-known gardener. The front garden of their house is now a city park. Once two stories, the house was struck by lightning in 1934, causing a fire that burned the second story which was never replaced.

Other small towns you might want to visit in Thoroughbred Country include Bamberg, which has a large historic residential district of fifty-two properties around the area of Railroad Avenue, as well as the "Cotton the World Over" mural on the side of the post office; Denmark, which hosts a Dogwood Festival the first weekend in April; Graniteville, a mill town known for its twenty-seven carpenter-Gothic-style mill houses called Blue Row; and Salley, noted worldwide for the Saturday-after-Thanksgiving Chitlin' Strut, a festival honoring an unsavory portion of the hog.

For More Information

Aiken County Parks, Recreation, and Tourism, 828 Richland Avenue, Aiken 29801. 803-642-7559.

Greater Aiken Chamber of Commerce, P.O. Box 892, Aiken 29802. 803-641-1111.

Thoroughbred Country, P.O. Box 850, Aiken 29802. 803-649-7981.

10

Upcountry

Native Americans lived in this mountainous region long before the American Revolution. The journals of early traders record visits in the 1600s. Carolina was established as a colony in 1670, and attention was turned toward the native population. In 1753 the British built Fort Prince George on the Keowee River to help protect the Cherokees from the warring Creeks, but also to help protect the settlers from the Cherokees. When the Revolution broke out, the Cherokees vowed allegiance to the British and Loyalists and fought with them against the patriots. That war resulted in the destruction of all the villages in this region of the Lower Cherokee Nation. After the defeat of the British, the Cherokee were forced to cede their land to the state of South Carolina.

Although the Upcountry has a rich history stretching back to the days of early Native Americans and many accompanying historical sites, this region—perhaps more than any other in South Carolina—attracts the outdoor enthusiast.

A state without an abundance of mountainous areas, South Carolina nonetheless has several impressive waterfalls. More than fifty waterfalls are found in the Upcountry, ranging in height from 40 to 700 feet. Reached by a fairly arduous 1.5-mile trail, a wooden deck has been built for visitors to view Raven Cliff Falls, in Greenville County above Caesar's Head, which drops 450 feet. Issaqueena Falls, located near Walhalla, is a lovely 200-foot cataract. At Whitewater Falls, two cascades plunge more than 400 feet each into Lake Jocassee.

Hiking in the Upcountry can be as easy as a stroll along a level path or as rigorous as a five-mile trek up Caesar's Head Mountain. Although the name Foothills Trail seems to indicate a nonstrenuous hiking track, this eighty-five-mile footpath is actually a wilderness adventure with a steep, rugged trail that winds over the mountain country ridges along the North Carolina/South Carolina line from Table Rock to Oconee State Park, passing through some of the most beautiful terrain in the Southeast. Hikers are afforded breathtaking views of thunderous cascades, hushed forests, and other natural splendors.

Rafting, canoeing, and kayaking are major adventures in the Upcountry where forty miles of the tumultuous Chattooga National Wild and Scenic River form the border between South Carolina and Georgia. The Chattooga, familiar to many as the setting for the movie *Deliverance*, offers some of the finest wilderness white-water experiences in the country. Section Three offers rapids such as Painted Rock, Screaming Left Turn, Rock Jumble, and the notorious Bull Sluice. Section Four features steep technical drops and culminates at Five Falls where rapids such as Corkscrew, Soc'em Dog, and Jawbone provide extraordinary challenges.

The Cherokee Foothills Scenic Highway (State Scenic Highway 11) begins off I-85 just over the Georgia/South Carolina line and wanders 130 miles along an ancient Cherokee and English and French fur-trader path through the Upcountry, eventually rejoining I-85 at Gaffney. As the highway passes through the heart of the foothills of the Blue Ridge Mountains, it brings the traveler in close proximity to twelve state parks, four recreation areas, three major lakes, and numerous historic and scenic attractions. Part of the route traced in this chapter will utilize Scenic 11.

Begin this driving tour at Anderson, located just south of I-85 on US 76/State 28. Although the town and county of Anderson—named for Revolutionary War leader Robert Anderson—had existed for years, their growth was slow until the emergence of the cotton mills in the late 1800s. A branch of the Greenville and Columbia line came into Anderson, as did the Savannah Valley line and the Piedmont and Northern electric railway, giving the community three bustling depots. Streetcars came to Anderson by the turn of the century, making it one of the first towns in the nation to offer such transportation. Anderson is known as the "Electric City" because it was here in the 1890s that engineer William C. Whitner devised means to transmit electricity over long-distance lines. Anderson's was the first cotton mill in the South to have electric power as well as the first electrically operated cotton gin in the country.

In addition to wandering around the sixteen-block area listed on the National Register of Historic Places, admire the work of local, regional, and national artists at the Anderson County Arts Center, housed in a historic Carnegie Library at 405 North Main Street (864-224-8811).

Examine the local-history exhibits and memorabilia at the Anderson County Museum in the old courthouse, Main and Benson Streets (864-260-4737).

The Anderson Jockey Lot and Farmer's Market, US 29 (864-224-2027), claims to be the South's largest flea market. Covering sixty-five acres and leasing space to fifteen hundred dealers, it may very well be.

Constructed in 1914 by Dr. Archer LeRoy Smethers, who in 1920 purchased and remodeled the old Johnson Female University as one of Anderson's first hospitals, River Inn, 612 East River Street (864-226-1431), is a lovely two-story Federal-style home offering bed-and-breakfast accommodations in three guest rooms with private baths. Guests will appreciate the warmth of the walnut-stained woodwork, beamed ceilings, and crown moldings. Although much of the front yard was usurped by highway widening, a commodious backyard invites guests to relax and enjoy the large shade trees. The warm and personal hospitality of the owners is manifested in many ways, one of which is a hearty full southern breakfast. As owner Pat Clark explains her menu, "You get grits whether you eat them or not."

Accommodations are also offered at Centennial Plantation Bed and Breakfast, 1308 Old Williamson Road (864-225-4448), a one-hundred-year-old farmhouse on ten acres, and at the Evergreen Inn, 1109 South Main Street (864-225-1109), which offers guest rooms, some with fireplaces, and a restaurant serving gourmet cuisine prepared by a Swiss-trained chef.

Retrace US 29 to US 76 and take it north past I-85. Then take State 28 to Pendleton. The entire town and surrounding area covering more than sixty-three hundred acres comprises one of the nation's largest historic districts and includes forty points of historic interest. Many of its buildings date back to the 1700s. Antique shops, art and gift shops, excellent restaurants, and charming bed and breakfasts make this quaint small town one of the most visited places in America. Both the county and town were named in honor of Judge Henry Pendleton of Virginia, who stayed in South Carolina after fighting with the patriot forces during the Revolutionary War and who championed the cause of Upcountry representation in the legislature. In the early 1800s many wealthy planters and politicians built large summer houses in Pendleton to escape the heat of Lowcountry summers. Of that heady period, it was said ". . . the very name of Pendleton became a synonym for refined and beautiful women, and for elegant high-toned and chivalrous gentlemen."

Begin at the village square, a lively business district of shops and restaurants facing the village green where many special events are held. Hunter's Store, 125 East Queen Street on the square (864-646-3782), built in 1850, houses the Pendleton District Historical, Recreational and Tourism Commission and is the place to pick up a self-guided tape tour or self-guided walking tour brochure of the town's fifty historic buildings, to get brochures about the surrounding area, or to ask for advice about restaurants and accommodations. The commission's headquarters features an arts-and-crafts store, a bookstore, exhibit area, and research library.

Farmers Society Hall, on the village green (864-646-3782), is the nucleus of Pendleton. It was built in 1826 as a court-

Farmers Hall in Pendleton

house, but when the district moved the court elsewhere, farmers took over the building and have used it ever since. The building is the oldest farmers' hall in the country in continuous use. Farmers Hall Restaurant, operating in the downstairs of the building (864-646-7024), serves a wide variety of items. Optional outdoor dining is available on the tree-shaded patio.

At the other end of the village green is the 1860 Guard and Market House. The cannon on the green was used by Pendleton men during Reconstruction when they organized as the Red Shirt Party in support of gubernatorial candidate Wade Hampton III. The sundial was reputed to have been given to Francis Huger by the Marquis de Lafayette for Huger's attempt to free him from prison.

Pendleton offers numerous interesting places to shop. Drop into The Mercantile, 149 East Queen Street (864-646-9431), a country store with collectibles, coffee, candy, and local crafts. Mountain Made, on the square (864-646-8836), features handcrafts and antiques. Two antique shops you might want to check out include Grandma's Antiques and Things, 204 East Queen Street (864-646-9435), and Pendleton Antique Company, 134 East Main Street (864-646-7725). To the rear of Hunter's Store is the Hunter's Store Warehouse, built around 1880. Modernized with vast porches on both floors, it now houses a series of shops and offices. The captain's walk on the roof is original and was a favored place from which to view the Blue Ridge Mountains.

Two gorgeous sister plantations recall the early 1800s when wealthy Lowcountry planters built homes in the Upcountry and moved to its more healthful climate for the summer. Both are open on Sunday afternoons April through October or by appointment, so call ahead. Ashtabula Plantation, State 88 (864-646-3847 or 864-646-3782), built in the 1820s by a family from Charleston, has been restored and furnished with period items. Woodburn Plantation, located on US 76 (864-646-3782 or 864-646-3655), the stately four-story mansion of Charles Cotesworth Pinckney, lieutenant governor of South Carolina between 1832 and 1834, contains period furnishings and historic memorabilia. Woodburn is adjacent to the Pendleton District Agricultural Museum, US 76 (864-646-3782). Cherokee artifacts and pre-1925 farm equipment, including a cotton gin that predates Eli Whitney's, an 1876 thresher, and a reproduction of the original McCormick reaper, as well as small hand tools are displayed. Nearby on US 76, stop at the Old Stone Church. The church is no longer in use, but its cemetery is the resting place of many area pioneers including Revolutionary War hero General Andrew Pickens who helped in building the church in 1797.

Among Pendleton's many special yearly events, one of the most popular is the Historic Pendleton Spring Jubilee, a festival of arts and crafts, entertainment, antique shows, historic home tours, museum exhibits, and great food, which coincides with the spring opening of the Agricultural Museum and Ashtabula and Woodburn plantations.

For such a small town, Pendleton offers a rich variety of good places to eat. Country Kettle, Mechanic Street across from the village green (864-646-3301), is a restaurant that serves lunch cafeteria style and specializes in fresh vegetables and pies. Granny Zuercher's Old-Time Bakery, Mechanic Street (864-646-3907), dispenses all kinds of breads and desserts.

In addition, Pendleton affords visitors a choice in historic accommodations. Liberty Hall Inn, 621 South Mechanic Street (864-646-7500), is a country inn built in the 1840s. What began as a five-room summer residence grew into a large family home, which at one point operated as a boarding house. Each of the ten guest rooms is furnished with antiques, original art, and local crafts. Liberty Hall stands on four acres of woods, lawns, and gardens that invite leisurely strolls. The inn also operates a restaurant that serves four-course dinners and an excellent selection of wines. More lodging is offered at the 195 East Main Bed and Breakfast, downtown (864-646-5673).

Continue north on US 76/State 28 to Clemson. Clemson University, the centerpiece of the town, owes its existence to the son-in-law of statesman John C. Calhoun. Many of the significant sites in this lovely southern town are on the campus or connected with the university. Begin at the University Visitors Center at Alumni Hall (864-656-4789) to learn more about the sights on campus.

Fort Hill, also known as the John C. Calhoun Mansion, in the center of the campus (864-656-4789) was the orator's plantation home during the last twenty-five years of his life. One of the South's most noted statesmen, Calhoun served as vice-president under both Andrew Jackson and John Quincy Adams and as a U.S. senator. The oldest part of the house was erected in 1803, but when the Calhouns acquired it in 1825, they enlarged it to its present size and named it Fort Hill in honor of an old fort built on the land in 1776. Combining both Federal and Greek Revival styles, the house is characteristic of Upcountry plantation design. Later, Fort Hill became the home of Calhoun's daughter, Anna, and her husband, Thomas Green Clemson, who willed the house and the eleven hundred acres of plantation land to the state in 1888 for the purpose of establishing a land-grant college. Now a National Historic Landmark, the mansion features fourteen spacious rooms furnished in pieces that belonged to the Calhoun and Clemson families, as well as white-columned piazzas, separate kitchen and office buildings, and a spring house.

Poke your head in at Uniquely Clemson, Newman Hall on campus (864-656-4789), to taste and buy some of the university's famous ice cream, blue cheese, and other agricultural products to take home with you.

In the late 1950s a small parcel of the Fort Hill estate was set aside to preserve a camellia collection. By 1973 forty-four acres had been developed into a public garden known as the Horticultural Gardens of Clemson University. In 1987 the Forestry Arboretum and adjoining university land were consolidated to form the 270-acre Clemson Botanical Garden. In 1992 the South Carolina General Assembly designated it as the South Carolina Botanical Garden, Perimeter Road (864-656-3405). It is considered to be the state's most diverse garden.

The 270-acre garden includes several thousand varieties of native and introduced ornamental plants arranged in trails or gardens—the Azalea and Camellia Trails, the Miller Dwarf Conifer Garden, and the Wildflower, Fern and Bog Gardens. In the two-acre Flower and Turf Display Garden are annuals, herbaceous perennials, and turf grasses appropriate for the southern landscape. Log cabins, farm implements, and a grist mill in the Pioneer Garden, which is marked in Braille, give visitors a look into the past. A pagoda situated on a reflecting pool in the Meditation Garden creates a tranquil area. The arboretum itself includes more than one thousand species of trees. Miles of trails through the gardens crisscross streams by way of footbridges and wind through native woodlands. Recent additions include the three-acre Vegetable Garden, the backyard Compost Garden, the four-acre Wildflower Meadow, and a Xeriscape Garden that promotes water-conserving plants and landscapes.

Relocated to the gardens is Hanover House (864-656-2241 or 864-656-2475), built in 1716 by a Lowcountry Huguenot family. Paul de St. Julien planned the first story of the house to be brick, but he ended up using all his kiln bricks in constructing the basement and triple-flue chimneys, so he had to complete the house with cypress timbers whipsawed in a reverse shiplap to act as gutters for waterproofing. He chose the name "Hanover" in honor of George Louis, Elector of Hanover, who ascended the British throne as George I and had befriended the French Huguenots. The house faced annihilation in the 1940s because it was located in the path of the hydroelectric plant planned to impound the Santee and Cooper Rivers. The School of Architecture, at what was then

Clemson College, dismantled the house and reconstructed it near the campus. Furnished to represent the 1700s, Hanover House interprets the lifestyles of Lowcountry rice, indigo, and cotton planters.

In addition to strolling, birdwatching, or jogging in the gardens, educational and cultural events draw visitors all year. There's a nature walk the first Friday morning of each month. Special events include a winter lecture series and the Spring Celebration in April, which blends art with nature using music, dance, storytelling, theater, nature walks, live animals, and more.

A college town can usually be counted on to provide a variety of good places to eat, and Clemson is no exception. The Vintage Cafe, 405 College Avenue (864-654-3900), specializes in prime rib, steaks, seafood, pasta, grilled chicken salad, and southern desserts. Nick's Tavern and Deli, 107-2 Sloan Street (no phone), is downtown Clemson's oldest tavern and deli. The eclectic atmosphere features several collections: beer bottles and beer memorabilia, post cards, and auto-racing relics. The eatery, which is within walking distance of the campus, offers extensive appetizer, deli, and beer menus.

There's never a lack of things to do in or near Clemson. See if there is a performance by the Clemson Little Theater, which performs at the Pendleton Playhouse (864-646-8100). The organization produces three plays a year. In December the Fort Hill and Hanover House Holiday Celebration features both historic houses decorated for the season. To find out more about the event, call 864-656-2475.

From Clemson, take US 76/US 123 to Seneca, a town created at the emergence of the Southern Railway line in the 1870s. Seneca, an Indian name, is taken from the Seneca tribe that settled here briefly before being overcome by the Cherokees.

The entire historic district of residential homes is listed on the National Register of Historic Places, and the downtown commercial area features a mural depicting life in early Seneca.

Visit the Lunney Museum, 211 West South First Street (864-882-4811), housed in a California-style bungalow, to see exhibits such as an outstanding collection of antiques covering a period from the late-seventeenth through the early-twentieth centuries. A fine assemblage of Victorian furnishings, as well as vintage costumes, and Oconee County memorabilia are shown. Don't neglect to examine the house itself. In 1909 pharmacist Dr. William J. Lunney and his wife decided to build a house in an area of the stately Victorian mansions known as Silk Stocking Hill. The Lunneys, however, chose a different style—the long, low silhouette of the bungalow emphasized by wide, overhanging porches. Craftsmanship is evident everywhere from the hand-cut crown molding to the gleaming, knot-free sugar-pine floors to the half-inch-thick hand-beveled glass in the front windows. Visitors are struck by the apparent contradiction between the informal exterior and the more formal Victorian interior, but the explanation is simple—just as with most people moving into a new home, the Lunneys brought things with them and what they had was Victorian.

Switch gears to the modern era at Duke Power's World of Energy, 7812 Rochester Highway (864-885-4600 or 800-777-1004). On Lake Keowee beside the Oconee Nuclear Plant, the museum's animated displays, computer games, and the "Story of Energy" show how natural resources such as falling water, coal, and uranium are used to make electricity. Visitors can feel a seam of coal or enter a fission chamber to learn how energy is made from an atom. Get a behind-the-scenes look at operators training in a nuclear control-room simulator. In addition, there's a nature trail and views of Lake Keowee and the Keowee Valley.

Take State 59 south from Seneca to Fair Play, near the South Carolina/Georgia line. The old community is said to have gotten its unusual name from a fight between two men who responded to the crowd's shouts exhorting them to practice "fair play!" Stop at the Fair Play Welcome Center, I-85 and State Scenic 11 on the shores of Lake Hartwell (864-972-3731), to pick up some tour information. Lake Hartwell, the anchor of this region, straddles the Georgia/South Carolina border. One of the South's largest and most popular public recreation lakes, it was built by the U.S. Army Corps of Engineers, 1955–63, for flood control and as a hydroelectric project on the Savannah, Tugaloo, and Seneca Rivers. With 56,000 acres of water and 962 miles of shoreline, Hartwell is one of the top three most-visited lakes in the country. Not only does the lake provide just about every water sport imaginable, but the area is rich in historical lore handed down from the Cherokee Indians and the early Scotch-Irish settlers.

Take the Cherokee Foothills Scenic Highway, State Scenic 11, north to Lake Hartwell State Park (864-972-3352), a 680-acre park with numerous activities. Continue north on State Scenic 11 to State 28 and turn west to Walhalla, the gateway into the Blue Ridge Mountains. The town was created in 1850 by the German Colonization Society. The upper part of the county is largely a U.S. Forest. Oconee Station Historic Site, 500 Oconee Station Road (864-638-0079), is a 210-acre park on the Oconee Creek in the foothills of the Appalachian Mountains. The park contains two historic structures: a stone blockhouse fort known as Oconee Station and a two-story brick residence known as the William Richards House. The blockhouse was constructed around 1792, one of several in a chain of such buildings established during Indian hostilities. Oconee Station was the last of these blockhouses to be decommissioned when troops were removed in 1799. Adjacent to the blockhouse is the brick house built in 1805 by William Richards, an Irish immigrant who had established a successful trading post at Oconee Station. This house is considered to be the first brick house built in the northwest corner of the state.

Stumphouse Tunnel Park with picnic tables surrounds the closed-off entrance to the Stumphouse Tunnel, off State 28, an old railroad tunnel bored into the granite heart of Stumphouse Mountain. Unfortunately, no train ever roared through this tunnel because the builders, who had hoped to link Charleston and the cities of the Midwest, went broke in the 1850s before the track was laid.

A nature trail adjoining the tunnel leads to 200-foot Issaqueena Falls, a waterfall of Cherokee Indian legend. According to the story, the Indian maiden Issaqueena pretended to leap over the falls to her death to escape hostile pursuers, but actually took refuge behind them.

In salute to their German ancestry, the citizens of Walhalla present an annual Oktoberfest featuring German and American food, carnival rides, hot-air balloon rides, German music and dances, sky divers, and other entertainment. To learn more about the festival, call 864-638-2727.

Liberty Lodge, 105 Liberty Lane (864-638-0940), offers bed-and-breakfast accommodations in a nineteenth-century Victorian manor with spacious rooms and open porches. The twelve acres surrounding the house offer walking trails and quiet areas in which to relax.

Retrace your route to Walhalla and turn northeast on State Scenic 11. Turn south on State 130 to Salem. Devils Fork State Park, 161 Holcombe Circle (864-944-2639), a park primarily used by water-sports enthusiasts, nestles along the shores of Lake Jocassee against a picturesque backdrop of the Blue Ridge Mountains. The name Devil's Fork was used as early as 1780 for an area creek. Although the origin of the name is unknown, it refers to the meeting of the Corbin, Howard, and Liber Pole Creeks to form Devil's Fork Creek. Perhaps the early settlers thought the three creeks merging into one resembled a pitchfork—a symbol of the Devil. Jocassee, after whom the lake was named, was an Indian maiden who was said to have drowned herself in the lake over the murder of her lover; the lake was known by the Native Americans as the "Place of the Lost One." The crystal-clear waters of the lake, 7,565 acres, are the only ones in the state offering both trophy trout and small-mouth bass, making it extremely popular with fishermen. Wildflowers, including the rare Oconee bell, are found in profusion, and peregrine falcons, a federally endangered species, have recently been reintroduced.

You can find pleasant accommodations at Sunrise Farm B&B, Sunrise Drive off State 130 (864-944-0121), located on a seventy-four-acre cattle farm, the last part of a one-thousand-acre turn-of-the-century cotton plantation. Lovingly restored, the house is filled with antiques. The adjacent June Rose Garden Cottage contains a fully equipped kitchen/living area with a sleeper sofa and a separate bedroom. Guests particularly enjoy the rocker- and wicker-filled wrap-around porches.

Return to State Scenic 11 and proceed to Sunset. Located on the shores of Lake Keowee in the foothills of the Blue Ridge Mountains, the one-thousand-acre Keowee-Toxaway State Park, 108 Residence Drive off State 11 (864-868-2605), features impressive rock outcroppings and numerous sparkling mountain streams. The land, which once belonged to the Cherokee, still yields arrowheads, pottery shards, and other artifacts, many of which are displayed at the park's museum and in outdoor kiosks. According to Cherokee legend, the name *Keowee* means "land of the mulberry groves" and *Toxaway* means "land of no tomahawks." Today, although there are no mulberry groves in evidence, the area provides a place of solitude and serenity. Keowee-Toxaway provides three trails for visitors. The elevation of the Raven Rock Hiking Trail, which is more than four miles in length, changes more than three hundred feet, providing a challenge for both the novice and experienced hiker. The Natural Bridge Nature Trail, a loop off the Raven Rock Hiking Trail, is an easy-to-moderate hike. The Cherokee Interpretive Trail is a short path connecting the interpretive center and the four kiosks.

Go east on State Scenic 11 and then south on US 178 to Pickens. The town is named for General Andrew Pickens, who with Francis Marion and Thomas Sumter, was one of the great Revolutionary leaders in South Carolina. General Pickens helped establish Pendleton and resided near there after the war. The railroad led the way in early development of the town.

Visit the Hagood-Maulin House and Irma Morris Museum of Fine Arts, 104 North Lewis Street (864-878-6799), not only a significant historic home, but also the repository of an important art collection. James E. Hagood built the house in 1856 in Old Pickens, fourteen miles west of the present town. That structure probably consisted of four rooms with an exterior porch connecting the dining room and kitchen buildings. In 1868 the house was dismantled, moved, and reconstructed in present-day Pickens. Later additions were made by Mrs. Frances Hagood Maulin, daughter of James Hagood. "Miss Queen," as she was known, was the social leader of Pickens and lived in the house until 1954. For many of the years of her residency, the old soldiers of the Confederacy had a reunion on her lawn each July 3. Mrs. Irma Hendricks Morris, an authority on seventeenth- and eighteenth-century antiques, then bought the house and began restoring it. After her retirement, she traveled extensively in Europe collecting fine furnishings and art, much of which, combined with locally made furniture from the Oolenoy Valley Cabinetmakers, is displayed in the house.

Housed in a 1903 jail, the Pickens County Museum, 307 Johnson Street (864-898-5963), is really two museums in one:

an art museum, featuring the paintings and crafts of local and regional artists, and a history museum, with relics and mementos of county history. The building is a treasure in itself with its unusual brick patterns, crenelated turret, copper roof, and barred windows.

Built around 1825, Hagood Mill, US 178, which is still operational, is one of the few mills in the state that retains many of its original components. Tours can be arranged through the Pickens County Museum.

Return to State Scenic 11 and turn east. The Upcountry's best-known landmark is the rounded dome called Table Rock, now part of a Table Rock State Park, 246 Table Rock State Park Road off State Scenic 11 (864-878-9813). Table Rock is an easily seen landmark which the Cherokees used in finding their way. Legend grew among them that the flat mountain top was a dining table for the Great Spirit—giving it the name it bears today. Developed in the thirties by the Civilian Conservation Corps (CCC), the park boasts rustic stone cabins with fireplaces and screened-in porches, a bathhouse, and the Table Rock Lodge Restaurant, which offers a panorama of the lake and Table Rock and Pinnacle Mountains. The most challenging hiking trails in the state park system, as well as a nature center, are among the many attractions awaiting visitors. One trail leads to the top of Table Rock Mountain while another leads to the summit of Pinnacle Mountain. A two-mile trail connects them, completing a ten-mile network passing through a variety of mountainous terrain with several waterfalls. The Carrick Creek Nature Trail includes short sections of both of the other trails and is less strenuous. The Pinnacle Trail also serves as an access point for the Foothills Trail.

North of Table Rock State Park on State 39/199 is Sassafras Mountain, at 3,554 feet the highest point in South Carolina. From the summit, four states can be seen: Georgia, North and South Carolina, and Tennessee.

Along State Scenic 11 near Table Rock State Park is a collection of rustic log cabins—each a shop or restaurant—creating a small village called Aunt Sue's (864-878-4366). In 1984 Aunt Sue and Uncle Lloyd and their family built a gift shop which they operated from July to September and then returned to their home in Florida. The following year they decided to move to the area permanently and added the Ice Cream Parlor, which also serves deli lunches, and two more gift shops. Several more shops have been added since. Although they aren't really related, each of the other shop owners is known as Cousin So-and-So. Today the complex includes the Souvenir House, the Christmas House, the Candle House, the Rock House, the Garden House, the Wood House, and the Stamp House in addition to the restaurant. About 80 percent of the time, Cousin Phyllis can be found on the porch entertaining visitors with her organ music.

Next door to Aunt Sue's is Mountain Home Antiques and Country Collectibles, State 11 (864-878-5197). Contained within the hundred-year-old former blacksmith's home are a wide variety of furniture and accessories, books, glassware, toys, tools, and jewelry. The shop is closed in January and February and is open weekends only in March and December, daily the remainder of the year.

A modern house built in the Victorian style to serve as a bed and breakfast, the Schell Haus, 117 Hiawatha Trail off State 11 (864-878-0078), offers six comfortably furnished rooms and suites. Tucked into a small clearing in the Blue Ridge Mountains, the establishment boasts a swimming pool, as well as some rooms with whirlpools and spas. Enjoy the spectacular scenery from rockers on the wrap-around porch or get closer to nature by exploring one of the hiking trails.

Return to State Scenic 11 and almost immediately turn north on US 276 to Caesars Head State Park, 8155 Geer Highway (864-836-6115). An excellent park for nature enthusiasts and photographers, Caesars Head is part of the Mountain Bridge Wilderness and Recreation Area. A bumpy six-mile road leads to the summit of 3,208-foot Caesar's Head Mountain, the second highest spot in the state, located on the North Carolina/South Carolina border. Near the park headquarters is a scenic overlook of nearby valleys, Table Rock and Pinnacle Mountains, and other distant Blue Ridge peaks. The park's Raven Cliff Falls is one of the highest waterfalls in the eastern United States, dropping an astounding four hundred feet.

Retrace your route to State Scenic 11 and turn east to US 176, where you will turn south to Inman. Hollywild Animal Park, Hampton and Little Mountain Roads (864-472-2038), houses one of the largest private collections of rare and exotic animals in the Southeast, including many "celebrity" animals from movies and TV commercials. Travel through the seventy-acre outback where hundreds of animals roam freely and experience the thrill of being surrounded by several herds, many of which will eat right out of your hand. Christmas at Hollywild features a spectacular drive-through exhibit of thousands of lights depicting sparkling holiday themes.

Return to State Scenic 11, turn east, and proceed past Chesnee. A 1781 battle at a drover's shelter called "Hannah's Cowpens" is remembered at the Cowpens National Battlefield, near the intersection of State 11 and State 110 in the northwest corner of the state (864-461-2828). Fought during the waning months of the southern campaign of the American Revolution, the Continental forces under Brigadier General Daniel Morgan outwitted a much larger force of British troops under General Banastre Tarlton. It was all over in less than an hour. This was the first and only time the military maneuver called double envelopment was used successfully on American soil. The British defeat at Cowpens was another link in a chain of British disasters in the South that led ultimately to the defeat at Yorktown. The park features a walking trail; a road tour; and a visitors center with exhibits, memorabilia, and a multimedia presentation. During the Battle of Cowpens Reenactment each January, living-history encampments and tactical demonstrations mark the pivotal battle. In October the Overmountain Victory Trail Marchers arrive in conjunction with a celebration at Kings Mountain National Battlefield Park. (See Old English District chapter.)

Continue east until State Scenic 11 ends at I-85. Turn northeast to Blacksburg. A much-anticipated yearly event, the Ed Brown Rodeo, held the first weekend in August, is a full-scale rodeo with bareback riding, saddle bronc riding, calf roping, steer wrestling, women's barrel racing, rodeo clowns, and much more. For more information, call Ed Brown at 864-839-6239.

Retrace I-85 south to Gaffney. The Peachoid, along I-85, which looks like the world's largest peach, but which is in reality Gaffney's water tower, is one of the most-gawked-at and most-photographed water tanks in the country. Directions are often given in reference to the landmark. For example, when someone asks where Atlanta is, they will be told that it is "190 miles south of the Big Peach." It took five months to design and mold the steel for the project. The water tower, which holds one million gallons, is 135 feet tall from top to bottom; the peach is seventy-three feet in diameter; the stem alone is twelve feet long and eighteen inches in diameter; and the huge leaf is sixty feet long, sixteen feet wide, and weighs seven tons. It is only appropriate that the town's water tower should depict the important agricultural product. Peaches first came to this country from China in the 1600s. By the middle part of the century, South Carolina was producing peaches in the Lowcountry; by the middle of the 1800s, growing peaches was a profitable business in the state, and peaches were planted in the piedmont section in the 1920s. Although Georgia is known as the Peach State, by 1946 South Carolina had outproduced Georgia in peaches and continues to do so today.

Continue southwest on I-85 to Spartanburg. Although long inhabited by Native Americans, the first European colonists came to what became Spartanburg County in 1785. These first settlers were primarily Scotch-Irish who came by way of Pennsylvania, Maryland, and Virginia. Spartanburg's long history as a center for trade and commerce began almost as soon as the county was formed. By 1789 pioneers had moved into the area in sufficient numbers to warrant a courthouse and jail. Stagecoach routes crossed the district, and some of the stagecoach inns still stand: Price's Tavern, the Price House, and Foster's Tavern. It is said that Spartanburg began with a Wild West atmosphere where election days were often marked by inebriation and street fights. The town and county were named for the Spartan Rifles, the Revolutionary War militia whose victory at the Battle of Cowpens led to the eventual British surrender at Yorktown. Agriculture has always played an important role in Spartanburg County's economy: first cotton production, now peach production. By 1850 the public square was a trading center for farmers of the region. Another boom period began with the expansion of the railroad between Spartanburg and Columbia, and by the turn of the century, the city was the crossroads of five railroad lines. At the same time, the textile industry began to grow. Spartanburg boasts many South Carolina firsts: first commercial airport in 1927, first radio station in 1930, and the first children's theater in 1972.

Thirteen Spartanburg County sites have been designated on the National Register of Historic Places. The city has a commercial historic district of Victorian architecture and several historic neighborhoods. The Spartanburg County Historical Association has produced a booklet describing a Downtown Walking Tour. It is available from the Spartanburg Regional Museum on South Pine Street or from the Spartanburg Convention and Visitors Bureau at 105 North Pine Street (864-594-5050).

Downtown's Morgan Square is anchored by a statue honoring Revolutionary War hero Daniel Morgan. One of Spartanburg's landmarks is the Town Clock Tower, located on the west end of Morgan Square at West Main and South Spring Streets, which contains both the clock and the town bell. The bell was first situated in the tower of the Opera House and City Hall and then was relocated to the new courthouse. During the bicentennial celebration in 1976, the tower was erected in the square.

You're guaranteed to find something that sparks your interest at the forty-six-thousand-square-foot Spartanburg Arts Center, 385 South Spring Street (864-583-2776), which houses four art galleries, the Science Center, the Art Association School, the Dance Center, Youth Theater, Little Theater, and Health Resource. The Youth Theater is South Carolina's oldest, full-scale children's theater.

From antique dolls to historic battlefields, numerous permanent exhibits and collections at the Regional Museum of Spartanburg County, 501 Otis Boulevard (864-596-3501), detail the area's proud heritage. At the museum you can learn more about the Battle of Cowpens, the founding of Spartanburg, Spartanburg County, and the Upcountry.

Believed to be the oldest house in Spartanburg is the 1790 Jammie Seay House, 106 Darby Road (864-576-6546). While the house is closed as we go to press, it is expected to reopen sometime during 1998. It is built in part of hand-hewn logs on a fieldstone foundation. The pipe-stem chimney, also made of fieldstone with brick at the top, is a style commonly found in

Virginia, but quite unusual for the Upcountry. Jammie Seay was born in Virginia in 1750, and as a Revolutionary War soldier, he fought in several battles in Virginia and Pennsylvania before migrating to South Carolina. He received the land grant on which he built the house in 1784. It remained in the family until it was transferred to the Spartanburg County Historical Association in 1974. Meticulously restored, the house is furnished in pieces appropriate to the period.

An island of green in the midst of the city, Hatcher Gardens, Reidville Road (864-582-2776), is a haven for birds and wildlife, as well as a center for the preservation of flowers, shrubs, and trees. Plantings include more than ten thousand plants, with particular emphasis on those native to South Carolina.

Although Spartanburg features many elegant restaurants, one casual local landmark eatery is a "must-see" experience for visitors—the Beacon Drive-In, 255 Reidville Road (864-585-9387). It is the second largest drive-in restaurant in the country and one of the few still using curb hops. The restaurant claims to be surpassed only by the U.S. Navy in the consumption of iced tea. Serving breakfast, lunch, and dinner, the fast-food restaurant features a one-hundred-item short-order menu on which the generous portions of most items are described as "a-plenty"—for example, fries a-plenty.

South of Spartanburg on US 221 is Roebuck. Walnut Grove Plantation, 1200 Ott's Shoals Road (864-576-6546), is located on land granted in 1763 by King George III to Charles Moore. The manor house, which has double-shouldered chimneys and clapboard-over-log construction, is authentically restored and furnished. The landscaped grounds include the Rocky Spring Academy, the first school in the area; a kitchen house filled with eighteenth-century gadgets and utensils; a blacksmith's forge; a smokehouse; a barn sheltering a Conestoga-type wagon; a doctor's office; an herb/flower garden; a nature trail; and a family cemetery.

Continue south on US 221 to Woodruff. The Price House, 1200 Oak View Farms Road, at the junction of Hobbysville, Oak View Farms, and Old Switzer Roads (864-576-6546), is an elegant plantation house built in 1795 by early entrepreneur Thomas Price. Fashioned from bricks made on the premises and laid in Flemish bond, the house has a steep gambrel roof and unusual interior end chimneys. It has been beautifully restored and furnished.

You can enjoy the tranquil beauty of the perennial and annual gardens at Nicholls-Crook Plantation House Bed and Breakfast, 120 Plantation Drive (864-476-8820). The gardens, which feature a white-rock courtyard similar to those of the Lowcountry, are planned in keeping with the eighteenth-century Georgian-style house and highlight heirloom species as well as improved varieties of nineteenth-century originals. Other than for bed-and-breakfast guests, tours of the gardens are by appointment.

Retrace State 146 to State 101 and go north to I-85. The BMW Zentrum Museum and Visitors Center, I-85 (864-968-6000), at North America's only BMW manufacturing plant, chronicles the history of the company in the automotive, motorcycle, and aviation industries and production of BMWs. Plant tours are arranged by reservations.

Turn west on I-85 to Greenville. After European settlers began moving into the area in 1777, Greenville became primarily a resort for Lowcountry planters; but after Reconstruction, the textile industry began to flourish, with mills and villages springing up on the western edge of the city. In 1915 Greenville held its first Textile Exposition and became known as the Textile Center of the South. Since then the area's economy has diversified.

One of America's finest university art collections, the Bob Jones University's Gallery of Sacred Art, 1700 Wade Hampton Boulevard (864-242-5100), is well regarded by art connoisseurs around the world. The gallery contains thirty rooms displaying representative works of Flemish, Dutch, German, French, Italian, English, and Spanish masters from the fourteenth through the nineteenth centuries. Among the works are paintings by Botticelli, Titian, Tintoretto, Rubens, Van Dyck, and Rembrandt. In addition, the museum houses collections of Russian icons, some of which bear inscriptions indicating that they were presented to the czar or a member of his family in commemoration of a special event; Renaissance furniture, including several choir stalls; a collection of linen, silk, and satin vestments made for the imperial chapel in Vienna; and the Bowen Bible Lands Collection of items relevant to biblical times. Among its exhibits are several life-size mannequins modeling Biblical costumes, four-thousand-year-old Egyptian and Syrian vases, an eighty-foot-long Hebrew Torah scroll written on gazelle skin, and a model of Solomon's temple. Located in the Jerusalem Chamber of the Mack Memorial Library is the university's collection of rare Bibles. The room is a reproduction of the chamber in London's Westminster Abbey where parts of the King James version of the Bible were translated. Tours of the galleries are self-guided, but audio tour tapes may be rented.

Hanging in the university's War Memorial Chapel is the largest assemblage anywhere of the paintings of Benjamin West. A Philadelphian, West was taught the use of color by Native Americans and used hairs from the family cat to fashion his brushes. After studying in Italy, he settled in England, was appointed official history painter to King George III, and became one of the founders of the Royal Academy. These gigantic paintings were part of a theme for a proposed chapel at Windsor Castle and revealed the evolution of religion. Due to the deteriorating health of King George III, the project was never completed and the finished paintings were returned to West.

If you have a hankering to see more art, American works from colonial times to the present are exhibited at the Greenville County Museum of Art, 420 College Street (864-271-7570). The museum's southern collection is recognized as one of the country's best representations of regional art, and the museum has an impressive assemblage of contemporary works.

A yen for Japanese art can be satisfied with a visit to the Nippon Center and Restaurant Yagoto, 500 Congaree Road (864-288-8471). An oasis of quiet elegance in the midst of a busy commercial area, the center is constructed in the Shoin Zukuri style of architecture dating back to the Muromachi period. Exquisite materials including thirty types of wood as well as craftsmen and gardeners were imported from Japan to construct the center, which accentuates the finest in Japanese craftsmanship. Completed at a cost of thirteen million dollars, the center contains authentic Japanese artwork including a thirteenth-century silk screen. Surrounding the building are Japanese rock gardens carefully raked into patterns that depict the earth and sea. The center hosts Japanese festivals, holidays, celebrations, tours, and tea ceremonies; it offers fine Japanese dining in traditional tatami rooms, at the sushi/sashimi bar, in a Teppanyaki area, or in a more American setting. Reservations are suggested.

Bed-and-breakfast accommodations in a 1920s Federal-style house are offered at Pettigru Place, 302 Pettigru Street (864-242-4529), where some of the five guest rooms and suites feature whirlpool baths.

Among Greenville's many festivals, the premier event is the Freedom Weekend Aloft, the nation's second-largest hot-air balloon event, held each Memorial Day Weekend. More than two hundred thousand spectators gather to enjoy food, fireworks, crafts, and big-name entertainment. Call 864-232-3700 for more information.

Take State 253 north from Greenville to Paris Mountain State Park, 2401 State Park Road off State 253 (864-244-5565), where you can get back to nature at one of the oldest protected areas in the state. The park is well known for its stands of large trees, several of which are state champion trees.

Retrace State 253 to US 25 and go south to US 123 where you will turn west. Take State 93 west. Between Easley and Liberty is Golden Creek Mill, 201 Enon Church Road (864-859-1958 days or 864-843-6320 evenings). Built with parts salvaged and assembled from several old mills, Golden Creek Mill provides visitors with an opportunity to tour the historic structure and to watch the grinding of grits, cornmeal, and wheat flour. Nestled on the wooded banks of a branch of the Twelve Mile River, the mill was built in 1825 as a grist mill, but in 1835 it was converted to a cotton gin and press. The concrete and materials for the dam were made on the premises. A century-old fourteen-foot overshot waterwheel, one of the largest in the country, is still used to power the antique milling equipment. Adjacent to the mill is a Country Store, Art, Photo, and Literature Museum, that traces all phases of grist-mill history.

The Upcountry is a haven for outdoor enthusiasts, but the region overflows with attractions for the tourist more interested in historic sites, arts and crafts, museums, and festivals. The Olde English District and the Old 96 District are easily accessible from the Upcountry.

For More Information

Discover Upcountry Carolina Association, P.O. Box 3116, Greenville 29602. 864-233-2690 or 800-849-4766.

Anderson Area Chamber of Commerce, P.O. Box 1568, Anderson 29622. 864-226-3454.

Anderson County Parks and Recreation Department, P.O. Box 789, Anderson 29622-0789. 864-260-4150.

Clemson Area Chamber of Commerce, P.O. Box 202, Clemson 29633. 864-654-1200.

Clemson University Visitors Center, 103 Tillman Hall, Clemson University, Clemson 29634. 864-656-4789.

Greater Seneca Chamber of Commerce, P.O. Box 855, Seneca 29679. 864-882-2097.

Pendleton District Historical, Recreational and Tourism Commission, 125 East Queen Street, Pendleton 29670. 864-646-3782 or 800-862-1795.

Index